LIBRARIES FOR THE NEW MILLENNIUM

Implications for managers

LIBRARIES FOR THE
NEW MILLENNIUM
Implications for managers

EDITED BY

David Raitt

BOURNEMOUTH

1998

LIBRARIES

LIBRARY ASSOCIATION PUBLISHING
LONDON

Published by
Library Association Publishing
7 Ridgmount Street
London WC1E 7AE

Library Association Publishing is wholly owned by The Library Association.

First published 1997

British Library Cataloguing in Publication Data

A catalogue record for this book is available from the British Library.

ISBN 1-85604-257-X

Typeset in 10/13pt Caslon 540 and 11/12pt Zapf Humanist by Library
Association Publishing.
Printed and made in Great Britain by Bookcraft (Bath) Ltd.

CONTENTS

INTRODUCTION

The focus of this book is on how and why libraries and information centres are finding it necessary to change direction and diversify in order to adapt to the threats and challenges posed by the Internet, consumer online, interactive television services and the like – in other words, how they will face up to the Information Society. There is little doubt that the face of libraries everywhere is changing. The growing ready availability of personal computers, in companies and in homes, in schools and universities, means that individuals have a more convenient tool to gain instant access to a host of different kinds of information. Conventional publishing is being pressed by instant electronic publishing. Anyone can do it. These factors impinge on education and knowledge: learning can now be obtained from non-conventional sources.

For libraries to stay in the game, they will not only need to become learning centres and make their collections and stock available electronically over the World Wide Web and other online services to people who want to get their information and knowledge from their office or home, but they will also have to contend with documents in new media. This all means an enhancement and augmentation of library and information services, making them more community-based (and this can be the community formed by all the people in an organization as well as those in a given city or region) and bestowing added-value upon them. This implies new roles and skills for library and information staff, who will need to investigate the future of library and information services and develop new ones both before and as the need arises, as well as re-examine organizational objectives and pricing structures. It means looking at the Information Society and deciding exactly what the library is going to become and what role it is to fulfill.

The objective of this book is to take libraries into the new millennium – a few years hence – and see what impact today's changing world would have on them at that time. The reader is thus presented with an eclectic collection of individual papers giving diverse views and ideas on how various types of library might evolve and be managed in the future and how people – readers, users, customers – might get their information and knowledge. The styles of the authors are quite different and, while I have made comments and suggestions pertaining to the intellectual coverage, I have been content to leave the chapters much as they are from an editorial point of view so that the individuality and personality of each author comes through to add his or her own distinctive contribution to this book.

The book is aimed at senior library and information service managers and decision makers (although this is not to say that other library and information professionals as well as library students should not find it useful) and covers issues and topics relating to: decentralizing the librarian and putting him or her where the user is; how libraries and information centres should be regrouping and consolidating their positions by offering new and extended services and resources; how far libraries have come and what developments they have taken into account in their planning in the face of the Internet threat; the impact of electronic information resources on both library staff and users; the challenge of digital library projects to understand more fully their future context; the importance of the information society for public libraries; the prospectives for artificial intelligence and expert systems in a library environment; how managerial issues, structures and techniques are affecting university libraries; the role of electronic documents in libraries of the future; education and training of future information professionals; and the ramifications and impacts of tomorrow's eclectic information and knowledge systems on an equally diverse mass user population.

This book is more than just a collection of chapters on electronic or digital libraries at the turn of the century. Many people, myself and the authors here included, have attempted to define the electronic library and have written about what it might be like – but it is evident that there is much more to be considered than the library itself. There is the whole organizational framework, the policies and the strategies, the technologies available, the staff and users and the social and economic milieu in which the library will operate. It is these aspects and issues that the papers in this volume explore in different ways.

Grygierczyk, for instance, tries to answer the question of whether there is a method for setting up a comprehensive scientific digital library at the end of the 20th century by describing an electronic library project at the University of Utrecht in The Netherlands. The strategic policy for the digital library construction, plus case studies and lessons learned are discussed. She concludes that because the digital library is a dynamic process, the construction of it can never be completed.

While other authors look at future libraries in a wider context, i.e. their interaction with the outside world, Barker focuses on the importance of electronic documents within future library systems and the tools to create, distribute, maintain and use them. Such media aspects have the effect of leading to information-on-demand and mobile computing and technologies which empower the end-user.

Like Barker, Lancaster, who has written much on electronic libraries and the future of libraries, concentrates this time on narrower issues, namely the potential of artificial intelligence and expert systems technologies in emerging digital library environments. While they may have their advantages in certain areas, they are not without their dangers and they are no substitute for the expertise and intuition of the skilled librarian.

On the other hand, Griffin discusses the recent advances in digital library research by looking at the activities of the Digital Libraries Initiative in the USA. To achieve the goals of such digital libraries, R&D means looking beyond technologies into social, legal and economic issues and contexts. Such a process is offering unparalleled interaction between researchers from different disciplines.

Steele looks at general information access trends and their impact on the organization and staff of academic libraries. He concludes that a more client focused and devolved budgetary structure to establish improved services in the digital era is called for.

Also in the area of academia, Walton and Edwards investigate how selected academic library and information services in the UK have strategically managed their services in times of change. Results from the Impact on People of Electronic Libraries project (IMPEL2) are used to show how libraries are reacting to a multiplicity of management and resource issues which they are now facing and will continue to face in the future.

Taking a somewhat different angle, Klobas identifies the roles that libraries might play in new millennium organizations, i.e. knowledge-based and learning organizations. By examining the changes in business thinking and practice that have provided opportunities for these roles, she shows how such organizations might better meet the need for people in information roles.

Batt asks what a public library is and what the Information Society is. Armed with his own definitions and conclusions, he then examines what the public library of the 21st century will be like, what services will be offered and what its role will be. The public library has to be placed at the heart of the Information Society and this requires vision and resources.

Following through on the theme of the Information Society, White looks at mass market information services and the role and impact they will have on access to information by consumers and businesses. Such services are often overlooked by information professionals, but the fact that they are reaching out directly to domestic end-users means that the library and information community has to take them into account.

All of the above chapters have implications for education and training. Like Walton and Edwards and White, van Brakel also considers information and the marketplace. The introduction of the Internet, new-user interfaces and technologies are changing the information environment, necessitating a completely different approach to the education and training of information professionals. Van Brakel looks at new developments the Internet has brought about and discusses the goals and actions required to bring information science education in line with tomorrow's realities.

The authors, specially selected from around the world to provide an interesting and balanced view, were each asked to write on a given theme, which I felt would cover the many facets of libraries in the new millennium. They were also asked to suggest, in so far as they saw them, the implications for library managers of what they had to say in their chapters. Most included this aspect in a separate section, but others chose to weave the implications throughout the text – going even further in some instances to include implications for the librarian and even the library user, as well as lessons learned.

What is perhaps surprising is that there are few common implications throughout all of the chapters. This is partly due to the individual topics covered by each, but it also reflects the opinions of the authors and does point to the fact that there are many factors the library manager has to be aware of. Since it could be argued that a library is a library is a library then, whether it is a public, academic or special library, the implications will still be valid from one context to another. Taken together, though, the sum of all the implications provided by each author does constitute a valuable and thought-provoking resource and a helpful guide for library managers and their staff.

Although many of the authors pointed to the impact that the Internet is having and will continue to have on library and information users, other major implications that libraries of the new millennium will have on library managers were mentioned. For instance, there is little doubt that to build a dynamic digital library of the future requires a proper project organization with a well-conceived framework and adequate funding and support from the library's governing authority and the public it will serve.

While libraries might be advised to go with the flow of technology and telecommunications, there is still a need to match technologies with users – even to the extent of getting into the design of suitable technologies. But the librarian has to beware of emphasizing technology to the detriment of information content and business acumen and expertise. This latter is something the new-age librarian has to cultivate – s/he cannot afford to ignore the threat of mass-market consumer information systems. This may mean becoming even more client-focused and involve learning a new vocabulary and language, for greater understanding and assessment of the potential of digital techniques and resources and for communicating, i.e. making users aware of new services to be offered and for promoting/marketing one's own information skills. These skills include knowledge transfer, policy making, and information organization and analysis.

The librarian is not quite (yet?) a Jack of all trades but s/he will need to be flexible, creative and intuitive to be able to create and deliver quality information services to customers (no longer just mere users) quickly and efficiently. Users want to see the worth or value of services being offered them; thus it behoves a library to invest in the emerging and future information needs of the community at large. This implies that librarians have to keep themselves well informed of all new developments both within the library and information field and in the outside world. It also entails encouraging interaction among staff so that they can understand each other's role and work and thus tacitly offer back-up and support. And, just as important, all this has implications on education and training – not only of existing information professionals, but even more so on future generations of library school students who will become the library managers of the new millennium.

I trust that readers will find the thoughts and ideas expressed in the chapters of this book of benefit when planning their libraries for the new millennium. I am deeply grateful to those potential authors approached who actually spent their time and energy in preparing these original contributions. I am confident that readers will view their efforts as both valuable and worthwhile.

David Raitt

BIOGRAPHIES

David Raitt graduated in library and information science at the end of 1967 and became a librarian at the Royal Aircraft Establishment in Farnborough, England. In 1969 he went to work for the European Space Agency in France, then Italy, as an information scientist responsible for online marketing, customer liaison and education and training throughout Europe, as well as database and user interface design. Transferring in 1979 to The Netherlands, he was in charge of the Library and Information Services at ESTEC, ESA's large R&D establishment, where, in addition to running the library, he provided a technology watch and multimedia information and training support to European astronauts. In 1992 he was reassigned internally to the post of System and Programmatics Engineer in the Systems Studies Division at ESTEC where, among other duties, he is responsible for coordinating, assessing and supporting activities in advanced information and knowledge management systems, coordinating academic research studies and young graduate trainee programmes, and carrying out strategic analyses and studies of space activities over the long term.

   A well-known and respected information personality, invited to speak and lecture all over the world on leading-edge information technologies, Dr Raitt has also had consultancies with Unesco, FID and the Commission of the European Communities on a wide range of library and information topics. Dr Raitt is Chairman of the International Online Information Meetings held in London each December and has also been Chairman of similar meetings held in Hong Kong, Mexico and Moscow. He is Editor of *The Electronic Library*, a journal he founded in 1983 which covers the applications of technology in information environments. He has also been involved in organizing other conferences throughout the world and is on several editorial boards. He has authored many publications in the information science and technology field. He has a doctorate in communications, library and information science and is a Fellow of the Institute of Information Scientists, The Library Association and the Royal Astronomical Society.

Philip Barker is Professor of Applied Computing and Research Director for the Human-Computer Interaction (HCI) Laboratory within the School of Computing and Mathematics at the University of Teesside. His research group undertakes HCI studies into end-user interface design, mental models and the development of methods to support the effective and efficient use of computer technology by both individuals and work groups within organizations. Professor Barker is particularly interested in the use of performance support systems, electronic book production, book-related metaphors and digital library systems.

Chris Batt, Borough Libraries and Museum Officer for Croydon, has been involved with IT in public libraries for over 25 years and has written and spoken widely. He is the author of the standard study on information technology in UK public libraries, which has now reached its fifth edition. (Sixth edition in process!) The study includes a survey of all 168 library authorities in the UK and has achieved 100% response rate in each edition. In 1993 he wrote a study on the future of public libraries for the Comedia report, Borrowed time; this study suggested how libraries might look in 20 years time. For the past 10 years he has written the Cutting Edge column on IT in *Public library journal* and is a frequent contributor to conferences in the UK and Europe.

Catherine Edwards is Research Associate in the IMPEL2 Project, Department of Information and Library Management, University of Northumbria at Newcastle. She joined the IMPEL team in 1993 having spent the previous six years in the library of a newspaper which was then entering the electronic era. She was research assistant on the IMPEL1 project, then coordinator of its successor, IMPEL2. IMPEL2 takes a qualitative approach to the study of organizational and cultural change in the growing electronic environment of Higher Education in the UK.

Stephen M. Griffin is a Program Manager in the Division of Information, Robotics and Intelligent Systems at the National Science Foundation (NSF), USA. He is currently Program Director of the Digital Libraries Initiative, sponsored jointly with the Department of Defense Advanced Research Projects Agency (DARPA) and the National Aeronautics and Space Administration (NASA). Prior to his current assignment, he served in several research divisions, including the Divisions of Chemistry and Advanced Scientific Computing, the Office of the Assistant Director, Directorate for Computer and Information Science and Engineering, and staff offices of the Director of the NSF. His responsibilities included program planning, development, analysis and assessment. He has initiated numerous activities directed at building topical research communities, and support and coordination for new areas of interdisciplinary research. He has been active in the Federal High Performance Computing and Communications Program (HPCC), authoring and editing HPCC publication material and serving as Executive Secretary of the Information Infrastructure Technologies and Applications Working Group. His educational background includes degrees in Chemical Engineering and Information Systems Technology. He has additional graduate education in organizational behaviour and development and the philosophy of science. His research interests are in topics related to interdisciplinary communication.

Natalia Grygierczyk was born in Cracow and finished her studies in Russian and Computational Linguistics at Utrecht University in 1987. She has worked at Utrecht University since 1988 as a project manager and has headed projects in areas of management information provision and administrative computerization. She has been a project manager of Electronic Library Utrecht since 1995.

Jane E. Klobas is coordinator of the Information Management specialization in the Master of Business Administration degree offered by the Graduate School of Management (GSM) at the University of Western Australia. She has worked as an information management consultant, advising senior managers on information management policy and practice; as a management educator; as a library and information science educator; in library and information service management; and in human resource management. Her interest in organizational knowledge management began in the early 1980s when she developed and managed a diverse information service for an Australian petroleum company.

F. Wilfrid Lancaster is Professor Emeritus in the Graduate School of Library and Information Science at the University of Illinois where he has taught courses relating to information transfer, bibliometrics, bibliographic organization and the evaluation of library and information services. He continues to serve as editor of *Library trends*. He was appointed University Scholar for 1989–92. He is the author of 11 books, six of which have received national awards, and has three times received Fulbright fellowships for research and teaching abroad. From the American Society for Information Science he has received both the Award of Merit and the Outstanding Information Science Teacher award. Professor Lancaster has been involved in a wide range of consulting activities, including service for Unesco and other agencies of the United Nations. He has recently compiled a new book, *Technology and management in library and information science*, and a report for the Special Libraries Association on potential applications for artificial intelligence and expert systems within libraries.

Colin Steele is University Librarian at the Australian National University in Canberra, a position he has held since 1980. Previously he was Deputy Librarian of the Australian National University from 1976 to 1980 and Assistant Librarian at the Bodleian Library, Oxford from 1967 to 1976. He is the author/editor of a number of books including *Major libraries of the world* (1976) and *Changes in scholarly communication patterns* with Professor D. J. Mulvaney (1993). He is on the board of a number of international journals, including *The Electronic Library* and the *Journal of librarianship and international science*. He is a member of the Editorial Board of *The new review of information and* *library research* since 1996. He has been an invited speaker at a number of major library and IT conferences in the USA, UK, South Africa and China. In 1995 he gave the Follett Lectures in the UK, the first Australian speaker to deliver this prestigious series. In March 1996 he was the invited Australian delegate to the OCLC International Research Directors Meeting. He is the nominee of the Chair of the Higher Education Council on the DEET (Department of Employment, Education and Training) Research Infrastructure Committee. He currently chairs cross-campus committees on Electronic Publishing and the Virtual University at the Australian National University.

Pieter van Brakel studied at the University of the Orange Free State and the University of Pretoria (UP). He obtained his Master's degree (Information Science) in 1975, and both a PhD degree (Information Science), and the Diploma in Tertiary Education in 1979. He was a Senior Lecturer in the Department of Information Science at UP from 1980, became an Associate Professor in 1982 and Professor in 1985. He transferred to the Department of Information Studies at the Rand Afrikaans University in October 1991. His teaching responsibilities include information technology, indexing, abstracting, thesaurus construction, and all aspects of online searching, including the Internet and World Wide Web. He is currently involved in various research programs, investigating the role of the World Wide Web to improve scholarly communication. He has published various refereed journal articles, of which eight were contributions in international publications. He is also on the Editorial Board of *The Electronic Library*.

Graham Walton is employed in the Information Services Department at the University of Northumbria at Newcastle, where he is Faculty Librarian for Health, Social Work and Education. His responsibilities include the provision of library and information services to over 7000 health, social work and education students. Library services at seven sites spread over 180 square miles are also part of his remit. Since 1993 he has taken on the role of Co-Director of IMPEL1 and IMPEL2 projects jointly run between the University Department of Information and Library Management and the Information Services Department. He has had active involvement in health sciences library groups and has been Chairman of Health Libraries North and the University Health Sciences Librarians group.

Martin White is a Principal Consultant with TFPL Ltd., based in London, providing market analysis and planning services to the information industry in Europe, and in North America through an office in New York. From 1982 to 1985 he was responsible for developing the electronic publishing activities of Reed Publishing, latterly as Executive Director of Reed Telepublishing Ltd. Over the period from 1985 to 1994 he managed IT, telecommunications and electronic publishing market research activities at Link Resources/International Data Corp., Logica and Romtec before joining TFPL in early 1995. He is a member of the editorial boards of the *International journal of information management* and of *EP (Electronic Publishing) journal*. He is a past president of the Institute of Information Scientists, and has authored a wide range of books, reports and papers on electronic publishing, information management and information technology.

1

ARTIFICIAL INTELLIGENCE AND EXPERT SYSTEM TECHNOLOGIES: PROSPECTS*

F. Wilfrid Lancaster

UNIVERSITY OF ILLINOIS, USA

Introduction

Possible definitions of the terms 'artificial intelligence' (AI) and 'expert systems' (ES) range along a scale: very strict at one end and very loose at the other. If a system has to 'behave intelligently' (e.g. make inferences or learn from its mistakes) to qualify as one having AI, few such systems exist in any application. On the other hand, if one accepts that a system exhibits AI if it does things that humans need intelligence to do, many more systems would qualify. One example can be drawn from the field of subject indexing. Many programs have been developed to select subject terms for documents, usually by extraction but sometimes by limited assignment. Most of these programs operate largely on frequency criteria or by matching words or phrases in the text with words or phrases highly associated with a limited set of descriptors or category codes. Such programs, in themselves, exhibit no intelligence. Nevertheless, they can be considered 'intelligent' by virtue of the fact that a human would need to use intelligence to perform the same task.

A strict definition of the term 'expert system' can be based on the structure/components of the system or, alternatively, on its performance. The former would insist that the system have all the necessary parts (knowledge base, inference engine, user/system interface), together with some necessary actions (e.g. explaining its own decisions), while the latter would require that the system behave at the level of the expert. A more relaxed definition would consider any system an expert system if it can help the non-expert perform some task at a level closer to that of the expert, whether or not all the essential components are in

---

* Work on this paper was supported in large part by the Steven I. Goldspiel Memorial Research Grant of the Special Libraries Association.

place. For example, the Hepatitis Knowledge Base, maintained for several years by the National Library of Medicine in the US, could be considered an expert system if it were used by general practitioners to make better diagnoses or select better treatments in this area, even though no inference engine was applied to it. If 'behave at the level of an expert' is an essential component of the definition of 'expert system', it is improbable that any such systems exist in any field. In this chapter, rather loose definitions of both terms are accepted.*

The history of AI/ES technologies to date can be divided roughly into three phases. The first was characterized by wild optimism regarding the problems that could be solved and the profits that could be made. This phase can be considered to extend through the 1960s, 1970s and most of the 1980s. The second phase, beginning in the 1980s, was one of disillusionment: the technologies had not lived up to their expectations in terms of the problems they could solve, were not as widely adopted as anticipated[1] and had not generated the profits expected. By the early 1990s, many of the larger companies had bowed out of the AI/ES field and many of the smaller ones, founded on these technologies, had either disappeared or had merged with other entities. By 1994 the field was virtually written off in some quarters.[2] Raggad[3] suggests that only around 10% of the medium-to-large expert systems implemented in industry could be considered a success.†

We now seem to be at the beginning of a third phase, characterized by a return to the enthusiasm or, perhaps, overenthusiasm of earlier years. The reason, of course, is the explosive growth of the Internet in general and the World Wide Web in particular. The Internet creates new applications, modifies existing ones, and facilitates collaborative projects in the implementation of systems. As Schmuller[5] points out: 'New companies (and new divisions within existing organizations) have sprung up: their goal is to infuse Web sites with intelligent capabilities and thereby help businesses acquire new customers and provide enhanced service. They also develop intelligent agents that streamline your interaction with the Web.'

---

* Expert systems technology, along with natural language processing, is generally considered to fall within the field of artificial intelligence even though intelligence is rarely present.

† Of course, not all writers paint such a negative picture. For example, Hayes-Roth and Jacobstein[4] imply that any failures that occurred were due mostly to factors beyond the technology itself, such as unreasonable expectations of what could be done and the problems involved in integrating the technology into existing organizational structures. Nevertheless, they acknowledge that there were only a 'few parts of it [the technology] that were mature enough or reliable enough for predictable commercial application'.

While the Internet may indeed have changed the situation in terms of the size of the market and the viability of various implementations, it does not change in terms of basic capabilities. Unfortunately, the published literature continues to include completely wild and unjustifiable claims, as in the following: 'AI will someday produce viable intelligent clones, capable of learning from natural language or broad enough in skill and knowledge to make "educated guesses" when confronted with questions from left field.'[6] Such extreme statements are more likely to appear in popular technical magazines than in the more scholarly literature. The fact remains, however, that the computing community's views of what has been achieved, or is likely to be achieved, almost always differ from the views of the practitioner community – those involved in the actual use of the systems. A typical example of this occurs in the field of medical diagnosis. A report from the American Association for Artificial Intelligence claims: 'These systems have achieved a high level of effectiveness, size, speed, and accuracy for tasks such as diagnosing diseases and suggesting treatments in human medical care . . .'[7]

On the other hand, Kassirer, editor of the *New England Journal of Medicine*, who has had many years of experience with such systems and participated in the development of several early prototypes, is less enthusiastic:

> . . . a major limitation to the improvement of these programs is a further expansion of their knowledge bases to include a larger and larger proportion of the diseases encountered by physicians. Most research groups have given up trying to accomplish this task, which is tedious, unrewarding, and endless because the currency of the program's knowledge base must be maintained as diseases become better understood and new diagnostic tests arise.[8]

Some writers do attempt to paint a more realistic picture of the capabilities and potentials of the more advanced technologies. For example, Bainbridge puts it this way: 'The phrase "expert system" conjures up images of an intelligent computer system that will outperform and, eventually, replace human experts. Such visions are far from reality and demonstrate a considerable misunderstanding of the nature of expert systems.'[9] And, from our own field, Weckert has said:

> . . . no machine can be made to function in the way that a human does, because of the different stuff of the hardware. For the same reason, in many fields of human expertise, no expert system will be as expert as the human expert. It may be that in the future truly expert systems will be built, but they will need to be constructed using hardware which is very similar, both [sic] in composition, form and structure, to humans.'[10]

He goes on to maintain that truly expert systems cannot be developed but useful systems certainly can.

Dreyfus and Dreyfus have probably been the strongest critics of artificial intelligence approaches in general: '. . . computers as reasoning machines can't match human intuition and expertise . . .'; '. . . human intelligence can never be replaced with machine intelligence simply because we are not ourselves "thinking machines" in the sense in which that term is commonly understood'; '. . . it is highly unlikely that expert systems will ever be able to deliver expert performance . . . we'd prefer to call them "competent systems" . . .'; and '. . . in any domain in which people exhibit holistic understanding, no system based upon heuristics will consistently do as well as experienced experts, even if those experts were the informants who provided the heuristic rules.'[11] They base their conclusions, in large part, on the fact that human expertise is very dependent on experience and intuition, and it is these human qualities, rather than codifiable knowledge, that computers can never provide. This point, also emphasized by other writers,[12] will be returned to later.

Fossland takes a somewhat different approach, arguing that it is more realistic to seek 'advice-giving' systems capable of helping in a wider range of problems than 'expert systems' that seek actual solutions to a smaller range; advice-giving systems are less 'brittle'.[13]

Applications in other fields

In the preparation of a research report for the Special Libraries Association in the US, the author has reviewed many hundreds of publications discussing artificial intelligence and expert systems in a wide variety of fields. Applications discussed cover virtually all aspects of human endeavour, extending as far as humanities research.[14] Expert systems have even been developed to aid in the development of expert systems.[15]

However, while thousands of 'systems' have been described in the literature (Durkin listed more than 12,000 expert systems in 1993[16]), only a tiny fraction of these were ever fully implemented in the sense of being put into day-to-day operation in some organization. The great majority existed only on paper or, at best, at experimental or prototype levels.

The few systems that can be considered fully operational required very substantial levels of investment in development and implementation. Systems of this type exist only in commercial environments where the benefits expected (increased sales, increased customer satisfaction, personnel reduction) appear to justify the costs of development and maintenance. Examples include 'help desks' for customer support,[17] target marketing,[18] and news distribution.[19]

The information service environment

Exaggerated claims for AI/ES technologies, and over-optimism regarding their potential contributions, are as prevalent in domains of direct relevance to libraries and librarians as they are in other fields. In particular, the report from the American Association for Artificial Intelligence (AAAI) claims that the AI community can have a significant positive impact on the Internet and, in the US, on the National Information Infrastructure (NII).[7] The study suggests several AI applications of relevance to the NII and, therefore, to the digital library, including intelligent interfaces, knowledge discovery services, and integration and translation services. These are all highly related and one application merges naturally into another, with all three falling into the 'intelligent agent' area.

These applications are described in the report in highly optimistic terms:

> . . . interfaces will need to be intelligent, adjusting automatically to a person's skills and pattern of usage. An intelligent interface to NII resources could help people find and do what they want, when they want, in a manner that is natural to them, and without their having to know or specify irrelevant details of NII structure . . . Integration and translation services might convert information from one format to another subject to semantic constraints. For example, a financial translation service would not just perform the unit conversion from Japanese yen into US dollars, but could convert from raw cost to total cost, including import duties, taxes, and fees . . . knowledge discovery services could track the creation of new databases and updates to existing repositories. These services could cross-index related topics to discover new correlations and produce summaries.

The report continues:

> Users should not be forced to remember the details of particular databases or the wide and growing variety of services and utilities to use them effectively. Instead, the system should support an understandable, consistent interface that tunes itself to the task at hand . . . Users should be able to form arbitrary questions and requests easily, without being limited by restrictive menus or forced to learn artificial query languages. Intelligent interfaces should accept requests in whichever modality (e.g. speech, text, gestures) the user chooses . . . Personal assistant agents should adapt to different users, both by receiving direct requests from the user and by learning from experience . . . intelligent user interfaces could act as assistants to both novice and expert users, helping them navigate the NII's labyrinth of databases and efficiently interact with advanced services. By responding to high-level requests in spoken language and other natural modalities, by communicating information both verbally and graphically, by automatically determining how and when to accomplish the goals of individual users, and by adapting to the skills and desires of those users, personal assistant agents will allow humans to benefit from information resources and facilities that might otherwise overwhelm them with their size, complexity, and rate of change.

And finally:

> Machine-learning algorithms . . . [offer] the promise of programs that examine giga-bytes of network-accessible data to extract trends that would otherwise go unno-ticed by people . . . machine learning techniques could lead to electronic news readers that learn the interests of each user by observing what they read, then use this knowledge to automatically search thousands of news sources to recommend the ten most interesting articles. Similar applications include building intelligent agents that provide current awareness services, alerting users to new web pages of special interest, or providing 'What's New' services for digital libraries.

While the more modest of these functions do seem attainable (and, indeed, have already been achieved to some extent by existing agents), others are beyond our present capabilities and, if one can believe such critics as Dreyfus and Dreyfus,[11] will remain so.

Such optimistic descriptions suggest that most of the problems faced by the user, or the librarian, in trying to locate relevant information in vast network resources (or, indeed, most of the problems grappled with by researchers in infor-mation retrieval over the last 30 or more years) are close to solution. A superficial browsing of the report might certainly give such an impression. A closer exami-nation, on the other hand, shows that the report is primarily a wish list – a call for significant levels of funding in areas where successes have so far been very lim-ited.

Careful study of the AAAI report shows that even this community recognizes the problems that exist, that successes have so far been modest, and that we are very far from being able to replace the human expert in any application:

> Building ontologies is difficult for three reasons. First, articulating knowledge in sufficient detail that it can be expressed in computationally effective formalisms is hard. Second, the scope of shared background knowledge underlying interactions of two agents can be enormous. For example, two doctors collaborating to reach a diag-nosis might combine common sense conclusions based on a patient's lifestyle with their specialized knowledge. Third, there are unsolved problems in using large bod-ies of knowledge effectively, including selecting relevant subsets of knowledge, handling incomplete information, and resolving inconsistencies . . . ontology con-struction is difficult and time consuming and is a major barrier to the building of large-scale intelligent systems and software agents.[7]

and, speaking of man-machine natural language communication: 'These abilities, in their most general form, are far beyond our current scientific understanding and computing technology.' And, finally, and most tellingly: '. . . these techniques often prove to be brittle and nonrobust under real-world conditions.'

Here they were referring to an unusually difficult task, computer recognition of visual images but, as stated earlier, very few 'real-world' applications, incorporating artificial intelligence and expert system technologies, exist in any field and it is likely to be a very long time before these technologies will make a significant contribution in facilitating the operations of the digital library.

To be really valuable, systems must be large enough, general enough, and robust enough to deal with real-world problems. Unfortunately, systems that work well at experimental or prototype stages, using limited data, rarely scale-up successfully to the handling of more general problems and more realistic volumes of data. This situation has been well addressed by Jacobs, at least for the area of text processing:

> Many of the more ambitious goals of artificial intelligence have proved unattainable because of the failure of the many small, successful systems to 'scale up'. The general use of technologies such as natural language interfaces and expert systems has done little to alleviate the basic difficulties and overwhelming cost of knowledge engineering. At the same time, emerging text processing techniques, including data extraction from text and new text retrieval methods, offer a means of accessing stores of information many times larger than any organized knowledge base or data base.
>
> Although knowledge acquisition from text is at the heart of the information management problem, interpreting text, paradoxically, requires large amounts of knowledge, mainly about the way words are used in context. In other words, before 'intelligent' text processing systems can be trained to mine for useful knowledge, they must already have enough knowledge to interpret what they read. The point at which there is 'enough', dubbed 'the crossover point' by Doug Lenat, is still a matter of debate, as no real program seems close to having enough knowledge to achieve general human-like understanding.[20]

Library applications so far

As in other fields, the literature of library science contains a plethora of descriptions of artificial intelligence/expert system applications: in cataloging, in selection/acquisition activities, in classification and indexing, in question answering, in database selection, in information retrieval, and in other areas.

Almost without exception, these have never moved beyond experimental or prototype stages, and most projects have been completely discontinued. Indeed, in some cases at least, the 'system' described existed only in the mind of the author. Furthermore, the few evaluations that have actually taken place (see Su and Lancaster,[21] as a rare example of an objective and rigorous study) indicate that the performance of systems in the library field has been uninspiring. It is necessary to look at the reasons behind this state of affairs before proceeding to a discussion of future prospects.

Many of these applications in the library field can best be referred to as 'solutions in search of a problem'. The developers, by and large, seem to have been naïvely optimistic regarding both system capabilities and system costs. The fact that software designed for expert system implementation was an inexpensive purchase appears to have misled many into the belief that expert systems could be put into operation cheaply. But the software is a trivial component of the total cost. Even for a system of very modest scope, the amount of effort needed for knowledge acquisition, and for reducing this to system form (rule-based, frame-based, case-based, or whatever), can be very great. Moreover, except under very unusual circumstances, the knowledge base thus created will not be static; in many cases it will require regular updating, another time-consuming and costly operation. Smith,[22] who has implemented expert systems in library applications in New Zealand, suggests that many library applications were a misuse of expert systems software: the shell was not used to develop a true expert system and few, if any, demonstrated any intelligence.

The truth is that the expert systems developed in the library field are little more than toys compared with operational systems in use in other environments. Systems that address significant problems successfully do not come cheaply. Allen goes so far as to suggest that these costs make expert systems an unattractive proposition for even commercial enterprises: 'The knowledge-engineering effort associated with traditional expert systems is too costly for the average customer service organization to undertake.'[23] He goes on to explain that this argues for the use of a case-based reasoning approach in such applications (help desks) because companies must usually maintain the necessary records (cases) anyway.

Whether viewed in terms of money or effort, a robust system designed to deal with real-world problems can be very expensive: eight to ten person years, or around $½m, just for the development work, is not unusual. A system known as Pharos, developed in the UK to advise businesses of European Community legislation that might affect their products, was said to cost £865,000 for development alone.

There is another, related matter that is frequently overlooked. Few librarians have the knowledge or experience needed to implement an expert system or to attempt to apply artificial intelligence techniques to library-related problems. In this they are no different from professionals in other fields. The systems that are successfully operating in other environments have not been developed by their practitioners alone but by the practitioners working closely with companies specialized in the field of knowledge engineering.

Applications of advanced technologies in the library of the future

In considering possible futures, it is necessary to make a distinction between librarians exploiting advanced technologies developed by others, and librarians involving themselves in the design and implementation of systems incorporating these technologies. Both topics will be dealt with. In looking at prospects, too, it seems sensible to emphasize the role of these technologies in a possible future digital library environment rather than one based primarily on printed resources.

The term 'digital library' can have several possible meanings. At one extreme, it could be merely a personal library of information resources maintained by an individual in electronic form: at the other extreme, it could be considered the totality of resources in digital form that can be accessed through networking capabilities. For the purpose of the present discussion, however, a digital library is more like a traditional library, at least conceptually; it is a library maintained by a university, corporation or other entity to serve a particular community of users.

The objectives of such a digital library are no different from those of a conventional library: to make available to users the information resources they need at the time they need them and to help users exploit these resources effectively and efficiently. In the digital library, however, most, if not all, of the resources will be in electronic form, and the great majority will be in a form that is 'accessible' rather than 'distributed.'

The library as a switching centre

Some see the library of the future as not having any 'collection' of its own. It would be a mere switching centre, referring users to potentially appropriate points in the vast network of resources accessible through the Internet or its successors. Others see the library as primarily a switching centre but having important value-adding functions: creating guides, indexes, annotations and other tools tailored to the needs and interests of the library's own community of users and designed to improve the intellectual accessibility of those network resources likely to have greatest relevance and value to this community.

More farsighted observers (notably Atkinson[24-5]) recognize that the library cannot survive as a mere switching centre, even a value-added switching centre. To justify its existence in the electronic world, the library must continue to perform one of the most important functions it now performs in the print-on-paper world: to organize the universe of resources in such a way that those most likely to be of value to the user community are made most accessible to this community, physically and intellectually. This implies that the library must act as an information filter, selecting the most relevant resources from the universe of network resources and downloading these to local storage/access facilities. Moreover, the downloaded resources will need to be organized intellectually and themselves made available to users at different levels or tiers of accessibility. Atkinson makes an important distinction between a 'control zone' of network resources extracted and controlled by the library community and an 'open zone' of everything else.[26]

The library as access provider

One library that has already gone a long way toward the adoption of collection development policies for electronic resources is the Mann Library at Cornell University, as discussed by Demas et al.[27] They identify various levels or 'tiers' of access, illustrated in Figure 1.1. Note that some high-demand items may be downloaded from the national network to the campus network while others are merely accessible from the national network on demand (possibly through the aid of 'pointers' provided locally).

Tier 1

Delivered over the campus network via the Mann Library Gateway. Anticipated high demand and need for quick response and manipulation time dictate the use of media and software which will provide very fast response time.

Tier 2

Delivered over the campus network via the Mann Library Gateway. Must be interactively available, but a relatively low number of simultaneous uses is expected and slower retrieval time acceptable. Therefore a slower storage medium, such as optical platter, may be acceptable.

Tier 3

Resources that can be delivered online via the Gateway on demand, but are not continuously available online. Tier 3 resources may be mounted on request for Gateway access or may be used in the library at any time.

Tier 4

Resources that are available in the library only (i.e. not delivered over the campus network), but that are available from many public access workstations within the library over a local area network.

Tier 5

Resources that are available in the library only, at single user stations.

Fig. 1.1   *Levels of access to electronic resources identified at the Mann Library, Cornell University. From Demas et al. (1995) by permission of the American Library Association.*

Based largely on this model provided by the Mann Library, one can now visualize the digital library as one providing various levels of access to electronic resources, as illustrated in Figure 1.2. Electronic resources in great demand (level A) are made permanently accessible through a campus or community network, while others (level B) can be accessed remotely via the network when needed (e.g. through the Internet). These are strongly linked to the library because the library may have been responsible for selecting the level A resources from the international network and downloading them to the corporate network. It may also have been responsible for building the indexes or providing the pointers that draw attention to the level B resources. Alternatively, the level B resources may be brought personally to the attention of individual users by reference librarians consulted face-to-face, by telephone or through electronic mail. The level C and D resources are not available through the campus network but must be used within the library through a local area network or a single dedicated workstation.

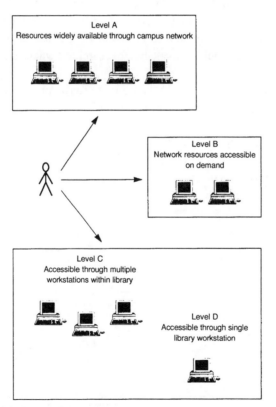

Fig. 1.2   *Possible levels of access to electronic resources provided by the library in an academic setting*

The library as filter

Some 15 years ago, in writing about the future of indexing and abstracting services, Lancaster and Neway visualized an online filtering system that would eventually bring relevant journal information to individual users.[28] The conceptualization is shown in Figure 1.3. It assumed that, given that journals exist in electronic form and include abstracts, acceptable 'accessing databases' could be built directly from the primary literature. A series of filters (really subject profiles) would be necessary to form major discipline-oriented and mission-oriented databases from all items newly added to all databases (i.e. not restricted to a particular set of journals). More refined filters would form more specialized databases from the first level databases. User interest profiles could then be applied to the second-level databases. An individual user, then, could log on to some system and be informed that X items, matching his or her profile of interest, have been published since the system was last used. The user may then view abstracts and, if required, get online access to the complete item. Rather than 'subscribing' to any one electronic journal, the filters would keep users informed of everything matching their interests, wherever published. At various levels, databases of abstracts would be available for searching when specific information needs arise.

The model of Figure 1.3 is highly appropriate to the present information environment made possible by the Internet although, as suggested earlier, it is probably the library community that should be most heavily involved in building the necessary filters, especially those closest to the individual user. Moreover, libraries will be concerned with filtering all types of resources and not just those that are the equivalents of the present journal articles.

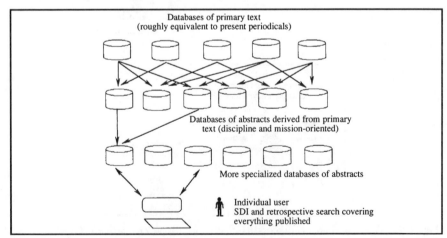

Fig. 1.3   *Filtering levels in a digital library environment*

In a highly developed digital information network, one can visualize a situation in which an individual builds a personal database by downloading from network resources the text and graphics of most direct interest. This individual may be supported by some form of institutional library (maintained perhaps by a university, college, or company) which has also downloaded from the broader network the text and graphics most likely to be of value to the institutional community. The situation is depicted in simple form in Figure 1.4. If an important role of the institutional library is to 'feed' the personal databases of its users in a dynamic way (e.g. through some form of profile matching), the most obvious evaluation criterion would relate to the frequency with which an individual needs to go beyond personal and institutional resources to satisfy a particular need. Presumably, if the institutional library was doing an excellent job, most of the individual's needs would be satisfied from his/her own database, some from the institutional database, and very little from the wider network resources.

It is clear that the vast expanse of poorly organized resources which are accessible, at least in a theoretical sense, through the Internet make the construction of effective filters a daunting proposition, whether at individual or institutional level. Moreover, we are assured that the situation will get much worse. The report from the American Association for Artificial Intelligence, dealing with the National Information Infrastructure, puts it this way: 'Current trends in semiconductor density, processor speed, and network bandwidth suggest that the infrastructure will be thousands of times larger than existing systems such as the Internet; the array of services supported by the NII will be unimaginably vast.'[7]

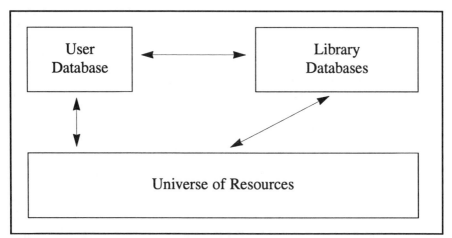

Fig. 1.4 *Interacting components in a digital library environment*

Implications for library managers

Whether or not one accepts them as truly 'expert' or as truly 'intelligent', it is quite obvious that information processing tools of ever-increasing sophistication will continue to be developed, and many will become commercially available. Some of these will be of direct relevance to librarians and other providers of information service. They will presumably include improved browsers and search engines for the exploitation of network resources, filtering agents to assist in the management of electronic mail and in the selective dissemination of information, powerful data mining programs, resource (i.e. database) selection tools, retrieval software applicable to the searching of databases internal to industrial and other organizations (especially better methods for the searching of large bodies of full text and of various types of images), and more user-friendly interfaces in general including, perhaps, some limited-application speech-based and pen-based interfaces.

Many of these relevant developments may occur in environments that are quite distant from the field we think of as 'library and information science' and they will be described in other literatures. For example, some of the more sophisticated approaches to interactive information retrieval, incorporating relevance feedback and ranked output, have been implemented in the customer support (help desk) application, while the more successful approaches to text processing tend to be associated with the news industry in general. Clearly, this is because these are multimillion dollar applications where substantial investments can be justified from a cost-benefit standpoint.

It should also be recognized that developments will occur in completely different areas that may still have some applicability in the operation of information services or in education and training activities. For example, expert critiquing systems seem well suited for use in training and retraining for 'reference work', and other computer-based approaches may be adapted for instructing library users in information-seeking skills.

In a technological environment that is constantly changing, and especially one in which library services can be expected to become increasingly 'digital', it is extremely important for librarians to keep themselves well informed concerning new products and new developments of the type referred to in this chapter. This is needed not only for the betterment of library services but also because the librarian may be in a good position to bring relevant new technologies to the attention of other parts of the organization (e.g. those responsible for the handling of a company's correspondence files, contract files, engineering drawings, image databases, and so on) and to participate in the evaluation of these technologies. Indeed, some writers (e.g. Raitt[29]) suggest that the assessment of new information technologies (in the broadest sense and not just those directly related to library services) should be a major function of the librarian of the future.

To what extent should librarians continue to involve themselves in the design and implementation of their own 'intelligent' or 'expert' systems? This question is difficult to answer definitively.

Of course, 'knowledge engineering' is an occupation that may sound glamorous to many librarians and, indeed, some have urged that librarians get involved in the design of more sophisticated systems rather than being merely the users of systems developed by others.[30-3]

Nevertheless, the fact that pitifully few systems developed within the library field itself have moved beyond experimental or demonstration stages does not encourage one to recommend that the directors of libraries should commit many resources to further work of this type. As pointed out already, the development and maintenance of systems robust enough to handle significant information processing problems is a very expensive proposition, and purchase of the necessary software is a trivial component of the total cost. Furthermore, the great majority of librarians lack the necessary expertise in this area. Knowledge engineering has emerged as a separate discipline and the companies that operate successfully in this field have achieved considerable experience in system development; their professionals are drawn from fields – e.g. computer science, psychology, linguistics – beyond our own. The knowledge engineering component of other professions is a specialization in its own right. The most obvious example is medicine – the typical practitioner in medicine is not a specialist in medical informatics and is not well qualified to develop sophisticated systems to support various aspects of health care. By the same token, most librarians would be well advised not to dabble in a field in which, in all probability, they lack the necessary experience and expertise. Nevertheless, like medical practitioners, they obviously must work closely with the knowledge engineers in any system development of direct relevance to library service.

There are other factors that need to be taken into account. The library-related activities that could most readily be taken over by computers tend not to be complex enough or critical enough: one could not justify the significant expenditures which would be needed to develop systems that would replace humans in performing the task, at least at the single library level. On the other hand, the most complex and most professional of tasks – those associated with the role of information consultant in the widest sense of the term – are not easily delegated to machines and are not likely to benefit substantially from technology in the foreseeable future.

Sparck Jones[34] is one writer who has stated the case most clearly. Discussing the information retrieval situation, she maintains that we should not overestimate the potential contribution of artificial intelligence. On the one hand, the sophisticated search, retrieval and evaluation activities associated with the work of skilled information intermediaries, especially those involved in information analysis functions, are well beyond the capabilities of present computing. On the other hand, the relatively shallow approaches employed by library users in typical catalogue or database searches are an inappropriate or unnecessary application of artificial intelligence.

Nevertheless, while one cannot encourage individual libraries to invest resources in standalone systems, there may be applications of sufficient importance to justify investment by the library community at large. That is, larger bodies such as consortia or professional associations may seek funding to address problems of collective interest. In such enterprises, it will be necessary for designated professional librarians to work closely with companies that are fully experienced in knowledge engineering activities.

It seems obvious that any such investment should look to emerging and future needs – problems and services associated with the digital library environment rather than that of print on paper. This suggests that the areas worth pursuing would be those related to the efficient exploitation of network resources on behalf of library users – e.g. improved tools for the implementation of current awareness services, for the evaluation of network resources, for the 'feeding' of personal electronic databases, for the creation of new composite documents from dispersed network resources, and so on. As mentioned earlier, Atkinson's distinction between a 'control zone' of resources controlled by the library community (in much the same way that they now control distributed artifacts through cataloguing, classification, indexing and related activities) and an 'open zone' of everything else is significant here. Artificial intelligence/expert system technologies may be applicable to some of the 'control zone' activities of libraries.

Of course, the commercial world is already producing search engines, intelligent agents, and other tools for the exploitation of networked resources. However, commercial interests, dominated by profit-making motives, do not always coincide with the interests of libraries and their users. Moreover, some library concerns, such as the consistent cataloguing of network resources, may not have much commercial appeal.

Conclusions

Basden[35] suggests that there are three possible levels of benefits associated with expert systems: feature benefits, task benefits and role benefits. Feature benefits refer to an improved way of using some feature or facility, such as a better interface for searching online catalogues or databases. Task benefits refer to an improved way of understanding some task, as in machine-aided approaches to indexing. Role benefits, on the other hand, refer to the ability to use sophisticated technology to perform roles not undertaken before or not possible before. So far, the library community seems to have focused on the feature and task benefits. Probably it would be better if future collective effort went into the possibility of using artificial intelligence/expert system technologies to achieve role benefits, perhaps to deal more deeply with knowledge discovery problems (as exemplified by Swanson's work on disconnected literatures[36]) or to exploit databases in forms of technological or social forecasting (Lancaster and Loescher[37]).

In concluding this chapter, it is necessary to point out that expert systems are not without their dangers. Weckert and Ferguson[38] raise some ethical concerns: reference librarians can make moral judgments (e.g. not to provide information on how to make a bomb or how to commit suicide), but inanimate systems cannot. It has also been pointed out that a significant barrier to the further development of diagnostic systems in the medical field is the possibility of misdiagnosis with attendant litigious consequences (Warner;[39] Bainbridge[12]). Of course, malpractice suits are less likely in the library environment than in health care. Nevertheless, one must be aware that such concerns do exist. Intelligent network agents may also present various technological dangers. Ordille[40] points out that agents operating within the Internet can damage servers and that, conversely, servers can damage agents.

There is, however, a more serious issue. A large component of 'expertise' is informal and experiential in character (Bainbridge[12]); the recorded knowledge, however detailed and comprehensive, still requires evaluation and interpretation. People do not become experts merely by having an expert knowledge base available to them. Indeed, the very availability of such a tool can be dangerous, for it puts decisions and actions that are properly the domain of the expert into the hands of the less qualified. To give a concrete example, an expert system applied to 'reference work' is no substitute for the experience and intuition of a skilled reference librarian. The system may help a library user, or an inexperienced librarian, to perform competently but not expertly. Over the longer term, too much reliance on technology could have very undesirable consequences – e.g. the truly expert reference librarian might disappear. This danger was well recognized by Dreyfus and Dreyfus: 'To the extent that junior employees using expert systems come to see expertise as a function of large knowledge data bases and masses of inferential rules, they will fail to progress beyond the competent level of their machines.'[11]

These various concerns, together with the fact that rigorous evaluations applied to decision-making systems (from those applied in library reference work to those applied to clinical diagnoses) have produced uninspiring results, strongly suggest that the library community should not be overly optimistic concerning the immediate potential value of these technologies.

Technologically advanced systems may have a useful role to play in the emerging digital library environment but it is important to recognize their limitations and the fact that they do not reduce our need to continue to develop our human expert resources. Horton was correct in pointing out that skilled human resources, rather than 'machines', are the real capital asset of the Information Age.[41] Harris has warned that the library profession may be losing control over its 'knowledge base' and abandoning its 'service ideal', leading to 'deprofessionalization' and the eventual demise of the profession.[42] We must not let over-reliance on technology, or over-optimism regarding its capabilities, lead us to settle for competence or mediocrity in place of true excellence.

References

1   Shao, Y. P., 'Expert systems in UK banking', *Proceedings (of) the 11th conference on artificial intelligence for applications*, Los Alamitos, IEEE Computer Society Press, 1995, 18–23.

2   'No more expert systems: the intelligent technology that got left behind', *Critical technology trends*, Report No. 3, March 1994.

3   Raggad, B. C., 'Expert system quality control', *Information processing & management*, **32**, 1996, 171–83.

4   Hayes-Roth, F. and Jacobstein, N., 'The state of knowledge-based systems', *Communications of the ACM*, **37** (3), 1994, 27–39.

5   Schmuller, J., 'The bottom of the tenth', *PC AI*, **10** (6), 1996, 8.

6   Rasmus, D. W., 'Groupware: reconnecting with human intelligence', *PC AI*, **9** (6), 1995, 27–8, 30, 32–4.

7   Weld, D. S., et al. (eds.), 'The role of intelligent systems in the National Information Infrastructure', *AI magazine*, **16** (3), 1995, 45–64.

8   Kassirer, J. P., 'A report card on computer-assisted diagnosis – the grade: C', *New England journal of medicine*, **330**, 1994, 1824–5.

9   Bainbridge, D. I., 'Expert systems in law: practice and promise', *International journal of applied expert systems*, **1** (1), 1993, 25–40.

10 Weckert, J., 'How expert can expert systems really be?', *Libraries and expert systems*, ed. by C. McDonald and J. Weckert, Los Angeles, Taylor Graham, 1991, 99–114.

11 Dreyfus, H. L. and Dreyfus, S. E., *Mind over machine: the power of human intuition and expertise in the era of the computer*, New York, Free Press, 1986, XI, 102–9.

12 Bainbridge, D. I., 'Computer-aided diagnosis and negligence', *Medicine, science and the law*, **39**, 1991, 127–36.

13 Forslund, G., 'Toward cooperative advice-giving systems', *IEEE expert*, **10** (4), 1995, 56–62.

14 Ennals, R. and Gardin, J.-C. (eds.), *Interpretation in the humanities: perspectives from artificial intelligence*, London, British Library, 1990, Library and Information Research Report 71.

15 Bramer, M. A. and Milne, R. W. (eds.), *Research and development in expert systems IX*, Cambridge, Cambridge University Press, 1993.

16 Durkin, J., *Expert systems: catalog of applications*, Akron, Ohio, Intelligent Computer Systems, 1993.

17 Acorn, T. L. and Walden, S. H., 'SMART: support management automated reasoning technology for Compaq customer service', *Innovative applications of artificial intelligence 4*; ed. by A.C. Scott and P. Klahr, Cambridge, Massachusetts, MIT Press, 1992, 3–18.

18 Anand, T. and Kahn, G., 'Focusing knowledge-based techniques on market analysis', *IEEE expert*, **8** (4), 1993, 19–24.

19 Hayes, P. J. and Weinstein, S. P., 'Construe-TIS: a system for content-based indexing of a database of news stories', *Innovative applications of artificial intelligence 2*; ed. by A. Rappaport and R. Smith, Cambridge, Massachusetts, MIT Press, 1991, 51–64.

20 Jacobs, P. S., 'Text-based systems and information management: artificial intelligence confronts matters of scale', *Proceedings of the 6th international conference on tools with artificial intelligence*, Los Alamitos, IEEE Computer Society Press, 1994, 235–6.

21 Su, S.-F. and Lancaster, F. W., 'Evaluation of expert systems in reference service applications', *RQ*, **35**, 1995, 219–28.

22 Smith, Alastair, Victoria University, New Zealand. Personal communication, November 1996.

23 Allen, B. P., 'Case-based reasoning: business applications', *Communications of the ACM*, **37** (3), 1994, 40–2.

24 Atkinson, R., 'Text mutability and collection administration,' *Library acquisitions: practice and theory*, **14**, 1990, 355–8.

25 Atkinson, R., 'Networks, hypertext, and academic information services: some longer-range implications', *College & research libraries*, **54**, 1993, 199–215.

26 Atkinson, R., 'Library functions, scholarly communication, and the foundation of the digital library: laying claim to the control zone', *Library quarterly*, **66**, 1996, 239–65.

27 Demas, S. et al., 'The Internet and collection development: mainstreaming selection of Internet resources', *Library resources & technical services*, **39**, 1995, 275–90.

28 Lancaster, F. W. and Neway, J. M., 'The future of indexing and abstracting

services', *Journal of the American Society for Information Science*, **33**, 1982, 183–9.

29   Raitt, D., 'The library of the future', *Libraries and the future: essays on the library in the twenty-first century*, ed. by F. W. Lancaster, New York, Haworth Press, 1993, 61–72.

30   von Wahlde, B. and Schiller, N., 'Creating the virtual library: strategic issues', *The virtual library: visions and realities*, ed. by L.M. Saunders, Westport, Connecticut, Meckler, 1993, 15–46.

31   Drabenstott, K. M., *Analytical review of the library of the future*, Washington, DC, Council on Library Resources, 1994.

32   LaGuardia, C., 'Desk Set revisited: reference librarians, reality, & research systems' design', *Journal of academic librarianship*, **21**, 1995, 7–9.

33   Brin, B. and Cochran, E., 'Access and ownership in the academic environment: one library's progress report', *Journal of academic librarianship*, **20**, 1994, 207–12.

34   Sparck Jones, K., 'The role of artificial intelligence in information retrieval', *Journal of the American Society for Information Science*, **42**, 1991, 558–65.

35   Basden, A., 'Three levels of benefits in expert systems', *Expert systems*, **11** (2), 1994, 99–107.

36   Swanson, D.R., 'Intervening in the life cycles of scientific knowledge', *Library trends*, **41**, 1993, 606–31.

37   Lancaster, F. W. and Loescher, J., 'The corporate library and issues management', *Library trends*, **43**, 1994, 159–69.

38   Weckert, J. and Ferguson, S., 'Ethics, reference librarians and expert systems', *Australian library journal*, **42**, 1993, 172–81.

39   Warner, E., 'Expert systems and the law', *High technology business*, **8**, 1988, 32–5.

40   Ordille, J. J., 'When agents roam, who can you trust?', *Proceedings of the first annual conference on emerging technologies and applications in communications*, Los Alamitos, IEEE Computer Society Press, 1996, 188–91.

41   Horton, F.W., Jr., 'Human capital investment: key to the information age', *Information and records management*, **16** (7), 1982, 38–9.

42   Harris, R., 'Information technology and the de-skilling of librarians', *Computers in libraries*, **12**, 1992, 8–16.

2

INFORMATION SERVICES FOR NEW MILLENNIUM ORGANIZATIONS: LIBRARIANS AND KNOWLEDGE MANAGEMENT

Jane E. Klobas

THE GRADUATE SCHOOL OF MANAGEMENT, THE UNIVERSITY OF WESTERN AUSTRALIA

Introduction

While the 1990s has seen many changes that affect libraries, these changes are but a subset of the changes that have affected the organizations served by libraries. On the edge of the new millennium, massive changes in business thinking are supported by technological advances that make new approaches to business and the organization of business possible. Librarians have the opportunity to play key roles in new millennium organizations. At the same time, organizations that use librarians effectively have the opportunity to turn the possibilities represented by the new business thinking and technological advances to sustainable advantage. These opportunities rest on true partnerships and seamless teamwork between librarians and their organizational colleagues. Many organizations that take advantage of these opportunities will find their librarians outside the library's walls.

This chapter identifies the roles that librarians might play in new millennium organizations, examines the changes in business thinking and practice that have provided the opportunities for these roles, considers alternative ways that organizations might meet the need for people in information roles, and considers the implications of the new information environment for business managers and librarians. Librarians in new millennium organizations will be knowledge managers and information analysts. They will perform a range of business roles. They will work as integral members of the business teams that need these roles, and many will work with those teams rather than in a library.

The new business environment and the demand for knowledge management

The 1990s has seen an extraordinary change in the way organizations are viewed and managed. Organizations may no longer be viewed as production-oriented entities, divided by function (human resource management, accounting, research and development, operations, marketing, service, etc.), and controlled by layers of management. Instead, management theorists see modern organizations as flexible structures characterized by a geographically dispersed workforce in which client-oriented work groups or teams, based around organizational processes, act autonomously to meet the organization's goals.[1-4]

Several terms have been used to describe the type of organization emerging from this change in management thinking. Each term conveys a vivid impression of the new millennium organization: it will be a 'knowledge-based organization', in which employees' knowledge is the organization's primary asset;[1, 5] it will be a 'learning organization', in which individuals, teams, and the organization itself continuously learn from the environment and from their activities, and act on what they have learnt;[6, 7] it will be a 'knowledge-based organization' in which products and services are customized and continually enhanced or changed to reflect what has been learnt from customers;[8] it will be an 'extended enterprise', in which customers, clients, suppliers, governments, shareholders, and other stakeholders are all included explicitly in the organization's definition of itself and its communication systems;[4] it will be a 'networked organization' in which computer-based communication networks permit widespread and rapid communication among all groups in the extended enterprise.[3] Network technologies, such as Internet technologies, will enable 'any time, any place' communication and access to information, unconstrained by time of day or physical location.[9-11] Managers have been presented with not only a new vision of organizations, but also the technology to support achievement of that vision.

Two features of the new business environment have resulted in a growing demand for information managers as we approach the new millennium: the focus on the role of learning and knowledge in organizations; and the convergence of information technology, telecommunications, and information resources in networked information resources. This demand is associated with the rise of 'knowledge management' as the focus of organizational improvement efforts. The new information managers may well be called 'knowledge managers'.[12] The rise of knowledge management has implications not only for managers and their organizations, but also for librarians as information providers and information managers in organizations, for the profession of librarianship, for the field of library and information science, and for educators. To understand these implications, we need to understand what is meant by knowledge management, to identify and to understand the knowledge management processes to which librarians contribute, and to acknowledge the roles that librarians and others might play in these processes in new millennium organizations.

Knowledge management in the new business environment

Knowledge management is concerned with the acquisition, transfer, and use of knowledge in organizations. While organizations have long been concerned with these processes, in the late 1990s managers (and, hence, organizations) are being urged to be more systematic in their knowledge management, to gain better value from the existing knowledge of members of the organization, and to deal more effectively with transfer of knowledge across organizational boundaries.

The organizational role of knowledge management has been tied closely to changes in organizational theory and the world economy by Stewart[5] who shares with many management theorists the view that we have now passed the 'industrial age' in which the focus of management was the control and production of physical goods. We are, instead, in the 'information age', in which the primary role of management is to develop the 'intellectual capital' of the organization. According to this view, the knowledge of its workers is the foundation of the organization's intellectual capital. Knowledge management aims to improve the organization, and its contribution to the economy, by increasing the organization's intellectual capital.

Within an organization, intellectual capital is increased when knowledge is acquired by learning from organizational activities, through research and development, or from existing sources of knowledge. Existing sources of knowledge include both knowledge from external sources, and knowledge already held within the organization. Knowledge held within the organization includes knowledge recorded in organizational documents, reports, and other recorded sources, and the knowledge of individual members of staff.

Examples of knowledge management activities: networked information systems for knowledge sharing

Many knowledge management activities are directed toward enabling the knowledge of individual members of the organization to be shared by others in the organization, or to 'know what we know'.[12, 13] At the time of writing, most work described in the information professions as knowledge management is concerned with development of computer-based information systems for knowledge sharing. This is a new development in organizations. It draws on the expertise of business experts, information management experts, and information technology experts. The aim is to build networked 'knowledge management systems' that provide access to the knowledge of organizational members, regardless of the geographical location of the person who holds the knowledge, or the time at which the knowledge is sought. Knowledge management systems are designed to record the knowledge of an expert in the expert's own words, to be updated each time new information comes to hand, and to enable interaction between groups of experts and between experts and other members of the organization who want to share their knowledge.

Knowledge sharing from computer-based knowledge management systems extends across traditional organizational boundaries to clients, customers, and others in the extended organization. Already, organizations are using the Internet to share knowledge with their customers. Several software companies have public knowledge management systems that make records of support questions and information available to Internet users. The Microsoft knowledge base[14] contains summaries of what support officers have learnt about the functioning of Microsoft products, including work arounds and fixes for apparent software bugs. The knowledge base is a searchable database which enables users of Microsoft products to search for answers to their support queries. Several companies share product knowledge about Lotus Notes and related products in public discussion databases accessible from the World Wide Web.[15] At these sites, customers can raise questions and respond to questions and statements made by others in the discussion. The record of the discussion includes knowledge shared between Lotus Notes staff and people external to the organization who are interested in or using the Lotus Notes software. NASA has a 'Lessons Learned Information System' which makes the lessons learned from their work, and that of others working with NASA, available to be shared among NASA staff and contractors, other US government agencies, and the space agencies of other countries.[16] Knowledge management systems enable knowledge to be shared, not just within an organization's walls, but also with members of the extended enterprise.

Knowledge transfer processes, including the sharing of existing organizational knowledge, are therefore key processes in knowledge management. The rest of this chapter will concentrate on these processes and the implications for librarians of organizational interest in knowledge transfer.

Knowledge transfer

Figure 2.1 illustrates the role of knowledge transfer within an organization. The figure shows that knowledge is acquired in order to be used. Knowledge may be acquired through research and development, organizational learning, and knowledge transfer. Knowledge transfer includes both the sharing of existing organizational knowledge and the acquisition of knowledge from external sources. Shared organizational knowledge and knowledge acquired from external sources contribute to the organization's intellectual capital in their own right, and also through their contribution to research and development and organizational learning. Both research and development and organizational learning, in turn, contribute to the organization's store of knowledge that may be shared.

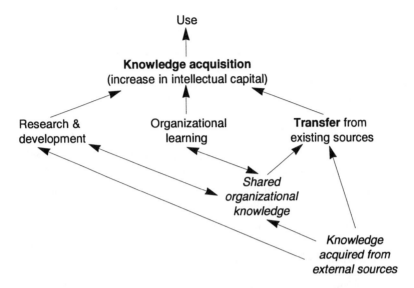

Fig. 2.1 *Knowledge management processes, and the role of knowledge transfer*

Information professionals are vitally concerned with knowledge transfer. Librarians have long been concerned with the acquisition of recorded knowledge from external sources. Information systems professionals, records managers (and, in many organizations, librarians and public relations professionals) have been concerned with sharing of recorded knowledge within organizations. Rather than processes with organization-wide impact, however, knowledge transfer processes have until now been seen as the separate domains of different functional groups. There has been little attempt to integrate knowledge transfer processes.[17, 18] Davenport and Prusak described one effect of this lack of integration:

> Librarians collect, categorize, and store largely textual information; information systems groups focus on largely quantitative or transactional information, and rarely do the twain meet. If an executive wanted to find out more about a customer or competitor who shows up in the latest weekly printout or terminal display, he or she must go to an entirely different source for the information, using different protocols for expressing the information requirement and accessing the source.[19]

Knowledge management enables organizations, managers and members of the information professions to view knowledge transfer as a set of related processes. This view provides new opportunities for organizations and members of organizations who seek and use recorded knowledge. It also provides challenges for the professions involved in knowledge transfer.

Knowledge and the knowledge transfer process

Several aspects of knowledge and the knowledge transfer process underlie the roles that librarians and other information professionals may play in knowledge transfer in the new millennium organization. Some key characteristics are introduced in this section.

Characteristics of knowledge

Knowledge transfer is a complex process that reflects the forms in which knowledge may be held, the sources of the knowledge, the limitations of human beings as communicators, and the organizational and wider social environment of the people who have and who wish to be recipients of knowledge. An understanding of these characteristics of organizational knowledge provides a background for discussion of activities in the knowledge transfer process. These characteristics are summarized in Figure 2.2, and discussed below.

Forms in which knowledge is held

The knowledge available to an organization can be classified as tacit knowledge or explicit knowledge.[20-1] Tacit knowledge is most easily recognized as the knowledge held by an individual 'in his (or her) head'. Tacit knowledge is unar-

```
the form in which the knowledge is held
    tacit (unarticulated and unrecorded) knowledge
    • explicit knowledge
        articulated, but not recorded
        • articulated and recorded
            physical records
            • electronic records


the source of the knowledge
    internal to the organization
    • external to the organization


organizational, social, and cognitive characteristics, including
    individuals' willingness to share knowledge
    limitations of human communication
        articulation
        • recording
```

Fig. 2.2 *Some characteristics of knowledge which affect knowledge management activities*

ticulated and unrecorded, and an individual might act or perform tasks without explicit reference to his or her store of tacit knowledge. A work group or organization can also have tacit knowledge. For a group, tacit knowledge is that shared understanding which underlies practices and behaviours but which is not recorded.

Explicit knowledge is knowledge that is articulated or recorded in a way that enables the knowledge to be transferred or shared. Explicit knowledge may be recorded in reports, books, technical papers, memos, minutes of meetings, databases, photographs, videos, sound recordings and other media. The record may be published or unpublished.

Sources of knowledge

Knowledge of value to an organization may be held externally or internally. Knowledge acquired from outside the organization is classified as 'external' knowledge until it becomes part of the tacit or explicit knowledge of the organization. All other knowledge – whether held only as the tacit knowledge of individuals or recorded, whether stored in an *ad hoc* manner or formally organized in a library, records management system, intranet, or other repository – is internal to the organization.

Organizational, social, and cognitive characteristics of knowledge transfer

Knowledge transfer is an imperfect process. People are not always willing to share their knowledge with others,[12, 22–3] and even if they are prepared to share their knowledge, they may not be able to articulate it adequately or in a language readily understood by potential recipients. The knowledge gained by the recipient from listening to or reading knowledge articulated by others is not necessarily the knowledge that the originator intended to transfer. Knowledge transfer is therefore constrained by social, political, and cognitive limitations. Organizations often rely on intermediaries such as consultants, knowledge engineers, librarians and information analysts to overcome some of these limitations. Computer-based systems, such as expert systems and knowledge management systems, also act as electronic intermediaries in the knowledge transfer process.

Activities in knowledge transfer

Activities in knowledge transfer reflect the form and source of knowledge to be acquired, and the availability of intermediate individuals and technologies to assist with knowledge transfer. There are five primary activities:

- articulation of tacit knowledge (know what we know);
- recording of knowledge (know that we know it);

- identification of sources of knowledge (know who knows what);
- organization of recorded knowledge;
- retrieval of recorded knowledge.

Articulation of tacit knowledge

Tacit knowledge must be articulated before it can be transferred. Knowledge may be articulated in conversations. When articulated but not recorded in this way, the knowledge remains tacit: it is part of the tacit knowledge of the originator, and contributes to the tacit knowledge of the recipient. To be shared more widely, the knowledge must be made explicit again in another conversation, or recorded in some form. Much knowledge management activity, including recording of knowledge in knowledge management systems, is aimed at enabling members of organizations to articulate and record information in such a way that it can be shared widely.

Recording of knowledge

A basic tenet of knowledge management is that, where possible, relevant tacit knowledge should be articulated and recorded in such a way that it can be shared readily among members of the organization. The tasks involved in knowledge management for an organization therefore include the articulation and recording of tacit knowledge so that it becomes explicit.

Recognition of the need to record organizational knowledge is far from new. Policy and procedures manuals, reports, databases, document management systems, and records management systems all record subsets of the knowledge accumulated by organizations. The format of the record is, however, changing from physical to electronic. For example, organizational intranets contain electronic records of documents formerly recorded only in print form.[24]

Identification of sources of knowledge

Sources of tacit and explicit, internal and external, knowledge must be identified if knowledge is to be transferred. Identification of sources of knowledge therefore involves both activities associated with location of published and other recorded sources of knowledge and activities associated with identification of individuals who have knowledge of value to the organization.

Librarians, records managers, and database managers have expertise in location of sources of recorded knowledge. At the time of writing, commentators on knowledge management tend to focus not so much on these well-recognized knowledge transfer activities but on new activities that aim to identify individuals from whom knowledge of value to the organization might be acquired.[12, 13]

Knowledge about tacit knowledge can itself be part of an organization's tacit knowledge base. For example, the librarians of many organizations know who in the organization is working on what projects and what information they have sought for their work. Unless the librarian's knowledge is recorded, it may remain tacit knowledge available only to those members of the organization who think to ask the librarian. Access to tacit knowledge can be aided by directories and other records of expertise.

There is, in addition, increasing recognition that both tacit and explicit knowledge can be acquired from outside the organization through formal environmental scanning and competitor analysis and from individuals' day-to-day information-gathering activities. These activities are seen by different organizations to be the role of individual members of the organization,[25] specialist competitor analysts drawn from the marketing field,[26] or librarians.[27–8]

Recorded knowledge from outside the organization is increasingly available in electronic forms. Individual members of the organization can access information distributed through the Internet (and other computer-based communication networks) if they have access to a desktop computer and any necessary accounts, and if they wish to gather information themselves. They need, however, to be able to identify appropriate sources of information, and to use those sources effectively to find the information they are seeking. While some members of the organization are comfortable using these sources themselves, others seek the assistance of intermediaries to help reduce perceived information overload. Librarians assist through training, by locating sources on behalf of the user, or through organizational activities such as establishing a specific menu or navigational framework to help individual users or groups of users structure their activities.

Organization of knowledge records for retrieval

While knowledge transfer is assisted by records of knowledge (and records of sources of knowledge), the mere recording of knowledge is insufficient for knowledge transfer. Records of knowledge must be organized in such a way that the records, and the knowledge they represent, can be retrieved and used. Two aspects of organization have become particularly important: the form in which the knowledge is recorded, and the way in which it is structured.

Information formerly distributed in print or graphical formats can now be distributed widely and inexpensively though networked information resources. Intranets are networked information resources that use Internet technology to make data, information, and the recorded knowledge of an organization available through World Wide Web browsers. We now have the potential to make all digitizable, recorded forms of organizational knowledge widely available to individual members of the organization using the same computer-based communication networks that deliver information from internal databases, external databases, and the Internet.

The issues associated with information organization for an intranet are, in many ways, similar to those associated with organization of knowledge from external sources. At first glance, they appear to differ in granularity: external knowledge is often packaged in documents which convey many ideas, while internal knowledge may be packaged in smaller chunks such as a database record, an e-mail message, or an item of correspondence, that conveys a single idea. This distinction does not stand up to close scrutiny, however, because individuals who seek to access recorded knowledge, from either internal or external sources, may seek any volume of knowledge ranging from a single idea or piece of information to the knowledge they anticipate will be conveyed in a larger document. Skills that are used by librarians to organize records of knowledge from external sources are therefore also valuable for organization of records of knowledge from internal sources.

Retrieval of knowledge

The primary purpose of these knowledge transfer activities is to enable individuals to obtain, to learn from, and to use, the knowledge available to the organization. All knowledge transfer activities are therefore directed toward enabling individuals to retrieve relevant knowledge from organizational sources. Retrieval of relevant knowledge includes both location of potential sources of knowledge and filtering of the relevant knowledge from among the potential sources. Knowledge management therefore includes use of intermediary information systems and information professionals such as librarians to assist with location and filtering of records of knowledge.

The scope of knowledge transfer

In summary, knowledge transfer requires the articulation, recording, organization, and retrieval of knowledge and/or information about knowledge. An organization's knowledge consists of the tacit knowledge of individuals and groups in the organization, and the organization's store of recorded knowledge. Existing organizational knowledge may be made available throughout the organization when the tacit knowledge of an individual or group is articulated, recorded, and organized for retrieval; and when recorded knowledge held by the organization is organized for retrieval. The organization's store of knowledge is increased when knowledge is obtained from sources external to the organization. While the individuals and groups who are to use the organization's knowledge might obtain it directly from its source, the complexity of knowledge transfer demands a systematic approach to knowledge management. A systematic approach requires expertise in articulation, recording, organization, and retrieval of knowledge. These activities, and the need to maintain and effectively use expertise in knowledge management, have become increasingly important to organizations as the potential for widespread distribution of knowledge records through computer-based communication networks becomes a reality. The next section examines the sources of knowledge transfer expertise.

Roles and responsibilities in knowledge transfer

Knowledge management involves three professional domains: the business domain, the information content domain, and the information technology infra-structure domain.[29] Members of organizations drawn from each of these domains play different roles in knowledge management. Business experts are those with expert knowledge of the business domain. Their role is knowledge creation, knowledge acquisition, and use of knowledge to achieve the organization's business goals. Information content experts include librarians, records managers, and database managers. They are concerned with acquisition, organization, and transfer of data, information, and knowledge that may be used by people in the business domain. Their primary responsibility is transfer of organizational knowledge.[18] They may acquire and transfer knowledge themselves if they are expert in the business domain, or they may act as intermediaries for others. The role of information technology experts is to provide the technical infrastructure that enables knowledge management process which meet the organization's needs. Expertise in all these domains is needed for effective knowledge transfer, as illustrated in Figure 2.3.

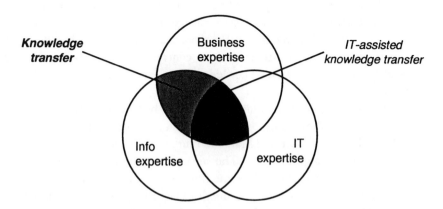

Fig. 2.3   *Three necessary domains of expertise for knowledge transfer*

While individual business experts (e.g. a research scientist or a financial analyst) also have expertise in the information content and information technology needed to acquire and share knowledge for their work, such expertise is likely to be limited to a specific aspect of the organization's business. Organizations that plan to share knowledge more widely need to pay specific attention to the information content domain, even when their business experts have subject-specific information expertise. As computer-based information systems play an important role in much modern knowledge management, organizations that plan to improve their knowledge management also need to pay specific attention to the information technology domain.

Knowledge management, information services, and librarians

Before returning to the role of experts in each of the three domains, it is worth considering in some depth the role of librarians as information content experts. Librarians have considerable skill and experience in knowledge management. They are experts in the organization and retrieval of records of knowledge. They provide an interface between the organization and knowledge developed, stored, and recorded outside the organization. Librarians have also long been recognized as having skills to contribute to management of existing organizational knowledge as participants in records management and data management processes in organizations.[30-1]

Management consultants and information systems advisers see a clear relationship between knowledge management and libraries. The Gartner Group is an information technology research company whose subscribers include the information technology managers and chief information officers of many of the world's largest business, government, and consulting organizations. In a 1996 research review, the Gartner Group predicted that organizational attention to knowledge management would bring about massive changes in the role of corporate libraries by the year 2001.[32] They predicted that there was a 70% chance that, during the five years to 2001, information resource centres (libraries) 'will be actively engaged in their organization's knowledge management or will face a slow and painful death'.

The Gartner Group predictions are supported by a study of changes in managers' attitudes to the libraries of America's largest corporations between 1990 and 1995.[33] In 1990, Prusak and Matarazzo surveyed business managers in 165 of the United States' largest firms.[34] The surveyed managers were those to whom the library manager reported. The same firms were asked to respond to a similar survey in 1995.[35] More than 10% of America's largest companies had closed their corporate libraries during the five years to 1995, and many of the firms that retained libraries had fewer library staff. Altogether, around 30% of the companies had closed or reduced the staffing of their libraries. Online database searching, the most highly valued library service in more than 70% of the organizations in 1990, was increasingly being done in the business domain rather than by librarians, and business domain-based searchers wanted to do more: when the business managers were asked what services they would like their libraries to provide in the future, more than half (53%) wanted online databases to be networked to end-users.

A dilemma for librarians

At the end of the 1990s, organizations have recognized the need for knowledge management, including systematic attention to knowledge transfer. Systematic attention to knowledge transfer requires the skills of experts in the information content domain. Librarians have such expertise, yet many libraries are closing or becoming smaller. Does this mean that there is no longer a role for librarians, or will librarians contribute to knowledge management in a different way, from outside the library's walls?

Several earlier works have proposed roles that librarians might play in an era of electronic information. A framework first proposed by Lancaster[36-7] and developed by Thompson[38] is used below to examine potential roles for librarians in new millennium organizations.

The end of libraries revisited

The situation at the end of the 1990s is remarkably close to the situation envisaged 20 years before the new millennium by both Lancaster and Thompson. They foresaw that, by the year 2000, large-scale electronic databases would have had such a profound effect on libraries that the nature of libraries would change, although the 'true tasks of librarians and libraries – the selection, the storage, the organization, and the dissemination of information – [would] remain what they have always been'.[39] As Lancaster and Thompson foresaw, we now have the technical ability to provide electronic access to material that formerly might have been limited to print, including graphics. If anything, the technical advances they foresaw have come about more quickly and have been seated more deeply into organizations and society. Databases are not just large-scale, but are also widely available through a uniform and relatively inexpensive interface from the Internet and intranets. The databases have the capability to record, not just formerly print-based formal records of knowledge, but records of individual knowledge in the form of words, pictures, sound, and video.

The effects on libraries foreseen by Lancaster and Thompson are summarized, with minor modifications to recognize the current technical environment, in Figure 2.4. The following paragraphs draw on the foregoing discussion of know-

access to electronic information for those who do not have their own physical access;

trained personnel to help users exploit electronic information resources;

a central location for high speed printing and reproduction of documents stored electronically;

collection, cataloguing, and indexing of local and special interest material;

construction of profiles of user interests to be matched against material added to databases;

free or low cost access for the community to documents and information available only for fee from electronic sources;

integration of print and electronic collections (an interim role, required only until all information sources are entirely electronic);

information services, drawing information from electronic information resources in response to users' questions;

some recreational and study material, but in a lower proportion than at present.

Fig. 2.4 *Predicted role of libraries in the year 2000 (based on Lancaster, 1978 and Thompson, 1982).*

ledge management processes, activities, and domains, and research into networked information resource use in the business domain,[40-1] to assess the extent to which the organizational roles foreseen by Lancaster and Thompson can be observed as we move close to the year 2000. (The proposed effect on access to recreational and study material, which is of little relevance in the corporate environment, has been omitted from this discussion.)

- **access to electronic information for those who do not have their own physical access**

Widespread access by individuals in organizations to desktop computers, and to the Internet, intranets, and/or other networked information resources, means that librarians in organizations will not have a significant role to play as providers of physical access to networked information resources in the new millennium.

- **trained personnel to help users exploit electronic information resources**

This role remains important, but will diminish as the information literacy of members of the business domain increases. Leading universities now offer courses in electronic information literacy as a foundation unit for undergraduates, and among information management core units for business students. As users develop skills in identifying, evaluating, and using electronic information resources, the role of librarians may be limited to the role of specialist information analysts for work teams. In this role, the librarian may either obtain specialist information on behalf of members of the team who have business expertise, or information on fields or from sources outside business experts' immediate area of expertise, or both.

- **a central location for high speed printing and reproduction of documents stored electronically**

As we approach the year 2000, this role too is diminishing. High-speed, low-cost, colour printers are becoming more prevalent. Most work groups in organizations can be expected to have ready access to a high-quality, high-speed, colour printer early in the new millennium. Where it is necessary to share printing and reproduction facilities, these facilities are likely to be found where they are found now, with other shared office facilities such as photocopiers and printers.

- **collection, cataloguing, and indexing of local and special interest material**

While the first three roles may be less significant in organizations than foreseen by Lancaster and Thompson, this role is much more significant – at least in the medium term. Organizational intranets are local electronic collections. Although the technology required to make information and documents available on an intranet is relatively straightforward, organizations are currently struggling with problems associated with how to structure intranets so that the information can be retrieved effectively without imposing information overload on users.

Librarians have information organization skills that can be used to structure information resources for the Internet, but several other organizational groups also lay claim to organization of local and special interest material. Information systems and computing groups and records managers have long dealt with internal information. Information technology professionals, in particular, are well placed politically to lead intranet developments, even though their primary expertise lies in the information technology domain. Their access to the information technology and high organizational profile makes information technology professionals the natural group for many organizations to turn to for intranet and Internet development. Moreover, information technology professionals have begun to publish formal models and frameworks specifically for structure and development of networked information resources, while library and information science professionals are lagging behind.[42] Nonetheless, information technology professionals are learning anew about the information content domain whereas librarians have a long tradition of theory, practice and service in this domain.

To some extent, the need for organization of internal knowledge may be relatively short-lived. Organizations are already discovering that they need to redesign their publication and communication processes to take advantage of the opportunities provided by intranets and knowledge management systems. The day-to-day work processes of individuals and teams that generate the data, information, or knowledge records in intranets and knowledge management systems now need to include maintenance of electronic information resources.[11, 12] Information organization and information management skills are therefore becoming essential for all individuals and work groups that generate organizational knowledge. Even if knowledge recording becomes an integral activity in the business domain, it will be necessary for organizations to develop and maintain policies and skills for recording and for information organization. Their experience with international management consulting firm Ernst and Young led two senior management consultants to propose that 'no technologies currently available can decide what information should go onto the [organization's information network], how different information bases should be structured, and what information is worth keeping around . . . Librarians are the most likely candidates for these roles, if they take up the challenge.'[43] Policy development and training will therefore remain important roles in information organization in the knowledge management era, but again there is no guarantee that these roles will be played by librarians, despite their qualifications and experience. Information technology professionals are already developing a public profile in these roles through widely cited case studies that describe their expertise.[44]

- **construction of profiles of user interests to be matched against material added to databases**

Recent developments in Internet 'push' technologies that deliver news stories and other information to the user's desktop based on a stored profile have raised user interest in profile development. The use of stored profiles is likely to be among the most common ways to interact with networked information resources in the new millennium. It will be in users' interests to develop profile construction skills. While librarians are the information domain experts in profile construction at present, this is another role that is likely to diminish as the information literacy of individual users increases in the new millennium.

- **free or low cost access for the community to documents and information available only for fee from electronic sources**

In organizational terms, this role might be interpreted as negotiation of licence agreements for access to external networked information resources. Such negotiation may be managed by a librarian, but need not necessarily be a librarian's role. Such negotiations are already managed by the individual or group responsible for negotiating other sales and supply contracts for many organizations.

- **integration of print and electronic collections (an interim role, required only until all information sources are entirely electronic)**

This role may continue for longer than Lancaster and Thompson foresaw, but integration is likely to be at the point of use – at a local, work group, level – rather than at a central or corporate level. Librarians may provide guidance on how integration may be achieved effectively. In organizations where users and information analysts have long been required to integrate information drawn from a wide range of sources, librarians may find it difficult to make inroads into this area in which business domain experts have developed information content expertise.

- **information services, drawing information from electronic information resources in response to users' questions**

This will be an important role for the information analyst, but widespread access to networked information resources means that the information analyst need not be located at a central service point such as a library.

In summary, then, the widespread availability of networked information resources and the consequent increased organizational need for information literacy among individual members of staff, provide a strong case for the end of libraries, although not for the end of librarians or organizational information and knowledge management policy.

Organizational options for management of knowledge transfer

'Knowledge management requires knowledge managers . . . to facilitate the creation, distribution, and use of knowledge by others.'[43] While the preceding sections show that librarians can contribute to these processes, they also show that members of other fields lay claim to similar expertise in knowledge transfer. Business managers are faced with the dilemma of where to obtain knowledge managers.

The domains of expertise framework shown in Figure 2.2 suggests that business managers have three primary options when they choose knowledge managers for new millennium organizations. They may employ business domain experts who also have information content domain expertise, information content domain experts who have business expertise, or information technology experts who also have business and information content domain expertise. Business experts and information content domain experts would be able to contribute effectively to knowledge management in modern organizations if they also have some expertise in the information technology domain, although such expertise can be obtained from information technology experts on an as-needed basis.

Knowledge transfer by business experts with information content expertise

Business experts with content expertise include business analysts, information analysts, and competitor analysts. While traditionally these experts were professionals such as chemists and lawyers with an interest in and aptitude for information retrieval, a wider range of organizations is now employing analysts who have a business degree with a specialization in information management or marketing. These new information analysts are employed for their range of analytical skills. Many have the skills to obtain, analyse, synthesize, and report on both quantitative and qualitative information gathered from both external and internal sources.

Several schools that teach a Master of Business Administration degree (including my own) now offer core units and electives in information management. These courses cover both the information systems and information science aspects of information management for organizations. There is a strong demand for business graduates who specialize in information management. This demand is widespread, at least in Australia and South East Asia, in business organizations of all sizes, in consultancies, and in computing service firms.

Knowledge transfer by information technology experts with business and content knowledge

A second option is to employ information technology domain experts with knowledge or expertise in the business and information content domains. Newspaper and World Wide Web advertisements for intranet and Internet development staff tend to emphasize computing or information systems background and skills, but few recognize the need for business and information content knowledge in these knowledge transfer systems.

While they do not have information content domain expertise, information systems professionals have some strengths in knowledge transfer. They often have stronger analytical skills, and a deeper understanding of information technology and of information system design and structure than librarians. Those with a business school background have greater business knowledge and a stronger business orientation than many librarians. Information systems professionals also have an aggressive public and business profile as the professionals most capable of managing information technology. This profile is supported by knowledge management consultants, many of whom are much more familiar with information systems than with the information organization and information retrieval skills of librarians. These strengths have resulted in many business managers assuming that computing and information systems professionals are also the most capable professionals to manage and analyse information resources. Despite this perception, information technology reseachers and educators believe that information and technology professionals have not yet proved to be particularly successful as managers of business information content because few have the business orientation required to successfully make the transition from the technical domain.

Knowledge transfer by information content experts with business expertise

The third option for organizations seeking expertise to guide their knowledge transfer activities is to employ information content domain experts with specialist knowledge of the organization's business, a business degree, or a broader business orientation. The librarians in many corporate information services are well placed to play such a role. Many corporate librarians have degrees in disciplines relevant to the organization's business (e.g. chemistry, law, geology) as well as qualifications in librarianship. While these librarians tend to see their careers in the information content domain, other librarians move from the content domain to the business domain.

Research teams in universities and other organizations with strong research and development arms have included information specialists for many years. Neway reviewed the history of information content experts as team members, and provided several case examples of information specialists working in research teams in a range of countries and research organizations during the 1970s and early 1980s.[45]

In the US, Europe, and Australasia, people trained as librarians are now working as integral members of work groups and teams in marketing, research and development, and consulting. In large US companies that continue to maintain a central library, these people may still be organizationally tied to the library and library career structures. Elsewhere, however, and particularly in smaller organizations that do not have the resources for a formal, corporate library or information service, organizations are appointing information analysts to positions where their work orientation and career structure is that of the group within which they work (e.g. [34]). Several small and medium enterprises in Western Australia have appointed information analysts who report to the chief executive officer, and who are seen by their managers as potential general managers rather than as career information specialists. This trend is not limited to business organizations. Leading academic libraries are also diversifying their services, with librarians working with teaching and research faculty.[46]

Implications

Attention from management theorists, consultants and information technology companies has raised the profile of knowledge management activities in organizations. New millennium organizations will pay close attention to systematic management of the acquisition, transfer, and use of knowledge from internal and external sources. Librarians have particular knowledge and expertise in knowledge transfer. There is, however, little evidence that librarians are well placed to take advantage of this opportunity to contribute to organizational success; instead, graduates of business schools – particularly those with an information systems background – are politically well placed to play significant knowledge management roles in the new millennium. At the same time, organizations remain in danger of focusing on technology rather than knowledge by hiring information managers and knowledge managers drawn from information technology fields rather than information content or business domains. The implications of these developments and trends will be felt by organizations, their managers, and the information professions. This section focuses on the implications for business managers, for librarians and library managers, and for the profession of librarianship and educators in the field of library and information science.

Implications for business managers

Knowledge management, although driven by management theorists and consultants, is a response to very real changes in the global economy and in organizations that are responding to those changes. Attention to organizational learning and knowledge management during the late 1990s will result in changes to the way work is done, and to the roles of librarians and other members of organizations who have traditionally been concerned with knowledge management. Managers who adopt the concepts of knowledge management need to make several practical decisions – the why, what, who, when, where, and how of knowledge management.

Effective knowledge management will require attention to three domains: the business domain in which knowledge is ultimately interpreted, evaluated, and used; the information content domain in which experts in transfer of knowledge from existing sources can act as intermediaries between large and diverse records of knowledge and the business experts who will use the knowledge itself; and the information technology domain in which information technology experts provide the infrastructure to support knowledge transfer. All three domains contribute to development and maintenance of organizational knowledge management systems, intranets and Internet sites, and to other knowledge transfer activities.

Managers should beware of emphasizing technology expertise to the detriment of information content and business expertise. Librarians have valuable knowledge and skills in knowledge transfer. An organization does not need a library to employ a librarian to develop policy, to train members of the organization in knowledge transfer practices and in information literacy, or to work as an information analyst or information content expert in a work group or team. Nonetheless, librarians cannot lay sole claim to information content expertise in knowledge management. A wise business manager will examine the knowledge and skills of individual librarians, information technology professionals, business-trained information analysts, and other information professionals to identify those individuals with the most appropriate knowledge and skills to contribute to knowledge management in his or her organization.

Implications for librarians

In the new millennium, librarians should expect to work among users of knowledge and information rather than in libraries. As the number of librarians employed within libraries declines, librarians have both the need and the opportunity to contribute to organizations in roles outside library walls. To take advantage of these opportunities, librarians should market their skills in knowledge transfer, in policy making, information organization and information analysis.

Librarians may also need to use a different language to promote their skills. They will need to be able to discuss knowledge management and knowledge transfer in the language used by business managers. For example, the concepts of library and information resource users, intermediaries and providers might be replaced by the concept of a team of organizational members who share activities in organizational knowledge transfer and use and who take different roles (knowledge user, intermediary, or provider) depending on the activities that they perform at any given time.

While librarians have the professional knowledge and skills to continue to play an important role in the interface between recorded knowledge and individual and organizational knowledge, few are well placed – geographically, or politically – to make this contribution to organizations. The continued success of librarians in organizational roles depends on their ability to adapt to the need to support individuals and work groups at the point of use, to become integral members of work teams, and to put a persuasive case to management for the role of information content domain experts in both day-to-day practice and policy making for knowledge management. If they are to compete successfully with members of other professions who are developing knowledge management skills, librarians will need to develop knowledge and skills in areas that business managers perceive to be librarians' weaknesses. For individual librarians, these areas might include business knowledge, business orientation, analytical skills, and an understanding of information technology and information systems.

Implications for library managers

The primary roles of library managers in new millennium organizations will be in policy making, and potentially also in training and staff selection. The term 'library manager' will therefore be a misnomer. Librarians who now aspire to be library managers might aspire to be chief knowledge officers or chief information officers in the new millennium.[22] As organizational structures change, these information content experts might act both as senior business managers and as senior information professionals. They are likely therefore to be drawn from among those librarians who have developed business knowledge and business orientation in addition to information content expertise.

Implications for the profession of librarianship

A comparison of the observations made in this chapter with the review of information science theory published in Olaisen, Munch-Petersen, and Wilson[47] suggests that the roles to be played in the new millennium are those of the broader field of information science rather than those of librarianship. Several factors underline the value of moving the focus from librarianship to information science: the reduced role of libraries, the organizational recognition of the need for experts in information and knowledge management regardless of the original form and source of the knowledge of interest, and the low political power of librarians compared with other information professionals.

It may be time to proclaim information science, rather than librarianship, the theoretical foundation of the information content domain in knowledge transfer. Business managers seeking information content experts may more easily be persuaded that an information scientist, whose professional focus is information use and knowledge transfer, is a more valuable member of a learning organization than a librarian, whose professional focus is perceived (albeit not necessarily correctly) to be management of a central physical repository and location of external records of knowledge.

Regardless of the proclaimed professional and theoretical background of information professionals who play knowledge management roles in new millennium organizations, the need for information professionals to work as integral members of business teams has implications for education. Information content professionals, whether described as librarians or information scientists, will need to develop skills in areas of relative weakness if they (and the organizations in which they work) are to take advantage of their information content expertise in the new millennium. Graduates with business knowledge and business orientation, and skills in both information resource management and information technology management, will be highly valued in the new information environment.

Conclusions

The prominence of knowledge management at the end of the 1990s provides a new opportunity for librarians to contribute to the organizations they serve. It also carries with it a serious threat for librarians: the threat that other, better placed, members of organizations will extend their roles to incorporate those that have been played by librarians in the past. The current focus on knowledge management may prove to be the event that defines the nature of corporate librarianship as we move into the new millennium. Whether or not knowledge management is a 'management fad', it is symptomatic of a massive change in management thinking. It reflects a real change in the emphasis of organizations from industrial production to service provision, and it is backed by the organizational power of international management consultants and widely read management theorists who write in influential management journals and magazines.

The new management thinking provides business managers with opportunities to develop flexible organizations that are able to respond quickly to changes in the environment. These opportunities can be taken only if business managers are able to leverage organizational knowledge effectively. While the current focus is on the role of information technology in knowledge management, organizations run the risks of repeating their earlier mistakes of relying on technology to fix information problems. Business managers who employ *information* specialists will, on the other hand, be well placed to operate effectively in the new information environment.

Librarians can take advantage of the opportunity provided by knowledge management by promoting themselves as knowledge managers and information analysts, unbounded by library walls. By positioning themselves as members of business teams with specialist knowledge and information handling skills, they will be well placed to play key organizational roles in the 21st century.

Acknowledgments

Many of the ideas advanced in this paper have been clarified in discussions with colleagues, students, and past students in the Faculty of Economics and Commerce at the University of Western Australia. I thank you all for sharing your knowledge, from which I continue to learn.

References

1   Drucker, P. F., 'The coming of the new organization', *Harvard business review*, January–February, 1988, **66**, 45–53.
2   Grindley, K., 'Price Urwick / *The Australian* computer opinion survey', *The Australian*, 1 April, 1997, 27, 31.
3   Nohria, N. and Eccles, R. (eds.), *Networks and organizations: structure, form, and*

action, Boston, MA, Harvard Business School Press, 1992.

4   Primozic, K., Primozic, E. and Leben, J., *Strategic choices: supremacy, survival, or sayanara*, New York, McGraw-Hill, 1991.

5   Stewart, T. A., *Intellectual capital: the new wealth of nations*, New York, Doubleday, 1997. Excerpts available on the Internet at <http://members.aol.com/thosstew/>.

6   Garvin, A. P., Berkman, R. and Bermont, H., *The art of being well informed*, Garden City Park, NY, Avery Publishing Group, 1993.

7   Senge, P. *The fifth discipline: the art and practice of the learning organization*, New York, Doubleday, 1990.

8   Davis, S. and Botkin, J., 'The coming of knowledge-based business', *Harvard business review*, **72** (5), Sept/Oct, 1994, 165–70.

9   Bullen, C. V. and Bennett, J. L., 'Groupware in practice: an interpretation of work experiences', *Computerization and controversy: value conflicts and social choices*, ed. by C. Dunlop and R. Kling, Boston, MA, Academic Press, 1991, 257–87.

10 Cronin, M. J. (ed.), *The Internet strategy handbook*, Boston, MA, Harvard Business School Press, 1996.

11 Klobas, J. E., 'Information infrastructure: organizational capability for online information provision', *Online Information 96, 3–5 December, London*, Oxford, UK, Learned Information, 1996, 73–84.

12 Davenport, T., 'Some principles of knowledge management', *Strategy and business*, **2**, Winter 1996, 34–40.

13 Prusak, L., 'Money talks but information speaks loudest', presentation to *knowledge management equals success for big and small organisations*, Australian Library Week seminar organized by the New South Wales Branch of the Australian Library and Information Association, ABC Ultimo Centre, Sydney, Australia, 8 May 1996.

14 Microsoft Corporation, *knowledge base*, <http://www.microsoft.com/kb>.

15 See WWW sites accessible from <http://www.lotus.com/discussions>.

16 National Aeronautics and Space Administration, *lessons learned home page*, <http://envnet.gsfc.nasa.gov/ll/llhomepage.html>, and links from this page, especially: United States, Department of Energy *Department of Energy lessons learned*, <http://www.tis.eh.doe.gov/others/ll/ll.html>.

17 Best, D. P., 'Business process and information management', *The fourth resource: information and its management*, ed. by D. P. Best, Hampshire, England, Aslib/Gower, 1996.

18 Davenport, T. H. and Prusak, L., 'Blow up the corporate library', *International journal of information management*, **13**, 1993, 405–12.

19 *Ibid.*, 407.

20 Nonaka, I. and Takeuichi, H., *The knowledge-creating company*, New York, Oxford University Press, 1995.

21 Polanyi, M., *The tacit dimension*, London, Routledge & Kegan Paul, 1966.

22 Davenport, T. H., 'Saving IT's soul: human-centred information management', *Harvard business review*, **72** (2), Mar–Apr, 1994, 119–31.

23 Constant, D., Kiesler, S. and Sproull, L., 'What's mine is ours, or is it? A study of attitudes about information sharing', *Information systems research*, **5** (4), 1994, 400–21.

24 Cortese, A., 'Here comes the Intranet', *Business week*, 26 Feb,1996, 46–54. Also available on the Internet at
<**http://www.businessweek.com/1996/09/b34641.htm**>.

25 Garvin, D. A., 'Building a learning organization', *Harvard business review*, **71** (4), July–August, 1993, 79.

26 Stanat, R., *The intelligent corporation*, New York, AMACOM, American Management Association, 1990.

27 Choo, C. W., *Information management for the intelligent organization: the art of scanning the environment*, Medford, NJ, Information Today, 1995.

28 Walker, T. D. (ed.), 'The library in corporate intelligence activities', *Library trends*, **43** (2), special issue.

29 The concept of three designs proposed here draws heavily on the ideas proposed in: Choo, C. W., 'The intelligent organization: mobilizing organizational knowledge through information partnerships',
<**http://128.100.159.139/FIS/ResPub/IMIOart.html**>, not dated, accessed 1997.

30 Debons, A., King, D. W., Mansfield, U. and Shirley, D. L., *The information professional: survey of an emerging field*, New York, Dekker, 1981.

31 Klobas, J. E., 'The application of the librarian's skills to information handling', in J. Henri and R. Saunders (eds.), *The information professional: proceedings of a conference, Melbourne, Australia, 26–8 November 1984*, Centre for Library Studies, Murray-Riverina Institute of Higher Education, 1985, 170–7.

32 Stear, E. and Wecksell, J., 'The information resource center in 2001', *Monthly research review*, MRR-1096-32, The Gartner Group, 1 October, 1996.

33 Matarazzo, J., 'Money talks but information speaks loudest', presentation to *Knowledge management equals success for big and small organisations*, Australian Library Week seminar organized by the New South Wales Branch of the Australian Library and Information Association, ABC Ultimo Centre, Sydney, Australia, 8 May 1996.

34 Prusak, L., Matarazzo, J. M. and Gauthier, M., *Values of corporate libraries: a survey of senior managers*, Washington, DC, Special Libraries Association, 1990.

35 Matarazzo, J. M. and Prusak, L., 'Valuing corporate libraries: a senior man-

agement survey', *Special libraries*, **81** (2), 1996, 102–10.

36   Lancaster, F. W., *Towards paperless information systems*, New York, Academic Press, 1978.

37   Lancaster, F. W. (ed.), *The role of the library in the electronic society: proceedings of the 1979 Clinic on Library Applications of Data Processing*, Urbana-Champaign, University of Illinois Graduate School of Library Science, 1980.

38   Thompson, J., *The end of libraries*, London, Clive Bingley, 1982.

39   Thompson, *ibid.*, p. 118.

40   Klobas, J. E., 'Networked information resources: electronic opportunities for users and librarians', *Information technology and people*, **7** (3), 1994, 4–17. Also published as Klobas, J. E., 'Networked information resources: electronic opportunities for users and librarians', *Internet research: electronic networking applications and policy*, **6** (4), 1996, 53–62.

41   Lamb, R., 'Informational imperatives and socially mediated relationships', *The information society*, **12** (1), 1996, 17–37.

42   Bieber, M. and Isakowitz, T. (eds.), 'Designing hypermedia applications', *Communications of the ACM*, **38** (8), 1995, special issue.

43   Davenport and Prusak, *op. cit.*, 409.

44   Davenport and Prusak, *ibid.*, refer in particular to: Orlikowski, W., 'Learning from Notes: organizational issues in groupware implementation', *The information society*, **9**, 1993, 237–50.

45   Neway, J., *Information specialist as team player in the research process*. Westport, CN: Greenwood Press, 1985.

46   Newton-Smith, C. and White, S., 'A librarian without a library: the role of the librarian in an electronic age', In *Synergy in Sydney: the sixth Asian Pacific specials, health and law librarians conference and exhibition, 27–30 August 1995; Sydney*, Sydney, Australia, Special Libraries Section, ALIA, 1995.

47   Olaisen, J., Munch-Petersen, E. and Wilson, P. (eds.), *Information science: from the development of the discipline to social interaction*, Oslo, Scandinavian University Press, 1996.

3

THE INFINITE LIBRARY: PUTTING STRATEGIC POLICY INTO PRACTICE

Natalia Grygierczyk

UNIVERSITY OF UTRECHT, THE NETHERLANDS

Introduction

Is there a method for setting up a comprehensive scientific digital library at the end of the 20th century? Is there a method that offers a realistic prospect of bearing fruit long into the next century? Is there policy that can help generate such a method? And if so, what should this policy be based on? Can our experience with practical situations lead to conclusions or even to the formulation of useful guidelines?

This chapter is about finding answers to these questions by describing the Utrecht Electronic Library Project. Basically, it is not a single project. As a matter of fact, it consists of some 40 subsidiary projects which are all systematically coherent and interdependent. These subsidiary projects all focus on the establishment of a scientific electronic library for the students and staff of Utrecht University. The project as whole has a budget of Dfl 2,100,000 (approx. £700,000) and a duration of three years. With a project staff of about 60 people and a target group of more than 25,000 students and 3000 academic staff, it is one of the most extensive of its kind in The Netherlands. The reader will find a description of the strategic policy at the foundation of the digital library's construction, a series of practical cases plus the lessons learned from them and, finally, an overview of general implications for library managers or managers of similar projects.

> Finally a free, calm day opens before you; you go to the library, consult the catalogue; you can hardly repress a cry of rejoicing, or, rather, ten cries; all the authors and the titles you are looking for appear in the catalogue, duly recorded. You compile a first request form and hand it in; you are told that there must be an error of numbering in the catalogue; the book cannot be found; in any case, they will investigate. You immediately request another; they tell you it is out on loan, but they are unable to determine who took it out and when. The third you ask for is at the

bindery; it will be back in a month. The fourth is kept in a wing of the library now closed for repairs. You keep filling out forms; for one reason or another, none of the books you ask for is available.[1]

The events in Chapter 11 of Italo Calvino's *If on a winter's night a traveler* are not, of course, the fault of careless library staff, nor are they caused by an incomplete classification system. They are the intricate forgings of a criminal organization secretly dispersing plagiarisms, cribs and mutilated imitations of original works. However, although these fabrications belong to the realm of literary fiction, they seem acutely familiar.

Let us make a mental voyage into the year 2050. Optical-fibre cables and quantum-leap processors constitute the structure of The Global Library, a repository comprising a colossal digital collection amounting to the volume of at least 25,000,000 complete Britannicas. The Global Library literally encompasses the entire world and has no main entrance. At any given moment it provides any person with unimpeded access to its contents. Wherever you are, whatever you wish to read in whatever language, it is all available to you. The long-awaited, just-finished Talio Loncilva novel; the spectacular outcome of inquiries into the internal properties of thunderstorm cloud systems, revealing measurements for which sophisticated methods were deployed on four different continents; the latest results on the treatment of the hard-metal syndrome, a disease which particularly claims victims between the ages of 70 and 80; your own correspondence with colleague scientists on the relationship between black-hole evaporation and the possible existence of a wormhole in Galaxy 998WS45. All this is available, it is at your fingertips, accessible within a blink of an eye. Without having to browse through dreary catalogues, without being afraid of missing crucial information because of an erroneous code, a wrong signature, because of not properly entered data or of not knowing the author's name. The disheartening 'out on loan' has become a thing of the past, a phrase in a dictionary.

A sceptical observer, to whom all this may sound a bit like inflated propaganda once again depicting some Utopian vision, may want us to harken to the admonitions of those contesting the digital library. In an almost Old-Testament-like fashion the bibliophile opposition are warning us of an unmitigated menace. Our heritage, they say, is in danger of becoming brittle and vulnerable. It is no longer durably documented. It is no longer permanent, no longer safe within the boundaries of a static two-dimensional space warranted by the long-established white paper leaf. In digital form our heritage will become volatile, virtual, ephemeral. Merely a current of electrons and magnetic polarizations that may suddenly change direction. By adding a fourth dimension, that of time – they warn – we may involuntarily induce the possibility of changing the content of texts at any given moment, abolishing the original as such.

> You start to explain to him the reason for your visit. He understands at once, and doesn't even let you continue: 'You, too! The mixed-up signatures, we know all about it, the books that begin and don't continue, the entire recent production of the firm is in turmoil, you've no idea. We can't make head or tail of it any more, my dear sir.' In his arms he has a pile of galleys; he sets them down gently, as if the slightest jolt could upset the order of the printed letters. 'A publishing house is a fragile organism, dear sir,' he says. 'If at any point something goes askew, then the disorder spreads, chaos opens beneath our feet. Forgive me, won't you? When I think about it I have an attack of vertigo.' And he covers his eyes, as if pursued by the sight of billions of pages, lines, words, whirling in a dust storm.[2]

Owing to current technological developments the images Italo Calvino left us in 1979 have since become a metaphor for the fate of our digital collection. Still there are more analogies. For example, the one depicting an ever expanding chaotic universe of increasing non-catalogued information, where only chance can help you find what you are looking for. Or the one describing the philistine rage of toppling all the bookcases in all the libraries.

Recent trends concerning the future of our libraries have been observed with awe and discomfort. Not surprisingly, since the formula of preserving and cataloguing information in the secure conventional way has proved to work remarkably well since the age of Alexandria, whereas in the new digital libraries the staff are desperately struggling to initiate procedures bearing an awkward resemblance to the conventional methods. They are feverishly engaged in cataloguing electronic information sources on the Internet using strict numeric codes, each of which refers to a different field. Electronic documents are being copied and saved in special servers managed and administrated by the staff themselves. In order to control the rampant disorder they adapt methods that have hitherto never failed in the traditional library. And simultaneously they are building firewalls, typical IT safeguards, around their universities. We mention these objections related to the real or imaginary drawbacks of recent technological developments as a counterbalance, as arguments for the sake of objectivity. But we choose not to go into them here.

In the next section we wish to make a plea for the potential of various new means and channels of information distribution in the era of the ubiquitous Internet. We are making an effort to depict the present and future perspectives advantageous to science from the viewpoint of the university library. Furthermore, we want to describe the outline of an approach that has been tested in practice, a project that has been designed to yield successful results by using existing technologies. First the strategic policy is described. Attention is drawn to the method of formulating a policy which is based on problems and wishes as expressed by our users. There follows a summary of our starting points with respect to the construction and expansion of the digital collection as well as to its accessibility via an information retrieval system.

The strategic framework: the method

> Reader, we are not sufficiently acquainted for me to know whether you move with indifferent assurance in university or whether old traumas or pondered choices make a universe of pupils and teachers seem a nightmare to your sensitive and sensible soul.[3]

What does the scientist need to do in order to write a paper, an article, a series of lectures? What sources does she seek to find and read? How does she acquire her books and is she interested only in books or in other information sources as well? Does she occasionally consult the catalogue? Does she ever surf the Internet? Does she come across any information while looking for files containing bibliographic references? No, she does not, or only rarely. Why – may we venture to ask?

Well, simply because she does not have the time for a laborious study of all these complicated systems. She does not grasp the enigmatic codes on her computer screen. Surely you do not expect her to waste precious time when she has an article to finish.

But then, does she use any dictionaries? Does she look up the sources referred to in the article and, if so, does she read them? No, again she does not. She merely copies fragments out of books and periodicals. OK, how many? And could she perhaps tell us how she usually employs these snippets in her article?

This scientist is one of many to whom we pose these questions. And let us not forget our students. We need to know the same from them. Their answers provide a fairly good impression, a basis for making a generalization on common procedures of scientific research and, of course, on the process of teaching and learning. It is our objective to trace the bottlenecks obstructing them in the act of finding and using information. Information needed for scientific and tutorial activities.

We believe that the starting point in the design of a digital library should always be a well-conceived user survey to reveal the existing problems of information supply. At the same time, these problems need to be related to the process of scientific research and education. (For an extensive methodology based on users' activities see also Devadason and Lingam.[4]) This survey is essential, since it is the primary task of the library to support students and staff in these matters. Moreover, a carefully conducted analysis will also result in a list of priorities. This analysis should involve several other aspects, for instance the present state of technology, emerging standards and trends, and bench-marking (i.e. well-tested examples elsewhere). Only then is defining a strategic framework for a comprehensive project of digital information supply justified.

A similar method was employed at Utrecht University in order to formulate a policy that would subsequently serve as the project's framework. This approach appeared to have a number of advantages. The policy from which several subsidiary projects were to be derived later would not take the shape of a basic idea only to be put into words and consequently concealed in an administrative memorandum. On the contrary, this policy was to be made operational in a series of subsidiary projects. It was clear from the outset that each project should have its *raison d'être* in the requirements expressed by its future users. In addition we aimed to avoid devising methods and applications that had already been successfully realized elsewhere. And finally, though quite importantly, the projects' coherence would facilitate and provide for the exchange of results.

So what is the strategy formulated in this manner like? Is it feasible considering the current state of technology, or is it not perhaps a bit meretricious? In short, is it realistic? This strategy is explained in the following section, with the focus on the two most significant components of the digital library: the collections and the retrieval of information.

The strategic framework: the collections

> He then returned to his carrel for his own research. He contemplated writing a Petite Histoire of Russian Culture, in which a choice of Russian Curiosities, Customs, Literary Anecdotes, and so forth would be presented in such a way as to reflect in miniature la Grande Histoire – Major Concatenations of Events. He was still at the blissful stage of collecting his material.[5]

The material is already available. Currently there are innumerable digitized articles cross-referencing to each other. You do not need prepare yourself for a bibliographic quest in order to find their references. You can just scroll them up and down on your screen. In addition to texts, you are also able to consult still and moving images, sound and music, you can explore the different means of communication in non-western cultures which have the same important function as language. You have access to dozens of databases crammed like cocoons fostering preprints that will not appear as articles in paper magazines until one or two years from now. Throughout the global network vast amounts of data on measurements are entered at different places all over the world from where they are sent to a central database to be collected and analysed in their totality.

Digital collections have existed for a number of years now, and the prospect is that in 50 years they will be fairly complete. But for now we have to be content with the fragments and pieces of a future aggregate. For example, several publishers issue digitized journals, though they fail to cover the entire field. There is

a growing number of universities that have decided to launch electronic magazines themselves. In this case, too, we are dealing with a more or less at random
group of authors. As employees they belong to the university only in an administrative sense, whereas as scientists they are *part* of a discipline. Several projects
have been launched for the digitization of manuscripts, incunabula and books,
but they comprise only a fraction of our total cultural legacy. Needless to say the
creation of a digital collection is still at a germinal stage; the collection's imperfection lies mainly in its incompleteness. The function of the – scientific –
libraries as nurseries cannot be underestimated in this phase. It is their duty to
take care of the collections related to the university's disciplines in order to make
these collections as accessible as possible to scholars and students.

Ideally, a continuous concern of a library is to build and preserve a complete
and first-rate collection which is in complete accordance with the requirements
of departments and institutes. So far there are no discrepancies with traditional
library functions. The difference becomes obvious – we are still in a period of
transition – firstly, in the manner in which these tasks are to be executed and secondly, in the costs accompanying the process.

To start with the latter. Over the past years these costs have nearly doubled.
For instance, libraries order subscriptions for both paper and electronic versions
of magazines. Currently, most publishers are not inclined to provide free electronic versions to libraries who already subscribe to paper versions. Even worse,
the extra cost sometimes amounts to 50% of the original subscription price. (A
rather curious circumstance considering the fact that electronic versions normally
consist of pure data, i.e. no layout, retrieval software or data management by the
publisher. Basically this medium requires less effort from the publisher than
paper magazines. Scientific publishers apparently regard 'electronic data dump'
as an extra revenue source.) Additional costs are incurred for maintenance and
storage of electronic information and for training of library staff to handle the
material. Meanwhile the traditional library process must continue as well.

As for the manner of performing tasks and services, the traditional selection
criteria also apply to the gathering of electronic material, for instance via the
Internet. But the specific methods of searching and selecting need to be adapted
and modified. New skills and infrastructural facilities are indispensable in this
respect. Nevertheless, the actual complication only rears its head after this stage;
while substantiating the availability of the electronic sources and securing the
continuous, durable quality of information collected.

In a nutshell, these are some examples of problems that complicate the
process of electronic collecting: the incompleteness of digital collections, the
extra costs, and the new demands on the library and its staff. Accordingly the
strategic policy of the Utrecht University Library, partly sparked off by these

problems, mainly focuses on the following aspects:

- Electronic publishing
- Digitizing the collection
- Expanding the collection via the Internet
- The integration of physical and electronic collections.

Electronic publishing

Let us go back to the year 1673, in the boiling month of July. Mr Newton has just received the latest issue of *Philosophical transactions*. He avidly turns the pages – 'Ah, an article by my much-esteemed colleagues Huygens, Halley and Leibniz. But I shall read them later. First I need . . .' – looking for responses to his article about his new theory on light and colours published last month. And yes, finally his eyes fall on a list of questions and comments made by his colleagues. There is even an article by his highly respected French colleague N., who aims to draw Mr Newton's attention to a possible error. 'Nay,' mutters the physicist. He reaches for the inkwell, sharpens his goose-feather quill and commences writing a reply – which is published in the same journal a month later: 'If therefore N. would conclude any Thing, he must shew how white may be produced out of two uncompounded Colours: which when he hath done, I will further tell him, why he can conclude nothing from that.'[6]

The scientific magazine evolved in the 17th century from the growing need for a swifter exchange of ideas. Scientists wanted a prompter and broader access to research results. Pray, what has become of the position and the role of the scientific magazine at end of the 20th century? First we should perhaps have a quick glance at the financial aspect of scientific publishing. How much do universities pay for their scientific journals? In other words, looking at it on a global scale, how much do they pay for the publications written by their own staff? To begin with, they spend money on salaries, on fees for reviewers and authors. They pay the purchase price of the article in the form of the journal subscription price. Plus the extra fees for reproduction and loan (at least in The Netherlands), usually a percentage of the subscription price. But that is not all: many publishers charge their authors for a publication in a prestigious journal, and, of course, there are also charges for preprints or offprints. In short, the universities not only reimburse the publishers for the costs of their publishing activities (compiling, graphic design and distribution), they are also charged for the contents they have paid for themselves.

Certainly, this is a simplification. The actual matter is somewhat more complex. Naturally the extra value added by publishers also lies in the solid scientific reputation many journals have built up over a long period of time. Still another case is the copyright. This right is not deposited with the universities but with the authors, who commonly are quite willing to transfer them to the publisher without any further demands. Nonetheless, this arrangement remains a rather peculiar circumstance, a situation that, due to rising prices and monopolizing will eventually become unaffordable.

It becomes even more peculiar if one calls into mind the initial need for faster interchange of information and for a more expeditious availability of research results, the basic idea from which scientific magazines originated 350 years ago. In many instances it takes one to one and half years before an article submitted to a journal is published. This is one of the reasons, besides improved technology, why universities are growing more and more interested in arranging so-called preprint servers. These servers contain among others recently written articles and papers awaiting publication in a scientific journal. Its eventual publication may then be considered as a final proof of quality.

Unfortunately, certain publishers respond rather harshly to the electronic distribution of preprints by simply prohibiting it by observing stricter copyright rules. One of the conditions for publication is the transfer to the publisher of all rights pertaining to distribution, including electronic diffusion. In this way publishers obstruct the interchange of ideas among scientists, basically denying the *raison d'être* of the journal itself. In the end it will even become absurd to prolong the publication of the journal. The periodical will altogether lack any ground for continuation.[7]

In spite of fierce attempts by publishers to discourage efforts to initiate electronic publishing, there is enough reason to experiment at least with the possibilities. In comparison to the complications related to tactile paper, this kind of publishing has become much easier over the past years. Peer reviewing, for instance does not need to take place prior to publication, requiring assiduous organizing and always causing considerable delay. Instead the review could be done afterwards, for instance, by introducing a procedure of electronic quality assessment by colleagues.[8]

Of course, these endeavours do not, at least in the short term, attempt to resolve the problem of the fragmented availability of electronic collections or the extremely high charges linked to them. In the longer term it is quite conceivable that the unbalanced relationship between scientists employed by the university and their commercially orientated publishers will change. Thus the completion of the collection would no longer be hampered by the high rates now charged for the diffusion of scientific output. We might even dare to look forward to the swift communication so common in the 17th century.

Digitizing the collection

In some respect universities are museums. They cherish invaluable manuscripts, precious old prints and magnificent archives lovingly collected by professors. Sometimes they even arrange exhibitions, putting on display priceless objects that are usually preserved in deep vaults and safes where daylight is not allowed to penetrate. The Utrecht University Library, for example, possesses the famous Utrecht Psalter, one of the oldest and most beautiful psalters in the world, originating from the 10th century AD. It may not come as a surprise to know that this remarkable manuscript has already been digitized on CD-ROM.[9]

The advantages of a digitized old collection are obvious – no limitations as to availability or loan periods, and no restrictions with respect to opening hours or physical conditions of the reading room (depending on the kind of keeper, visits may be quite nerve-wracking). Add to this the blessing of an improved method of preserving our cultural heritage plus the benefits of sophisticated retrieval methods, and one does not need to be persuaded anymore. At the same time, the digitization of any item, whatever its volume, contributes to the completion of the total global collection.

In our projects on digitization we follow three points of departure:

- A mere electronic version of the paper form by means of a scanner is not adequate. In order to fully exploit the added value of the medium the material must undergo a qualitative enrichment by the appending of cross-references to related and explanatory sources. This is to be done by establishing hyperlinks (for instance to dictionaries and encyclopedic information) and by adding advanced – not simply linear – retrieval methods. This is one of the minimal requirements a digital collection should meet.
- The selection of material to be digitized should occur on the basis of clearly formulated conditions. The most important criteria are a clear correlation with education and research at Utrecht University and the cultural significance of the material.
- The digitization of the library's own collection should amount to the digitization of the entire library service. The process should not be limited to the mere digitization of information sources. Even in a very modest case, involving only a small part of the collection, the entire library service should be 'digitized', for the adaptation of the library structure and organization round this source is crucial to the availability of electronic information. (Consider, for example, the difference in maintaining an electronic information source as opposed to a book or paper magazine, or the battle against computer viruses versus moulds devouring paper books.) Less obvious, but something that should not be forgotten, is the implication that library staff functions will be redefined: staff will be required to acquire new skills.

Expanding the collection via the Internet

Of course, we should not shy away from using the Internet, especially considering the scientific information it puts at our disposal. Not only is that information available in abundance, it is often the most up-to-date, highly useful and of impeccable quality. Nevertheless, there are some drawbacks. The information may be highly volatile; it could disappear without warning; it has not officially been certified, unlike articles that have gone the paper way after passing the stage of scrupulous and time-consuming peer reviews. This last has, in fact, proved to be a most useful point of departure for traditional methods of collecting. Owing to their procedures involving painstaking peer reviews some publishers may boast of an outstanding reputation built up through the course of many years. It is precisely this circumstance that has been beneficial to universities and publishers alike.

Why should this basis be different in the four dimensions of cyberspace? Currently, there are a number of very reliable servers. In this respect, Ginsparg's preprint databases in high-energy physics are among the most quoted examples. As such they form a strong argument against all sceptics – of which there are quite a few to be found at the library – who hesitate to trust any other method than the conventional one. Gingsparg's success will persuade and inspire other initiatives, so we can expect the number of similar reputable servers to multiply before long.

The second starting point, the safeguarding of the durable quality of digital collections, is related to the first. Some complications will be resolved spontaneously, especially that of volatility. This will happen in much the same way as the problems concerning the selection of high-quality information are resolved. Respectable servers will be careful to maintain their reliability. In this constellation the library plays an important part, too. It should aim at solid agreements for document and data management at selected servers, even if this implies fees or licensing.

The integration of physical and electronic collections

Suppose you were a physicist sitting at your desk. You would like to have a look at the latest research reports on magic numbers in helium clusters. So you switch on your computer and put your question to a database. It provides you with a list of articles in the *Chemical physics letter* and several book titles. You read the abstracts on your computer screen. One of them seems to be very noteworthy and you turn to the full-text version. A bit later you have another glance at the titles. Another treatise sparks your interest; it is on classical rare-gas clusters. Unfortunately, the treatise is not available in an electronic form. So you divert to the library's catalogue. The book appears to be in your own library's collection. The only thing you have to do now is to order it on-line. Within an hour the book will be right on your desk.

In many libraries this is, of course, still a fantasy, though perhaps not for long. This example illustrates the premise that electronic and paper collections must be integrated complementarily. It is therefore quite crucial to think of the digital library not as an isolated, virtual building. It should not be regarded as an entity unrelated to the traditional physical collection, since this collection has been gathered, administrated and disclosed for hundreds, sometimes thousands of years, thus holding the vast reservoir of our knowledge.

This integration implies the interconnection between primary and secondary information, between full-text files or multimedia electronic files and bibliographic sources referring to actual books and magazines and their physical location. The user will profit from this principle because it is now possible to look for information about a certain subject without having to indicate a specific source or collection in advance.

The strategic framework: information retrieval systems

> The universe (which others call the Library) consists of an undetermined, and perhaps infinite number of hexagonal cells, in the centre of which are large ventilation shafts fenced by low balustrades. Each hexagon provides a view of higher and lower storeys, infinitely.[10]

How many years would a scientist need to travel, how many libraries would he need to visit, before he had collected all the information available on a certain topic? And still, after all this time he must start his quest afresh, because in the years elapsed thousands and thousands of new books would have appeared.

Jorge Luis Borges' library is almost perfect, except in one dimension. Its spatial infinity is at the same time it greatest insuperability. The electronic library surmounts this problem by conquering space in a different way. Being able to search through the accumulated physical and digital collection and retrieve the required information at the speed of light is probably the most remarkable asset of a library integrated into a network. Basically it should be feasible to browse through all the material available in cyberspace – a downright impossibility in physical reality. To this end, all libraries must be integrated into one global network. Their collections must be complete and their documents need to be extensively cross-indexed. The final requirement then would be an information retrieval system.

Oddly enough, the greatest asset of digital information supply – the power to gather all relevant data within seconds – is also the biggest imperfection of all current information retrieval systems. After accepting our search question the most popular types of so-called search engines pretend to browse every corner of the world and then present us with thousands and thousands of 'relevant' documents. Unfortunately these retrieval systems offer only false certainty.

These search engines usually operate in a misleading fashion. Firstly, they do not explore the latest material. Sometimes they even gather data that has not been updated for months. At the moment there is not even any reliable information about the frequency with which the search engine robots browse the documents they have indexed before. Secondly, most systems operate only within their own domain. Thirdly, they explore only html documents. Fourthly, it is unclear how their method of ordering according to relevance is determined. And finally, many users are not aware of the most serious flaw, that they falsely claim to be precise and complete. Fortunately experts at many research laboratories and universities are engaged in improving IR systems. The prospects for developing an adequate agent that complies with the most important requirements are said to look bright.

Naturally, the university libraries are also experiencing the deficiencies of current IR systems. There are several alternatives that can be used to maintain a high level of service, including the provision of electronic information. A scientific library could of course employ the right number of technologically trained reference librarians needed to answer every individual question. This would probably result in a large crowd considering the population of 25,000 students and 3000 academic staff at Utrecht University. We therefore think it wiser not go into the matter of costs or the amount of time necessary to gather the requested information.

Another suggestion would be to develop an integrated model of several existing IR systems (partly) available on the market. During the past few years Utrecht University has been working on this option in cooperation with a software engineering firm and a number of national research centres. We adopted the following principles:

- searching for information independent of technical structures;
- an information retrieval system dependent on the type of user and usage.

Searching for information independent of technical structures

Let us first look at reality as it is. Suppose you were engaged in medical research on spontaneously epileptic rats. Suddenly you have an urgent question. You turn to a database containing abstracts from the magazine *Brain research*. You examine the next database, one that is not linked with the first. But it appears you are unfamiliar with the latter. It takes quite some time before you understand the system and the function of several keys and buttons. You formulate and reformulate your question over and over again. You start searching in the catalogue. Desperately you turn to the Internet. Finally, you have a look at your watch and sigh deeply.

Can we apply the information technology and all it promises to avoid time-consuming quests for the information sources? We think so, for instance by designing an information retrieval system that enables you to browse several databases (if required) by means of one search question. This system should operate on bibliographic files as well as full-text files and other sources relating to different disciplines. It must be able to go through files marked with different indexing techniques and it must cope with a dynamic, physically distributed and ever-expanding collection. In short, we need an information retrieval system that can be set into motion by a single entry question while sparing the user the technical quirks typical of certain databases.

An information retrieval system dependent on the type of user and usage

There is an additional requirement an information retrieval system should meet. The system must operate in accordance with the needs and wishes of the user. Suppose you were a barrister in addition to an employee of the university. You are in a hurry because you have a court session in two hours. You know there is ample jurisprudence for the case you are defending today and you also know where to find the information. But you do not want all of it and certainly no theoretical material, you just want a specific answer to a specific question. Further suppose that, after a successful session, you are inspired to write a paper on the matter. You would like to gather as much theoretical background information as possible, judicial information as well as all the relevant medical data. This time your wishes are of an entirely different nature to those of a few hours before.

This example suggests that for an information retrieval system to suit the demands of every individual university staff member and student it must also be highly flexible. It should be able to serve many different users who may have many different needs. The system interface should be flexible accordingly. As a lawyer you do not wish to analyse the mechanics of the system, nor do you feel the urge to study the inscrutable formulas your search question needs to be cast into. No, you prefer the use of vernacular language, mixed perhaps with a few specific legal expressions. (Put your modest request to a forum of reference librarians and they will overwhelm you once again with an avalanche of Boolean formulas, perhaps fascinating in their logical elegance but rather abstruse to you.)

Naturally, all the theoretical principles mentioned above must be put into practice. At Utrecht University we have been substantiating them in a series of 40 interrelated projects. So what are the complications, recurrent pitfalls, the envisaged and the unforeseen difficulties? What are our experiences, and what have we learned? Are there any lessons that reveal new and important ideas on how to build an electronic library?

Lessons learned

It cannot be stressed too often that in order to realize your policy in a series of subsidiary projects it is imperative to have a strategic framework. Without such a framework it is likely that your project will run aground, that you will fail to implement its outcome into your regular organization. Or worse, that it will culminate in a chain of unwelcome results. Yet even an elaborate strategic framework, based on user requirements, is but a step in the right direction. When building a digital library – or any other similar project for that matter – one ought to be prepared for quite a few irksome situations. Several of the most significant factors involved will be mentioned below. We shall illustrate them with a number of actual problems and cases faced in the course of our project. But prior to that a short description of the Utrecht Electronic Library Project's content will be given for the sake of clarity.

Context: Utrecht Electronic Library projects

We have mentioned the point that the user surveys, in which problems were assessed and analysed, provided a guideline during the definition phase of our projects. One could quite easily foresee that the larger part of these problems would be connected with infrastructure and the support during information searches. The first series of subsidiary projects dealt with the infrastructure in its most comprehensive meaning. The same user surveys were used to analyse the wishes of students and staff with respect to library services. In addition, the project management took into account a broad range of technical facilities as well as new standards and trends. These requirements, now in a specified form, led to a second series of projects, i.e. the new electronic library services.

'Infrastructure' project series

One of the most surprising conclusions of the user surveys and panel debates conducted among users in Utrecht and at universities in other countries was the assessment of a strong need for (electronic) information sources, while at same time – and this is the surprising fact – hardly anyone knew about the availability of existing facilities.

Lately, the price of information has increased sharply, not only in an absolute sense but also relative to the frequency with which it is used. This is particularly the case with electronic information. A peculiar circumstance. More information is being offered (at a steadily growing price), but users tend to neglect most of it. Still, this regrettable – some would say unacceptable – situation is a fact at many universities and institutions. The solution is self-evident. Better information, guidance and instructions on the availability of electronic information sources and its facilities, improved ergonomic interfaces, an efficient information retrieval system, the additional training of library personnel and unimpeded and uncomplicated access to all information sources. These objectives have already partly been realized in the subsidiary projects. Each of these projects has a specific guideline that defines its content in accordance with the leading principles of the project's framework.

On the one hand, the project aims to solve existing problems: on the other, these solutions must be sustainable, without neglecting dynamic developments in the field, i.e. an ever growing collection, changes introduced by information suppliers who tend to offer more and more platform-independent sources (like *SilverPlatter*), the expansion and improvement of user equipment, the libraries' independent management and maintenance of electronic information sources, and, last but not least, the consequences for library staff.

'Electronic library services' project series

The guiding principles for this project series were also derived from the user surveys. In this instance we concentrated on the users' wishes. The projects included:

- the digitization of traditional services: the filtering of information and electronic notification services (SDI); the electronic availability of the books' tables of contents;
- the digitization of the library's own collection: the (partial) digitization of special collections, old prints, impressions and manuscripts;
- the digitization of the university's scientific output: electronic publishing of theses, papers and articles.

In this case we also kept to a number of guidelines, in accordance with the points of departure as described in the strategic framework. For instance, a digital information source should not be a mere electronic copy of a paper one. Apart from linear scrolling it would be useful to indicate a desired topic. Besides text, pictures and statistics, one would also like to include moving images (films) and sound. Separate documents should be hyperlinked to related material within the library's own collection and beyond, but they should also refer to bibliographical sources and the printed material's location.

These projects must result not only in the digitization of material but also in a methodology for similar activities and decisions regarding the remaining parts of the collection. Finally, as has been said before, the (partial) digitization of the collection in fact amounts to a revision of the library organization. One cannot simply consider this operation as a mere adjustment or expansion of library and IT staff adorned with additional technical training courses.[11]

Some pitfalls (and how to get out of them): three lessons learned

Lesson 1: How some attempts to revive an obsolete technology are very rewarding

The objective of one of the subsidiary projects was to make the electronic library accessible from every working site on the campus. This goal was based on the express wishes of students and staff members. But how could it be achieved?

First we needed to address two points: what was the 'market situation' for electronic information sources?; we had to know what the terrain, the infrastructure at the university, was like.

The subscriptions (licences) we had, about 60 databases in all, could technically speaking be divided into two types: platform-dependent (CD-ROMs for DOS, Windows, Apple Macintosh or Unix), and platform-independent sources (predominantly online databanks) accessible via WWW browsers or Gopher. Presently most information offered by publishers is on platform-dependent sources, accessible only through DOS. They constitute about 90% of the total number of sources available at Utrecht University. However, this should not be a problem as 80% of our PCs are DOS-machines. Another fortunate circumstance was the set of the relatively modest hardware requirements. Simple Intel 386-type machines, purchased some five years ago and now mainly used as word-processors, are still good enough for receiving this type of electronic information. Why not connect all those faithful old boxes to the information sources on the network? Why had this not been done before? Why did we have to arrange a special project to this end?

The answer was rather banal. It was due to conflicting network software. The larger part of our electronic information sources were exclusively attainable through the so-called NFS protocol. Most faculties, however, had been using Novell, a protocol that cannot communicate with NFS. This meant, in contrast to platform-independent sources, that the use of platform-dependent sources was also limited by the type of network to which the computer was connected. How was this problem eventually solved?

There were several scenarios. The first was very simple. It could have been decided to do nothing, flatly refuse to spend a single penny on it, saying that provisionally these electronic services would be available only on specially equipped computers. The users just had to wait; wait until all the information providers started offering their products in a platform-independent form, i.e. via the WWW. There was of course a minor problem; by then the user would need quite a powerful computer, the latest high-end machine furnished with a top-notch processor plus lots and lots of RAM. If a department was unable to afford such a machine – well, too bad. Perhaps in the distant future there would be higher budgets instead of regular annual cut-backs.

The second scenario was somewhat more subtle. We could concentrate on configurations meeting the demands of predominant information sources (in our case DOS) and take into account the number of these machines in comparison to the total number of computers (i.e. 80%). And then we had to start the tedious process of trying to eliminate the incompatibility problem between the network protocols. In addition, we could attempt to realize platform-independent access for the happy few, the owners of powerful computers, in the expectation that their number was growing steadily. We chose this latter option and met with some difficulties, problems which, fortunately, we were able to overcome.

Ironing out the incompatibility between network protocols appeared to be a much tougher ride than we had anticipated. It was no trifle, we could not bridge the gap using some kind of ready-made translation program. To be frank, the project took us nine months. We will not bore you with our misery – all those erroneous and outdated test keys, faulty and incompatible drive letters – we would only like to mention a single significant and recurring problem.

We always tend to forget the human factor – it is never a matter of mechanics alone. Conflicting views, opposing proposals and alternative solutions – the stuff considerations are made of or the subjects of many, many time-consuming discussions. IT experts usually do not express much enthusiasm at the idea of a platform-dependent access to an electronic library. Why do they need to exert themselves by working on an obsolete solution? They assure us they have the knowledge, the technology to realize a state-of-the-art option.

Library staff, who know the wishes and needs of most users, take a different stance. They dread experiments with software, detest fast machines and the like, and are usually rather indifferent towards promises of technical innovations. It also works in the good old-fashioned way, so why bother? The faculties were the third party in this game. In the least bothersome case they were compelled to discuss all kinds of tailor-made solutions with their IT-departments time and again.

All in all, this did not enhance the progress of the project. But eventually, after nine months of patience we reached our aim, an aim that had seemed close before we began. Patience, it must be said, is the key word when dealing with problems. For solutions, though, the key word is perseverance. One must never forget the purpose of the project: to comply with the needs of the library's users, i.e. students, teachers and researchers.

Lesson 2: Why involving non-experts in a project can be valuable in the long term

One of the Utrecht Electronic Library Projects was centred on the electronic publishing of the university's own scientific output such as doctoral theses. The reason for this was clear. Firstly, we wanted to improve availability and search facilities for the convenience of staff and students. An electronic format would make this possible. Secondly, there was the factor of added value, like multimedia illustrations, cross-references, direct measurement results, significant data for conclusions etc. All that could now be added to the thesis in a single stroke.

Another important consideration was the costs Dutch graduates incur for printing the compulsory fifty copies of their thesis in order to send one to every university library. A waste of paper, money and storage facilities, especially if you take into account the comparatively low frequency with which most theses are read.

There were basically two options for the project organization. Firstly, we could employ one or two experts who would study the situation, then analyse and explore the needs. Next they would look for matching technological solutions and perform bench-markings to explore the possiblity of adopting different solutions realized elsewhere. Finally they would conclude the project by setting up a process of electronic publishing and printing on demand. Secondly, we could have exactly the same activities carried out not by specialists but by the regular library staff, thus getting them acquainted with their new tasks straight from the beginning.

The second option had both advantages and disadvantages. The positive aspects were that the staff would be involved in analysing the problems they were used to working with. They would also feel more committed to the project, which would certainly ease the assimilation of all project results into the regular organization. On the other hand, the whole project could take considerably longer, even twice the time, since the staff consisted basically of non-experts who still had to learn all the necessary technological know-how. But then again, any loss of time would certainly be made up for in the end, perhaps not during the project but in the period following its conclusion. We chose to apply this principle in many of the other subsidiary projects except in those requiring highly specialized expertise in the initial phase.

Lesson 3: How a complex project structure could lead to the simple implementation of results

Simple – that is about the last thing the Utrecht Electronic Library Project could be called. This is due to the great number and the composition of working groups, project groups, response groups, all of which are involved in the project apart from the steering group. The entire structure is complex but can be conveniently mapped in a comparatively transparent scheme. In short, the whole project is supervised by the steering group represented by the university librarian, the managing director of the Utrecht Academic Computer Centre and the general project manager. Their role is to control the project with respect to its main principles and aspects.

Next there are two project groups, each having its own group supervisor. One group deals with the infrastructure projects, the other with the new electronic library services. Both groups, in which department librarians, department automation services experts and staff of the Academic Computer Centre participate, check the plans and results presented to them by the 40 subsidiary projects. Their task is to advise and ensure the commitment of the participants.

Each of the 40 subsidiary projects has its own project leader and executives forming a working group. Their task is to actualize the objectives. In this respect they are accountable to the general project manager. The end-users and faculty automation services are represented in the response groups. They contribute to solving current complications and also take part in surveys and evaluations before, during and after the development of new services. Their role is to advise as well as to guarantee the overall commitment. Finally there are a number of user and advisory groups which are consulted *ad hoc* for certain types of projects.

Because of its complexity this structure demands a great deal of time and attention. This is especially true for the often time-consuming meetings and arrangements. Nevertheless all these efforts have paid off, notably with respect to factors like engagement and acceptance. The organization's emphasis on the particular factors of engagement and acceptance seems justified because of the university's decentralized management structure. This situation entails a large measure of independence of departments and faculties, not only with respect to training and research but also to automation policy. The relative financial and political autonomy of department and faculty libraries plus the facilitating role of the central library at Utrecht University, tend to complicate rather than expedite certain matters, such as the introduction of standard software solutions.

Implications for managers
Human resources and finance

It may seem self-evident, but the building of a digital library parallel to a conventional library (a process during which the existing regular services continue) is almost unfeasible without a specially appointed project organization, a well-conceived framework and additional funds. Earlier we defended the idea that the digital library should be an integrated part of the traditional library. For the sake of argument we wish to use a metaphor that is in clear conflict with this principle.

Let us think of the digital library as a real, new building. New staff are employed to find, order, disclose, maintain the material and to put it at the public's disposal. But the old building is still there, together with its own staff, its customers and procedures. We must keep in mind that this is a period of transition, when both libraries coexist, functioning side by side, both requiring effort and funding. The pace at which traditional activities can be dismantled is likely to be much slower than the rate at which new services may be introduced. Consequently, it would be rather unrealistic to expect from the library personnel an equally good performance of old and new tasks without a supporting structure.

Probing and experimenting in pilot projects

Unfortunately there are no handbooks, extensive check lists or limpid instructions that could assist you in building a digital library. This is quite understandable, in view of the increasingly rapid development of new technologies. Almost every guideline becomes obsolete as soon as it is in print. What should be done in this changing situation void of a solid mainstay, where your general knowledge of the whole discipline seems to lessen by the day?

A relatively safe and well-tested method in this case – at least in our experiences – is the launching of small-scale projects serving as trial balloons in the course of preparing large-scale regular services. These experiments should show whether certain technologies are applicable within a specific environment. It would become possible to judge whether they are realistic within a particular context with respect to their costs and the expertise available. In short, the introduction of a new digital service should be preceded by a series of well-prepared pilot projects in order to determine, study and test as many of the practical effects possible.

Framework

The reader may wish to object to the frequent emphasis on this demand for a strategic policy framework, quoting our assessment that these dynamic times are characterized by a blatant lack of a reassuring mainstay. In our view these two suppositions are not contradictory. A laboured strategic framework rests on several points of departure which must be valid today as well as tomorrow. The basics of acquiring knowledge and diffusing it, the fundamentals of scientific inquiry and evaluation, in short the essence of the learning and research process, will not change overnight, not even over a period of a hundred years. (To affirm this we only need to look back at the history of scientific research over the past 20-odd centuries.)

The project's strategic policy must indicate the disciplines on which the library needs to focus in order to support research and education. Yet it is better not to define the *way* this ought to be done within the policy framework. Rather it should be determined in short-term, flexible pilot projects (cf. Lesson 1 in the previous section as to the project framework's guiding principle on specific project decisions).

Safeguarding the results

Many IT projects achieve their apotheosis in the approval of a thick report simply brimming over with recommendations, schedules and diagrams. The report is then often put away for the next decade or so. To avoid such an unfortunate fate the results of each subsidiary project should be implemented in the regular organization and its branches. This implementation should form an integrated part of the project's final stage. This aim usually involves the description and introduction of the library and computer centre staff's altered tasks with respect to new services. Obviously, this is not possible without the unconditional support of the university librarian and the managing director of the computing centre. To that end, both managers must be appointed in the steering group as project supervisors. Furthermore, as has been pointed out already, involving personnel would work beneficially to this end (cf. Lesson 2 in the previous section).

Another way of safeguarding the project results is an intensive exchange of information between participants and future users. Aiming at an equally efficient and extensive method of providing information, all communication should follow structured channels in order to reach the proper groups at the proper time. This is particularly important in the case of decentralized organizations, a structure most universities are founded upon, since it is crucial to position the end-users and representatives of central and decentralized levels within the project organization (cf. Lesson 3 in the previous section).

Pragmatic aspects

Since setting up the digital library we have been striving to deploy our own resources as much as possible. The larger part of the research, the writing of the software plus explanation and instructions, has been carried out by the university's own experts, as have the evaluations of existing and future services. For instance, researchers from Ergonomics (Faculty of Psychology) conducted the user surveys, they also built the interfaces and evaluated the use of new software. Staff from Communication Sciences were also involved in writing instructions for software.

Since the start of the project information scientists from the Mathematics Department and Computer Centre experts have been responsible for the system design and programming. Linguists have been exploring natural language processing systems for the purpose of information retrieval. Additionally, this approach has proved to be comparatively cost-effective. The fees charged by the university's own facilitating organizations are a good deal more economical than the average commercial rates.

In addition, we checked all ideas and formulated plans during our definition study with our own user groups as well as with users outside Utrecht University.

We were not frugal of time and efforts devoted to the definition study, realizing that this would ultimately be unprofitable. A solid foundation and the minimization of risks with regard to wider-scale projects have confirmed this premise.

Conclusions

In this chapter a method of building a digital scientific library has been described. It may come as no surprise to learn that this method was designed so as never to be completed. The tangible image of the digital library as a modern building packed with computers is in fact not a suitable metaphor, not only because we are dealing with a global library, ubiquitous and diffuse, but also because its main distinction is its dynamics. The building will never be completed.

This may seem to be a somewhat overblown view. However, this is not the case because essentially we are dealing with something that cannot be achieved in the physical world – that is, creating a set of conditions to expand, alter and perfect the library, infinitely. These conditions, still, concern corporeal entities: the library staff and its organization. For that reason our project management thought it a proper idea to choose a different approach. Of course, the aspects of user requirements and user methods of working are also taken into account within the context of more traditional computerization projects, calling on the interactive and iterative method of system development. Yet the completion of these projects generally coincides with the supply and installation of a finished product. This relatively static approach usually does not altogether provide for the crucial function the staff has after the completion of the project.

It has become commonplace to suggest that a growing number of skills are required from the library staff, even to such an extent that they could well be called IT experts. This may be correct, but still the question remains how this change can best be arranged. In the Utrecht Electronic Library Project it was decided to opt for the active participation of personnel, even if this led to a longer-running programme. As we have pointed out, these projects involve the same people who, after the conclusion of the project, will be responsible for the new tasks and services. In our view this should facilitate the transition from project situation to the regular carrying-out of tasks. This approach also expedites the incorporation of innovative aspects, such as IT skills, electronic collecting of material and trend watching within the regular structure. This approach was formulated carefully. The construction of a digital library is a dynamic process occurring on a project base. Eventually this process should evolve into the regular working method of a learning organization.

At the beginning of this chapter I promised you not to go into the drawbacks and disadvantages of current technological developments. Nevertheless, I could not entirely avoid describing a few of the numerous recurring pitfalls and problems but we are convinced that they form complications of only a temporary nature. The foundations have been laid. The establishment of the global library, the greatest endeavour since Alexandria, is only a matter of years away. Somehow Jorge Luis Borges, the blind librarian, must have envisaged this prospect in the Library of Babel:

> He also alleged a fact which travellers have confirmed: *In the vast Library are no two identical books*. From these two incontrovertible premises he deduced that the Library is total and that its shelves register all the possible combinations of the twenty-odd orthographic symbols (a number which, though extremely vast, is not infinite): in other words, all that it is given to express, in all languages. Everything: the minutely detailed history of the future, the archangels' autobiographies, the faithful catalogue of the Library, thousands and thousands of false catalogues, the demonstration of the fallacy of those catalogues, the demonstration of the fallacy of the true catalogue, the Gnostic gospel of Basilides, the commentary on that gospel, the commentary on the commentary on that gospel, the true story of your death, the translation of every book in all languages, the interpolation of every book in all books.[12]

References

1   Calvino, I., *If on a winter's night a traveler*, London, Picador, 1982, 200.
2   Ibid., 80.
3   Ibid., 42.
4   Devadson, F. J. and Lingam P. P., 'A methodology for the identification of information needs of users', *IFLA journal*, **23** (1),1977, 41–51.
5   Nabokov, V., *Pnin*, Harmondsworth, Penguin Books, 1996, 63.
6   Newton, I., in *Philosophical transactions and collections, to the end of the year 1720, abridged, and disposed under general heads, in five volumes*, London, 1732. Volume I, Part I, 158.
7   Savenije, J. S. M., 'Nieuwe concurrenten voor de uitgevers: de schoenmaker en zijn leest.', Proceedings 6e Dag van het Document, Zwolle, Projectbureau Croll & Creutzberg, 1997, 71–80.
8   Waaijers, L., 'The science and art of information and libraries: practical implications', Interdisciplinary Research Conference Information Science, Delft, 1996.
9   Van der Horst, K. and Ankersmit, F., *The Utrecht psalter, picturing the Psalms of David*, Utrecht, Utrecht University Library, 1996.
10 Borges, J. L., 'Library of Babel', in *Labyrinths: selected stories and other writings*, Harmondsworth, Penguin Books, 1972, 78.
11 Grygierczyk, N., 'Down to earth in cyberspace. Buiding digital library: policy,

plans, practice and problems' in *Online information '96 Proceedings*, ed. by Raitt, D. and Jeapes, B., Oxford, Learned Information, 1996, 409–15.
12   Borges, J. L., *op. cit.*, 81–2.

4

ELECTRONIC DOCUMENTS AND THEIR ROLE IN FUTURE LIBRARY SYSTEMS

Philip Barker

UNIVERSITY OF TEESSIDE, ENGLAND

Introduction

This chapter discusses the growing importance of electronic documents within future library systems. It commences with a simple taxonomy and a brief description of the basic nature of libraries and the functions they are intended to perform. The role of new technologies (especially publication media) in libraries is then briefly discussed. Electronic documents are identified as an important component of future library systems; their potential uses and the problems associated with using them are described and discussed. The importance of metaphors as a basis for system design is outlined. The need for appropriate tools to facilitate the creation, distribution, maintenance and use of electronic documents is then addressed. Particular emphasis is given to the Internet and in-house intranets as publication media for electronic documents. The final part of the chapter discusses the implications of mobile computing equipment and the need for libraries to meet the requirement for 'information on demand'.

Some decades ago, in his 'systems map of the universe', Checkland[1] identified five basic types of system. He referred to these as natural systems, human-activity systems, designed physical systems, designed abstract systems, and transcendental systems. Within the hierarchy of natural systems, the human species occupies a unique and prominent position. It has established its prominence as a consequence of three fundamental evolutionary developments. First, its ability to support communication between individuals and groups of people using a variety of different forms of language. Second, its use of a range of archival media for the storage and processing of data and information. Third, the ingenious ways in which human beings have designed and fabricated various types of machine and support aids to enable human performance to be extended and augmented.[2, 3]

According to Checkland's taxonomy, libraries are examples of designed physical systems. As such, they are intended to be artefacts that support various types of human activity relating to the storage, retrieval and sharing of information. Of course, from a historical perspective, libraries have arisen as a consequence of some of the fundamental limitations of human memory – basically, our inability to remember (and recall) substantial volumes of factual or descriptive material over significant periods of time with high levels of accuracy and precision. Libraries (and the books they contain) are therefore essentially information and data storage facilities that have been designed and developed as a mechanism for augmenting and extending human memory – and fulfilling their curiosity.

From a 'human activity' perspective, the role of books (and the library systems that house them) and their evolution as memory aids can be seen by examining some of the types of 'information recall' problems that people often encounter. For example, the question 'What were you doing at 3 pm on 3rd September 1982?' automatically suggests the need for some sort of **diary** facility. Similarly, questions such as 'What is the meaning of the word cobra?' and 'What is the plural form of corpus?' create a need for a **dictionary** of some sort. Finally, questions such as 'How high is the Eiffel tower', 'How long is the Great Wall of China?' and 'What is the longest river in the world?' demand the need for various types of **encyclopaedia**. In the past such books have been routinely published on paper; as we shall discuss later in this chapter, there are now very many compelling reasons why they should also be published on electronic media.

As well as serving as 'memory aids', books and libraries also facilitate the sharing of information; they also serve a communication role, particularly from one generation of people to another. In this context, of course, it is important to realize that we can only visualize and understand what has happened in the past as a result of what has been documented about it. The ongoing archival of details of current events and activities is therefore of vital importance to future generations. Books and libraries (like museums) therefore have important 'monitoring' and 'informing' roles to play with respect to capturing various aspects of human culture and recording developments in science, engineering and technology.

Bearing in mind what has been said above, libraries have now become an important part of our everyday lives. They can exist in a variety of different forms and manifest themselves in many different ways, depending upon the publication media they employ and the nature of the end-user population they are intended to serve. Libraries may thus be intended for individual or group use; they may be private or public. Conventionally, those intended for group use can be classified into six basic types according to the size of the target population they are intended to cater for: departmental, institutional, organizational, branch, regional, and national. These libraries may be used to archive a wide range of resources such as books and other paper-based items, microfilms, slides, sound resources (audio tapes and CDs), videos, CD-ROMs for computers, and so on.

No matter what type of library is involved, the basic principles of operation are essentially the same. These involve:

- making available some form of storage facility where items can be physically stored;
- maintaining a complete catalogue of all the items in the system;
- providing appropriate index facilities to enable users to locate and retrieve items of interest – such as subject, author and keyword indices, and possibly, a KWIC index;[4]
- putting into place various 'monitoring' and 'management' mechanisms for 'tracking' the movement of items and realizing the acquisition of new materials.

Of course, the basic mechanisms listed here can be augmented and extended in various ways through the addition of various kinds of 'support service'. The nature and quality of these will depend upon a number of factors such as the type of library involved, the people it has to cater for and the environmental infrastructure in which it exists.

Undoubtedly, new information handling, storage and communication facilities are having a significant impact on the nature of library systems and the types of service that they need to provide for their clients. Naturally computers, in one form or another, are playing a key role in the developments that are taking place. Some of these developments will be discussed in later parts of this chapter.

We commence by exploring the use of 'new media' in libraries and then go on to discuss the potential uses of electronic resources. This discussion involves a consideration of electronic documents and the various forms these can take. Various issues relating to the use of in-house intranets (and the Internet) for the publication and dissemination of electronic documents are then discussed. The final part of the chapter outlines the implications for libraries of providing 'information on demand' through mobile computing equipment.

Media considerations

For several centuries, paper has always been the primary storage medium for use in conventional library systems. Because of its very attractive properties it is unlikely to be dispensed with in the foreseeable future. However, having said that, for several decades many 'new media types' have started to appear within libraries and in some cases have totally displaced the need for any form of paper. This section therefore looks at three important issues relating to the use of media in library systems. The topics to be discussed are: first, the roles that media can play; second, the types of transition and transformations that are starting to take place within libraries as a consequence of the introduction of new media; and third, the growing importance of paperless publishing and the implications this has for the creation of new types of publication. The final part of this section will briefly review some possible scenarios for the development of future library systems.

Basic roles for media in libraries

As was suggested earlier in this chapter, many new types of medium are starting to appear in and be used by libraries and library systems. For example, as well as conventional paper-based resources, we now see the use of numerous other media forms to support the storage and retrieval of sound collections such as the spoken word and music, image collections (both static and dynamic) and computer programs of various sorts. One of the main reasons for the appearance of these other media is that they offer many types of facility that paper-based storage cannot afford. This means that new and novel kinds of publication become possible, such as hypermedia electronic books, personalized newspapers and interactive catalogues, which previously were not feasible – because of either cost restrictions or technical limitations. Some of these possibilities are discussed further later in the chapter.

Bearing in mind what has been said above, it is important to examine the functions that media are likely to play within any given library system. Essentially, there are four primary roles that need to be considered: first, their role as a basic storage medium for information and data; second, the support they can provide for information searching and retrieval; third, their utility as a mechanism to facilitate the 'taking away' of information (through photocopying, borrowing, use of smartcards, and so on); and finally, the facilities that they can offer as a tool for the support of system administration and management.

The majority of conventional libraries use paper primarily for each of the functions listed above. However, computer systems are increasingly being used within library systems. Naturally, this has caused designers, authors, managers and researchers to think more deeply about the role of new media and the ways in which they might influence the publication and management of information. As is discussed in later parts of this chapter, the publication medium used for any given piece of work can significantly influence how it is stored, managed, retrieved and disseminated.

Libraries in transition

The types of transition that are taking place in library systems as a consequence of the incorporation of new technologies are reflected in a number of ongoing research and development projects that have recently been described in the literature.[5-7] Our own work in this area has involved the use of new technologies to facilitate the 'computerization' of a conventional, paper-based library system in order to create an equivalent electronic version. The library itself was intended to provide an 'Open Access Student Information Service' (OASIS) for students within an academic setting.[8]

We believe that the conception and subsequent evolution of our initial OASIS facility towards the electronic version that now exists, reflect the types of change that have occurred or are likely to occur in other types of library system. There are four essential steps: first, the establishment of a paper-based collection; second, the extension of the basic system to accommodate the use of new publication media (user perspective); third, the use of computer-based methods to manage the system (management perspective); and fourth, movement towards a totally electronic (digital) system. The extents to which each of these phases is realized will determine the ultimate nature and characteristics that any given library will reflect. A simple classification of library systems based on the realization or otherwise of these four processes is presented at the end of this section.

New books for old

In his book on 'paperless publishing', Haynes offers a number of attractive reasons for moving away from the use of paper towards the more extensive deployment of electronic media for the purposes of publication.[9] Of course, there are many different types of electronic medium that could be used to publish any given piece of work. Typical examples include: low-capacity magnetic diskettes; high-capacity portable hard disk units; solid-state disks of various kinds; optical disk systems (which include recordable, rewritable and read-only media); and computer network systems such as in-house intranets, private networks and publicly accessible nets such as the Internet. There is thus a rich range of media upon which to publish. Naturally, each medium will have its strengths and weaknesses and its advantages and limitations. Obviously, it is necessary to give careful consideration to the type of medium that is ultimately employed for any given publication since this could significantly influence its final properties and 'behaviour'.

As was suggested above, new media provide many opportunities for exploring new types of publication. One of the most popular of the recent developments in this area has been the 'electronic book'. An early example of such a publication was Shneiderman and Kearsley's electronic book 'Hypertext Hand On!'[10] This was distributed inside the cover of a conventional hardback book in the form of two 5¼ in. floppy disks; these had to be installed on to the hard disk of a host computer system before the electronic book embedded within them could be accessed. More recent examples of electronic books include: the extensive range of CD-ROM products that have been released by Microsoft (such as the *Encarta* encyclopaedia, *Musical Instruments*, *Dinosaurs*, *Ancient Lands*, and so on); the hyper-media electronic books that have been described by Barker[11] and Tan;[12] and the 'animated books' outlined by Gloor.[13] Some of the more recent developments in electronic book publication have recently been reviewed by Barker.[14]

Scenarios for future library systems

Bearing in mind the various media types that were discussed in the previous section and the extents to which they are likely to be taken up, Barker[7] has formulated a number of scenarios for possible future developments in library systems. He envisages four basic possibilities that involve the evolution of 'polymedia libraries', 'electronic libraries', 'digital libraries' and 'virtual library' systems, respectively. Each of these types of development is briefly discussed below.

The term polymedia is used to denote the use of several different, independent media for the storage of information and knowledge – paper, microfilm, compact disc, and so on. **Polymedia libraries** are thus envisaged as being institutions that store their material on a wide range of independent media types. Essentially, such libraries will therefore be similar to conventional libraries as we know them today. The organizational and management processes within these libraries will be, as they are now, basically manual in nature.

An electronic library is deemed to be one in which the core processes of the library become basically electronic in nature. Obviously, the most important way in which this is likely to happen is through the widespread incorporation and use of computers and the various facilities that they are able to make available, such as online indexes, full-text searching and retrieval facilities, automated record keeping and computer-based decision making. In addition, within an electronic library system there will be a conscious movement towards the more widespread use of electronic media (both digital and analogue) for the storage, retrieval and delivery of information. This will mean that libraries of this sort will be involved in an active and extensive computerization programme.

Digital libraries differ from the two previous types of library discussed in this section because all of the information that they contain exists only in a digital electronic format. Of course, the information itself may reside on different storage media such as electronic memory or magnetic and optical disk (compare the polymedia libraries that were discussed earlier in this section) but users will not necessarily perceive any differences between them. Because of the way in which information is stored, digital libraries do not, therefore, contain any conventional books. The major types of publication contained in this type of library will be various types of electronic document – similar to those that are discussed in the next section.

Obviously, in order to access digital information it is necessary to use either special purpose, multimedia 'reader' stations or some form of computer system. This equipment may be located within the confines of a communal public reading room or within individual rooms that are used for private study. The information can also be accessed remotely via telephone modems or by means of computer communication networks. Naturally, one great advantage of having information in digital form is that it can be shared instantaneously and easily at relatively low cost. Therefore, while a conventional library might only hold one or two copies of a book, a digital library could generate an unlimited number of copies 'at the touch of a button'.

Virtual library systems depend for their existence upon a rapidly maturing area of technology known as virtual reality or VR.[15] VR has often been described as the 'ultimate multimedia experience' – the simplest form of which is known as telepresence. Such experiences depend upon the ability of a computer and its associated interaction peripherals to create highly realistic simulations and surrogations in which users can become totally immersed. Currently, there is much interest in the development of virtual libraries and the use of VR within the other types of library that have been described in this section.

Two uses of virtual reality in library systems have to be considered: first, the provision of facilities to support this type of experience within a library; second, the creation of virtual libraries or virtual experiences – for example, the ability to browse around a library system without actually having to physically go to it. A good example of this latter approach can be found in the 'Treasures of the Smithsonian' surrogation that has been published on CD-I by the Smithsonian Institution.[16]

Although some virtual library systems are available in the form of packaged CD-ROM products,[17] the most advanced systems exist only within sophisticated computer systems that are supported by advanced telecommunications equipment, to facilitate remote access and sharing. Such libraries can be accessed using two-dimensional (2D) interfaces that are based upon the use of conventional computer workstations. The 'Book House' system described by Pejtersen[18] provides a good example of what can be achieved using this approach. Of course, greater degrees of realism can be achieved through the use of three-dimensional (3D) interfaces that involve the use of head-mounted displays and peripherals such as a 'data glove'. These facilitate the creation of a 'total immersion' environment and interaction based upon pointing operations and gestural communication. Using equipment of this sort it is possible to enter a virtual library, browse around its rooms and shelves, use an index or catalogue, select a book (by pointing to it and 'touching' it), open it and then read it. Of course, the only place where the book really exists is in the computer and within the minds of its readers.

Using electronic resources

Electronic resources have become an important aspect of each of the types of library described in the previous section. However, as has been described in some detail by Negroponte,[19] the most useful types of electronic resource are those that exist in digital form. Because of their importance, the remainder of this chapter deals primarily with this category of resource. Fundamental to the discussion that is presented is the concept of an **electronic document**. This section therefore commences by defining the meaning of this term. It then explains why such documents are so important within the context of future library systems. Various approaches to classifying electronic documents are then described and, finally, some of the issues relating to authoring and publishing these resources are outlined.

What is an electronic document?

Both the paper-based and the electronic version of my *Collins English dictionary* define a *document* as: 'a piece of paper, booklet, etc., providing information, esp. of an official or legal nature'. Documents in their various forms have become an important and essential aspect of our everyday lives. Such entities are used to document and record virtually every aspect of what we do – income tax returns, credit card transactions, bank transactions, travel activities, and so on. As well as recording information, documents can also be used for communication purposes – for example, a telegram, facsimile transmission and a sales invoice.

Within most organizations, documents provide a fundamental and necessary mechanism of communication. As a consequence of this, documents can assume a wide variety of different formats. They can also embed a number of different types of communication modality and can utilize a wide range of presentation and publication media. The majority of conventional documents have been published using the medium of paper. Of course, as a communication medium paper has many limitations. For example, it has limited bandwidth, it is unreactive and cannot dynamically adapt the information that it carries in order to meet the individual needs of specific readers. Because of these shortcomings paper often has to be augmented by the use of other media.

The advent of the computer has made possible the creation of many new types of document. Broadly, these are referred to as **electronic documents**. Such documents exist only inside a computer system in digital format. Documents of this sort are created using an appropriate 'authoring tool', stored in a computer's memory system and subsequently displayed using suitable audio and/or visual display technologies. According to Maunder, 'electronic documentation systems employ the same steps as traditional publishing systems, but with an electronic twist. Electronic documents are acquired in computer format and published by releasing them to a central database. They can then be distributed by floppy disk, CD-ROM, or communication link. Such documents can be browsed quickly using a computer'.[20]

Naturally, the motivation for wanting to use electronic documents stems from the many advantages that are associated with their use. Barker,[21] for example, suggests that one significant advantage of electronic documents over those that are based on the use of paper is that they can embed many more communication modalities than is possible with conventional documents. These include text, static pictures, sound, animations, motion pictures and various tactile modes of communication. Of course, there are many other advantages to be gained from the use of electronic documents. One considerable advantage over other types of document is that they can easily be transformed and processed by computers. Another advantage is the ease with which they can be transferred from one location to another by means of communication networks. Yet another advantage is the ease with which they can be personalized in order to meet the particular requirements of individual users or groups of users. Personalization depends upon the design and use of flexible, multi-level document structures. These can embed multiple *threads* through a knowledge corpus which can be adapted to meet the needs of particular types of user-profile or end-user stereotype.

Many other researchers have also discussed the advantages of electronic documents. Maunder, for example, claims that 'the cost of preparing, distributing and maintaining technical manuals can be cut with a practical approach to electronic documentation'.[20] Similarly, in his book, Gloor[13] suggests that 'hypermedia documents offer a uniquely integrated environment that cannot be simulated on paper'. Hyperdocuments[22] and various other types of electronic document will be discussed further in subsequent parts of this chapter. But first, it is necessary to classify the different types of electronic document that currently exist.

Types of document

Electronic documents can take many different forms. Consequently, there exists a number of ways in which they can be classified. One important approach depends upon the way in which their embedded information is intended to be processed by their users.[21] In this taxonomy, two basic strategies for organizing information are possible: linear and non-linear. Alternative ways of classifying documents can be based upon: the behaviour they exhibit; the 'media types' they embed; and the basic functions they perform. Each of these approaches to classifying documents is briefly discussed in the remainder of this section.

Linear and non-linear documents

In a linearly organized document the embedded units of information (sections, paragraphs, sentences, diagrams, sound clips, video sequences, and so on) are laid down in a way that assumes, in general, that they will be processed from start to finish taking each unit of information within the document in the order intended by its author(s) – just as in a film-strip or an audio recording. In contrast, non-linear documents are designed in a way that assumes information units will not be processed in any particular order. Indeed, the order in which specific items of information will be accessed will often depend upon the individual user involved, his/her current interests, experience, mood and information requirements. Although a *pseudo-linear* order can be imposed on a non-linear document, such an ordering is not the normal mode of usage. Non-linear documents are therefore ideally suited for browsing, serendipitous access to material, and retrieval strategies that involve 'jumping' from one location to another. Further details on the use of linear and non-linear documents can be found in Gloor,[13] Martin[22] and Barker.[11, 21]

A behavioural taxonomy

Depending upon the way in which they have been designed and the media upon which they are published, electronic documents can be made to exhibit many different types of 'behaviour'. Using this characteristic as a basis, Barker[23] has identified three broad categories of electronic document. He refers to these as 'static', 'dynamic' and 'living' documents, respectively.

Undoubtedly, the simplest examples of electronic document are those which are static in nature. As perceived by their users, such documents never change their form. They contain fixed information and, by definition, the way in which this is presented to users is always the same. Documents in this category are often just electronic emulations of their paper-based counterparts. Dynamic documents also contain fixed information but they are able to change their outward form and appearance – that is, the way in which their embedded material is presented to end-users. Unlike the previous two types of document, living publications are able to change both their form (outward appearance) and the information that they embed. Naturally, the publication of living documents depends critically upon the availability of a dynamically updateable publication medium such as a hard disk or a computer network facility.

Examples of the above three types of electronic document can be found in many of the numerous publications that are now commercially available on computer disk (for example, Lotus Organizer), on CD-ROM (as illustrated by the wide range of Microsoft multimedia products such as the Encarta encyclopaedia) and through the Internet (at various Web sites). Of course, living documents have the tremendous advantage that they can be updated and modified continuously. This means that they can always contain current and up-to-date information. In addition, documents of this sort can also be easily reformatted and restructured in order to meet the various and changing requirements of different individual users.

A media taxonomy

It is possible to classify electronic documents according to the various kinds of 'media element' that they embed. Using such an approach for the classification of electronic books, Barker[24] has identified ten basic taxonomic categories – which, of course, can also be applied to the more general situation of classifying electronic documents. The categories used in his original classification were based upon a document's use of:

- just one linear medium – linear text; sound; static pictures; moving pictures;
- more than one linear medium – multimedia, telemedia and polymedia documents;
- a single non-linear medium – hypertext or audio;
- multiple non-linear media – hypermedia and virtual reality.

Of course, any of these categories of document might also embed some form of 'intelligence' which enables them to self-tailor their content, appearance and end-user interface in dynamic and adaptable ways. Such facilities are often embedded in electronic questionnaires and other forms of data entry system, usually to facilitate error checking and to eliminate the need to ask any unnecessary questions. Some examples of the use of embedded intelligence in electronic documents will be discussed later in the section that deals with publishing on intranets and the Internet.

A functional taxonomy

Another simple way of classifying electronic documents, be they linear or non-linear, is by the basic function(s) they perform. Inherent in the use of this approach is the use of some form of embedded 'metaphor' – that is, the creation of a functional similarity or likeness that a given type of document might show to some related paper-based counterpart. Typical examples of the classes of document contained in the functional taxonomy include electronic books, journals, newspapers, magazines and newsletters, diaries and organizers, online catalogues. Associated with each of the categories in this taxonomy will be certain expectations about: the type of information that instances of a given class will 'carry'; the ways in which that information is organized; and the nature of the tools that will be available to access that information. Electronic books and journals are two of the most important categories in this taxonomy because they form the basic building blocks of the electronic libraries that were discussed in the previous section. Of course, there are many different types of electronic book – text-books, technical manuals, encyclopaedia, conference proceedings, and so on. Both Barker[11, 24] and Tan[12] have made extensive studies of electronic books. Barker,[4, 7] has also reviewed some of the more important research and development activities that have taken place in this area. A useful discussion on electronic journals has been presented by Rowland et al.,[25] while electronic newspapers have been discussed by Sargent.[26].

Authoring and publishing issues

The ways in which electronic documents are created and used can be significantly different from those used for conventional paper-based publications. The differences arise primarily for three basic reasons: first, the interactivity that electronic documents can exhibit; second, the much richer range of media that they can embed; and third, the new and novel features that electronic media can make available. In this section some of the important issues relating to the authoring and publication of electronic documents are briefly discussed. This discussion includes an identification of some of the general principles involved, the types of authoring facility that are necessary, the role of mark-up techniques and the types of medium commonly employed for publication.

General principles

The creation of an electronic document is normally undertaken as a three-step process involving design, authoring and publication activities. The design phase serves to identify the purpose of the document, its properties and its behaviour. Authoring involves developing the basic resources that are needed to create the document; it also involves testing, evaluating (in a formative way), integrating and synchronizing these resources in order to produce the final document. In the final stage, the document that has been produced has to be transferred across to the publication medium that will be used to make it available to others. Detailed discussions of multimedia and hypermedia authoring processes have been given by Gloor[13] and Barker.[11] The latter source provides a useful 'overview model' of the major steps involved in creating hypermedia documents.

Naturally, the way in which any given document is authored will depend upon the purpose it is to serve and the types of media element that it is to embed. It will also depend upon the type of 'authoring tool(s)' employed; this issue is discussed in the following section. The type of document that is being created will naturally influence the type of metaphor that will be used in the design process, and which may subsequently be embedded within the end-user interface to the publication.

Two other important considerations that have to be taken into account when creating electronic documents are the number of authors involved in the initial authoring phase and, if the document is a living publication, who is allowed to alter it. With large hypermedia documents group authorship is obviously very important from the perspectives of efficiency and effectiveness.[12] Group authorship will usually require 'version control' mechanisms to be invoked. Similarly, in living documents (that may allow users to make changes and add personal and/or public annotations) it will be necessary to implement various control mechanisms that prevent end-users from destroying the integrity and accuracy of stored material.

Types of authoring tool

As was mentioned above, the creation of electronic documents requires the selection of an appropriate 'authoring tool'. The type of tool, or toolset, employed will depend upon a variety of factors such as the types of document that are to be created, the medium upon which they are to be published, who they are being published for and whether or not any installation or organizational guidelines have to be observed.

The simplest approach to authoring is by means of some form of word-processing system. However, it is important to realize that each word-processor has its own way of storing the documents it creates. Mechanisms to facilitate the portability of publications is therefore important. This is discussed in the following section. Another possibility is to use a 'fully-fledged' multimedia or hypermedia authoring tool – such as ToolBook or HyperCard.[11] Naturally, tools of this sort although being more powerful will have similar limitations to word-processing systems. Special-purpose tools for creating interactive documents are also available – one of the most popular of these is Adobe Acrobat.[27] As well as these 'conventional' types of authoring tool, it is also possible to create electronic documents using tools that are intended for use on the Internet and the World Wide Web. Tools of this sort are discussed in more detail later in the chapter.

The role of markup

Nowadays, with the increased availability of computing resources and communications facilities it is imperative that electronic documents are both portable and 'technology independent'. Portability implies that documents that are authored on one particular type of hardware/software platform can be delivered on any other. One way of achieving this is through the use of an appropriate 'markup' facility.[12]

Over the years, various types of markup facility have become available. These include both proprietary tools such as Microsoft's rich text format (RTF) and international standards such as Standard Generalised Markup Language

(SGML), HyperText Markup Language (HTML) and HyTime (Hypermedia Time-Based Structuring Language). SGML and HyTime are attractive solutions to the portability problem because they are based on International Standards Organization (ISO) specifications. The importance of SGML is reflected in the comments made by Turner, Douglass and Turner when they write: 'The Standard Generalised Markup Language (SGML) is rapidly emerging as the single most important and powerful tool for the creation of "smart documents". These dynamically formatted files can be presented on paper or on screen; via CD-ROM; or electronically over networks and the Internet's World Wide Web. Smart documents can also be used and reused across multiple hardware and software platforms.'[28]

HTML is essentially an SGML application that represents a distinct mode of authoring and publication. It is a markup language whose tagging repertoire is extremely limited and whose primary purpose is to prepare hypertext documents for viewing on the World Wide Web or via an intranet server. It ensures the portability of hypertext documents on the WWW and that they are viewable anywhere on the Internet. HTML will be discussed in more detail in the following section.

As was mentioned above, SGML provides a document with flexibility and portability that is impossible to achieve with word-processing systems or page description utilities. However, in order to handle the **interactivity** and **multimedia** aspects of hypermedia documents, various extensions are needed. The HyTime standard has therefore been introduced as an application of SGML that extends its functionality. HyTime, like SGML, is an ISO standard. As is the case with SGML (for text-based documents), HyTime can be used to ensure the development of hypermedia documents that are portable and whose life span is potentially infinite.[28] The HyTime standard has been described and discussed in detail in DeRose and Durand.[29]

Publication media

Obviously, the medium upon which any given document is published will vary considerably from situation to situation. In general the choice will depend upon a variety of factors – cost considerations, equipment availability, the frequency with which a document has to be updated and the types of media element that it employs. Usually, when it is necessary to embed substantial volumes of video material, CD-ROM is probably the best medium to use at present. However, when a significant amount of updating is likely to be necessary a computer network facility may prove more beneficial. Sometimes a 'hybrid' solution that combines both CD-ROM and a network facility will be the most appropriate publication mechanism. A comparison of the relative merits of electronic publication media has been presented by Gloor.[13] He studied the use of two media

(CD-ROM and the World Wide Web) for the publication of conference proceedings in electronic form. Interestingly, despite the utility of the electronic proceedings, Gloor comments: 'Even in the emerging cyberspace society, a printed document may be superior to any hypertext'!

Intranet and Internet publishing

Over the last few decades, computer networking facilities have grown to a position of prominence as a mechanism to facilitate the effective and efficient communication of electronic data and information. Today, computer networks play a key role within virtually all organizations, within both the public and private sectors. Such networks form the basis for both in-house **intranet** services and globally accessible public networks like the **Internet** and the World Wide Web. Because of the growing importance of using these types of resource within library systems, this section deals with intranet and Internet publication. It begins by outlining the general principles involved, the basic mechanisms that are employed and the significance of HTML and related authoring tools. The techniques involved are then briefly illustrated by means of a simple case study involving the development of a **Book Reviews Online** system.

General principles

Electronic documents can be created, stored and accessed using virtually any form of computer system – provided it has the correct hardware/software support. However, if an isolated, stand-alone computer such as a PC is used, the ability to share these documents and distribute them to other users could be very limited. Bearing this in mind, the basic principle underlying the use of network facilities for the publication of electronic documents is that once they have been 'set up' within an appropriate library facility, they can then be made available for global access (within a defined domain) to other users. This can be done in a way that does not impose any restrictions on the time of day at which documents are accessed or the geographical location from which access is made. Of course, for security, privacy and integrity reasons, some form of access control may need to be imposed in order to restrict access to those having appropriate authority.

Although there are many different ways in which an electronic document library can be created, one of the most common and popular is that involving the 'client/server' approach, as implemented on the Internet and WWW. In this approach, a document collection is stored on and made available to users by means of one or more interconnected **servers**. The purpose of these is to 'service' requests for information from one or more **clients**. A special software package running on a client computer (called a **browser**) is used to provide the basic end-user interface to the document collection. A browser normally provides at the very least three basic functions: first, a mechanism whereby the location of a sought-after document can be specified, achieved by using its 'uniform resource locator' or URL); second, facilities for enabling a document to be viewed on the client machine; and third, facilities to search through a document and follow hyperlinks to other related documents. This latter process is often referred to as 'navigation'.

After a browser has sent a URL request for a document to a server, a copy of that document is transferred over the computer network to the client where it is stored locally in a storage cache. The time it takes for a document to be transferred depends upon a number of factors – such as the network traffic density at the time the request is made, the size of the document and the type of information it contains. Large, multimedia documents containing sound and video can take quite a long time to download. However, once an electronic document is installed in the client's local cache memory, subsequent interaction with it can be very fast indeed.

As discussed earlier in this chapter, the HTML convention is normally used to markup documents for use on the Web. Consequently, the browser that is used within a client computer will expect documents to be marked up in this way. However, because of the limitations of HTML with respect to handling multimedia/hypermedia documents (and materials that are not marked up in HTML), any given browser will normally have to be augmented by a number of **helper applications**. These are called upon by the browser as and when they are needed, in order to make available facilities that the browser itself cannot provide, for example, playing audio files, viewing MPEG video clips, reading documents that are marked up in SGML, and so on.

Publishing on networks

There are various ways in which a document collection can be made available via a computer network. The particular approach that is employed will depend upon whether the library documents are to be made publicly available or whether they are needed only to service the needs of a 'closed' user-group. In both cases, documents will be mounted on a server, but the purpose of the server (and the domain it serves) will be different. Servers that are intended to be used only for in-house purposes (to meet the needs of a particular group or organization) are said to constitute an intranet facility. On the other hand, servers that are intended to be used to provide global public access to documents will normally form part of the world-wide Internet service, which will ultimately form the basis of a future trans-global information superhighway.

Some of the different ways in which network publication can be used to improve access to electronic documents will be illustrated by reference to three recent projects. Each of these was intended to study the feasibility of and prob-

lems involved in using the particular approach that was adopted. The first project, called the TULIP project,[6] was initiated a few years ago by the Elsevier publishing corporation. This is a large-scale dissemination experiment which is
intended to study the problems of distributing learned journals in electronic form
to selected university sites in the USA. The second example involves the publication of a series of hypermedia conference proceedings on an Internet server.[13]
These proceedings can be accessed at the following URL:

<http://awi.aw.com/DAGS95>

The third example of a network publication is based upon our own work involving the development of an Electronic OASIS (described previously) using an
intranet facility.[8] This work involved converting conventional paper-based documents into electronic form and then making them available on an in-house
intranet server.

Of course, publishers themselves are also now exploiting the power of network
publication. For them, some of the main attractions of using computer networks
are for advertising new products, making available online catalogues, issuing
errata, and providing 'teleshopping' facilities (via online bookstores) whereby
books can be ordered directly using interactive electronic order forms. Some
examples of the ways in which publishers are now using network resources are
illustrated by the websites that reside at the following URLs:

<http://www.wiley.co.uk:80/electronic/hipr>
<http://www.birkhauser.com/hypermedia/hypermedia.html>
<http://www.mcp.com/que>

As well as being able to increase the availability of electronic documents, another
important reason for wanting to publish documents on computer networks is the
'new and novel' facilities that can be made available. Some of the more important
of these (some of which have already been mentioned previously) include the
creation of living documents; the ability to create dynamic documents and online
forms, the use of annotation facilities, group authorship, and the use of personal
profiles. The last facility is a very important one since it can be used to enable
users of an electronic library to tailor documents and the way in which they
appear and behave to the needs of individual users. In this context, the use of
'smartcards' would seem to have much to offer library users.[30]

Of course, each of the different sorts of library facility discussed earlier in this
chapter will need to respond in appropriate ways to the availability of network
publishing. There are two basic requirements that need to be considered: first,
how network resources can be used as a management tool to facilitate the running of a library through the use of online ordering, interactive interlibrary loans,

and so on; and second, the provision of facilities to enable users of a library to access collections of electronic documents that are held either locally or at geographically remote sites. These possibilities open up many exciting possibilities for future developments in library systems.

The basic principles of 'web publishing' have been described and discussed by numerous authors (see, for example, Gloor,[13] Tan,[12] Haynes[9] and Bodensiek.[31]) Naturally, one of the most fundamental requirements for getting involved in this area is an understanding of the HTML markup language and the types of facility that it can be used to provide.

Unfortunately, HTML has a number of limitations with respect to the level of interactivity and the degree of intelligence that can be embedded within an electronic document. Many of these shortcomings can be overcome by adopting the use of a new Web programming language called 'Java'.[32] This can be used to create various sorts of 'applet' that can be downloaded to a browser and which can give a document 'local' intelligence, greater interactivity and allow a wider range of dynamic behaviour.

A case study: Book Reviews Online

In order to illustrate the ways in which the HTML facilities described above can be used, this section outlines a simple case study. It involves the design and development of a 'Book Reviews Online' retrieval system that we have been creating as part of our digital library research programme.[33–4] The system runs on an in-house intranet facility and is based upon the use of a Netscape WWW browser.

As has been established previously in this chapter, books form a fundamental building block for virtually all library systems, both conventional and electronic. Unfortunately, there are now so many books and related documents in existence that no one could ever hope to read them all in just one lifetime. Reviews therefore constitute an increasingly important mechanism to facilitate the selection of books to read. In principle, a good book review will provide a precise and accurate summary of the content of a book. It will also specify the level at which the book is aimed and the style/approach that the author(s) have adopted.

When using an online book reviews system, users should be able to search for reviews of particular books of potential interest to them. They should then be able to check if their local library holds copies of the required books. If they are not available then facilities should be provided to enable a user to order copies of sought-after items by raising an electronic purchase order or by means of an interactive, form-based inter-library loan facility. Within this case study there is thus ample scope for the use of online forms for specifying both search criteria and 'buy or borrow' ordering information.

Obviously, the retrieval mechanisms that are used to obtain book reviews from an online database and search the online catalogue of a local library should allow users to identify target documents using any of the 'standard' attributes associated with books. That is, users should be able to specify one or more of a book's authors, its full or contracted title, a list of keywords describing its content, its publisher, its ISBN and so on.

Bearing in mind the above requirements, two basic 'proof of principle' prototypes were constructed.[33] The first of these involved multiple hyperlinking from reactive, screen- based attribute lists (embedded in a HTML document) through to the associated electronic reviews. This prototype was 'expensive' to update and maintain and became very cumbersome to use with respect to end-user interaction as the number of reviews increased. The second prototype was designed to overcome these limitations and involved the use of a simple interactive form that was serviced by a Common Gateway Interface (CGI) script running on the server. The script, which was written in the Perl programming language, extracted data entered into an online 'book review' form by its user and passed this data across to a search engine. This search engine, which was also written in Perl, was responsible for retrieving appropriate book reviews from the online database and presenting these to its user.

The second prototype proved to be very easy to maintain and use since it required no HTML knowledge on the part of its user. Individual reviews are simply copied across to a 'reviews directory' where they are stored as simple ASCII text files. When a search request is executed, the search engine performs a sequential search through every file held in the reviews directory. The names of all files that meet the search criteria for a given search are placed on a 'hit list' for subsequent display.

Mobile computing and information on demand

The basic functions of the various types of library described early in this chapter are twofold: to archive important information; and, subsequently, to make this information available to those who need to use it. In the past, people who wanted to access the information held in a library had to physically go to that library in order to consult the documents they were interested in. The use of digital electronic libraries now means that, in principle, this no longer has to happen since the information they contain can now be delivered to their users wherever they happen to reside. Nowadays, the phrase **information on demand** is often used to describe situations of this sort in which digital electronic information can be delivered to particular points of need at times and in ways that are determined by the specific requirements of individual consumers or client groups. As is discussed in this section, the advent of **mobile computing equipment** now makes the realization of this technique a practical reality.

The importance of information stems from the role that it plays in decision-making and problem-solving activities. Obviously, the availability of relevant information can significantly influence whether or not a problem can be solved, the speed with which a solution can be derived and the quality of the solution that can be obtained. In his discussion of problem solving and information availability, Barker[35] has identified four basic types of information: global, isolated, local and mobile.

Global information is information that is easily and widely accessible on a world-wide basis through electronic communication systems. These may be private or public networks and/or broadcasting systems of various sorts. Typical examples of global information are files of material that can be obtained from the Internet, using software such as ftp, for example, or downloaded from the World Wide Web. Obviously, global information may be either private (and possibly encrypted for use only within a closed user-group) or publicly available for general consumption.

As its name suggests, isolated information is information that cannot be accessed directly from a particular work setting. Such information can arise from three basic types of situation: information that cannot be accessed because it is not in electronic form; information that is in electronic form but cannot be accessed because of connectivity problems, which may be transient, temporary or permanent; and cases in which information is available online but cannot be accessed because of restricted access rights that may be imposed for financial, political, security or ethical reasons. Sometimes it may be possible to access certain types of isolated information using special techniques such as 'fax back' or by requesting a 'media mount' operation to be performed by personnel located 'back at base'.

Local information refers to material that is available to a decision maker at the location where s/he happens to be working, for example a public or private library or a workstation in a client's office. In this latter case, the computer equipment might provide access to an associated digital electronic library in the form of a collection of one or more CD-ROM discs or an in-house 'intranet' facility.[31, 36] This type of information is 'fixed' at the location where particular types of job-related decision have to be made.

Mobile information corresponds to material that physically moves about with a decision maker as s/he travels around from one location to another. It might exist as material that is embedded within the internal storage facilities provided by a portable notebook computer or a palmtop computing facility. Alternatively, it might consist of data contained on floppy disks, portable hard disks, solid-state disks or CD-ROM discs that are 'carried around' with the computer system. Obviously, certain types of information that might normally be regarded as isolated could be converted into mobile information by copying it across to a portable medium – provided it exists in a digital format. The particular subset to be cross-loaded would obviously depend upon the problems to be solved at the locations that are to be visited.

One of the major objectives underlying the philosophy of information on demand is that we should consider ways to minimize the amount of unavailable/isolated information and maximize the volume of globally available information, bearing in mind the limitations and/or possibilities offered by local and mobile material. Of course, one of the most important ways in which this can be achieved is through the more widespread use of electronic documents within a framework of digital library systems that can be accessed through the use of mobile computing equipment such as notebook computers and personal digital assistants.[35, 37]

In the work that we have been undertaking, we have been implementing the 'information on demand' paradigm using the concepts of living information and portable dynamic electronic libraries.[23] This work has involved two major stages: first, formulating a model that shows the relationship between the four types of information discussed earlier in this section; and second, using this model to formulate strategies for the creation of reconfigurable, flexible electronic library systems as a mechanism for making available collections of electronic documents that are relevant to the needs of any particular problem solving situation.

Much of the technology needed to implement the concepts described in this section is available today. As has been stated earlier, there is a wide range of 'pocket size' devices now available to facilitate the realization of the types of information sharing outlined above.[37-8] One of the most popular of these has been the Psion Organizer.[35] Through its solid-state disks and serial communication port, this hand-held computer enables its user to 'carry' a personal electronic library within his/her pocket. It also enables electronic documents to be sent and received using fax and e-mail. Many other types of bespoke, portable electronic book readers are also now starting to become quite well-established, such as the Sony DATA Discman,[39] for which there is a growing stock of commercially available electronic publications. Combined with the potential of smartcards for dynamically copying electronic books from a master library, these highly portable devices will place many new demands on libraries and library administrators.

Conclusions

Within virtually all areas of human endeavour, library systems form an important resource with which to facilitate the archival, dissemination and sharing of information. As is the case in most other types or organization, the advent of powerful, low-cost computer-based technologies is forcing system designers and managers to rethink their approach to providing the services and facilities that they offer. Obviously, the use of new technologies within libraries brings with it many exciting possibilities for the development of new approaches to information storage and access. Among the more important of these possibilities we must include the movement towards the more extensive use of digital electronic libraries, the availability of information that is 'medium independent', and access to information 'as and when' it is needed without imposing any restraints on the geographical location from which a request originates.

Fundamental to the effective and efficient use of digital library systems will be an underlying infrastructure of well-established, generic classes of electronic document. These document classes will form the basic building blocks for the creation of dynamic collections of library items that can be tailored to meet the requirements of individual users. The types of document that are available will encompass both the already familiar kinds of library item (such as books, journals and catalogues – in electronic form) and newer kinds of facility (like interactive newspapers, intelligent electronic books and living documents).

Undoubtedly, global access to these collections of electronic documents will be provided by an all-embracing information superhighway. This will enable libraries to be accessed from within the home, from a school environment, an office, an airport, a train or a car. Naturally, mobile computing equipment of the sort outlined in this chapter will provide a very important mechanism for facilitating access to the information networks of the future and the digital electronic libraries that support them.

Naturally, on-going technical and organizational developments of the sort described in this chapter are likely to have a number of important implications for users of libraries and for the people who manage them. It is therefore important to consider what would happen if there were to be a large-scale movement towards the creation of a single global electronic library, or a relatively small number of integrated regional libraries, in which all transactions were of an electronic nature and were conducted using documents and devices of the sort outlined previously in this chapter. Some of the important questions that would need to be addressed would include: How would such a transition influence the livelihood of small branch libraries as they exist today? What would be the future for librarians in terms of jobs and job skills if such a system was created? What would be the future of conventional books? What sort of new services might appear? Obviously, these are very important issues that need to be discussed and debated. Unfortunately, space does not allow them to be discussed here. Maybe these are topics for a future book – perhaps, an electronic one?

References

1 Checkland, P. B., 'A systems map of the universe', in *Systems behaviour*, ed. by J. Beishon and G. Peters, London, Harper and Row, 1972, 50–5.

2 Bagrit, L., *The age of automation, BBC Reith Lectures 1964*, London, Weidenfeld and Nicholson, 1965.

3 Barker, P. G., 'Emerging principles of performance support', in *Online information '95, Proceedings of the 19th Online Information Meeting*, Olympia, London, 5–7 December, ed. by D. I. Raitt and B. Jeapes, Oxford, Learned Information (Europe), 1995, 407–16.

4 Barker, P. G., 'End-user interface design for an electronic KWIC', in *Online Information '94, Proceedings of the 18th Online Information Meeting*, Olympia, London, 6–8 December, ed. by D. I. Raitt and B. Jeapes, Oxford, Learned Information (Europe), 1994, 191–202.

5 Fox, E. A. and Lunin, L., 'Introduction and overview to perspectives on digital libraries', *Journal of the American Society of Information Science*, **44** (8), 1993, 441–3.

6 Zijlstra, J., 'The university licensing programme (TULIP): a large scale experiment in bringing electronic journals to the desk top', *Serials*, **7** (2), 1994, 169–72.

7 Barker, P. G., 'Electronic libraries of the future', in *Encyclopedia of library and information science*, Volume 50, Supplement 22, ed. by A. Kent and C. M. Hall, New York, NY, Marcel Dekker, 1997, 119–53.

8 Barker, P. G., Beacham, N., Hudson, S. and Tan, C. M., 'Document handling in an electronic OASIS', *The new review of document and text management*, **1**, 1995, 1–17.

9 Haynes, C., *Paperless publishing*, Blue Ridge Summit, PA, Windcrest/McGraw-Hill, 1994.

10 Shneiderman, B. and Kearsley, G., *Hypertext hands-on! – an introduction to a new way of organising and accessing information*, Reading, MA, Addison-Wesley Publishing Company, 1989.

11 Barker, P. G., *Exploring hypermedia*, London, Kogan Page, 1993.

12 Tan, C. M., 'Hypermedia electronic books' (Draft PhD Thesis, University of Teesside, 1997).

13 Gloor, P., *Elements of hypermedia design – techniques for navigation and visualization in cyberspace*, Boston, MA, Birkhäuser, 1997.

14 Barker, P. G., 'Electronic books: a review and assessment of current trends', *Educational technology review*, **6**, 1996, 14–18.

15 Barker, P. G., 'Virtual reality: theoretical basis, practical applications, *Journal of the Association of Learning Technology (ALT-J)*, **1** (1), 1993, 15–25.

16 Smithsonian Institution, *Treasures of the Smithsonian*, CD-I produced by the

Smithsonian Institution in association with Philips Interactive Media of America, Washington, USA, 1990.

17   Bogaerts, W. F. and Agema, K. S., *Active library on corrosion*, Amsterdam, Elsevier, 1992.

18   Pejtersen, A. M., 'New model for multimedia interfaces for online public access catalogues, *The electronic library*, **10** (6), 1992, 359–66.

19   Negroponte, N., *Being digital*, London, Hodder and Stoughton, 1995.

20   Maunder, C., 'Documentation on tap', *IEEE spectrum*, **31** (9), 1994, 52–6.

21   Barker, P. G., 'Authoring hypermedia documents; a rationale and case study, *Journal of document and text management*, **1** (3), 1993, 191–214.

22   Martin, J., *Hyperdocuments and how to create them*, Englewood Cliffs, New Jersey, Prentice-Hall International, 1990.

23   Barker, P. G., 'Living books and dynamic electronic libraries', *The electronic library*, **14** (6), 1996, 491–501.

24   Barker, P. G., 'Electronic books and libraries of the future', *The electronic library*, **10** (3), 1992, 139–49.

25   Rowland, F., McKnight, C. and Meadows, J., *Project ELVYN: an experiment in electronic journal delivery – facts, figures and findings*, London, Bowker-Saur, 1995.

26   Sargent, G., 'Echo across the Web: a local newspaper on the Internet', *The electronic library*, **14** (4), 1996, 357–63.

27   Deep, J. and Holfelder, P., *Designing interactive documents with Adobe Acrobat Pro*, New York, John Wiley & Sons, 1996.

28   Turner, R. C., Douglass, T. A. and Turner, A. J., *Readme.1st – SGML for writers and editors*, New Jersey, Prentice Hall, 1996.

29   DeRose, S. J. and Durand, D. G., *Making hypermedia work – a user's guide to Hytime*, Dordrecht, Kluwer Academic Publishers, 1994.

30   Zoreda, J. L. and Otón, J. M., *Smart cards*, Boston, Artech House Inc, 1994.

31   Bodensiek, P., *Intranet publishing*, Indianapolis, QUE Corporation, 1996.

32   Anuff, E., *The Java sourcebook – a complete guide to creating Java applets for the Web*, New York, John Wiley & Sons, 1996.

33   Barker, P. G., *Book reviews online*, Working Paper, Interactive Systems Research Group, Human-Computer Interaction Laboratory, Middlesbrough, UK, University of Teesside, 1997.

34   Bouvier, E., 'WWW Book Reviews', (Final Year BSc Dissertation, School of Computing and Mathematics, University of Teesside, 1997).

35   Barker, P. G., 'Towards real information on demand', in *Online Information '95, Proceedings of the 20th Online Information Meeting*, Olympia, London, 3–5 December, ed. by D. I. Raitt and B. Jeapes, Oxford, Learned Information (Europe), 1996, 261–9.

36 IEEE, 'Digital electronic libraries', *IEEE computer*, **29** (5), 1996, special edition.
37 Rockman, S., 'Personal digital assistants, *Personal computer world*, **19** (4), 1996, 124–32.
38 Falk, H., 'PDAs: palm-size computing power', *The electronic library*, **14** (2), 1996, 167–70.
39 Sherman, R. J., 'The electronic book', *Journal of document and text management*, **1** (1), 1993, 95–100.

5

DIGITAL LIBRARIES AND THE NSF/DARPA/NASA DIGITAL LIBRARIES INITIATIVE*

Stephen M. Griffin

DIVISION OF INFORMATION, ROBOTICS AND INTELLIGENT SYSTEMS, NATIONAL SCIENCE FOUNDATION, USA

Introduction

This chapter discusses recent advances in digital libraries research and technologies and the implications for libraries. It argues for increased collaboration between technologists, librarians and domain scholars and a merging of perspectives in considering future research and development activities. The activities of the US Digital Libraries Initiative (DLI), sponsored by the National Science Foundation (NSF), the Department of Defense Advanced Research Projects Agency (DARPA), and the National Aeronautics and Space Administration (NASA) offer models for accomplishing these goals. The six projects have become highly visible and influential efforts in the digital libraries research arena. Implications for library managers responsible for planning are addressed and new directions are suggested based on experiences to date, technology trajectories and changes in institutional practices.

In recent years there has been explosive growth of interest in the development and use of digital libraries. Some of the contributing factors to this are readily apparent:

- base computing and communications technologies have become powerful, plentiful and economical, allowing for creation, collection and manipulation of digital information on a grand scale;
- international networking infrastructure has been put in place to support connectivity and interoperability at little or no cost to users;

---

* The material in this chapter represents the views of the author and does not necessarily reflect National Science Foundation policies.

- online information proliferates through global efforts to produce and convert information in digital form;
- common Internet access frameworks (i.e. World Wide Web) have emerged and become widely adopted.

Yet these factors alone do not explain the appeal and growing interest in digital libraries. 'Digital libraries' has also become a transformational metaphor for *thinking* about information, systems, people and interactions between them. This has supplied a new stock of concepts for technology discourse – new concepts for the management and use of information, which have inspired a profusion of new research and technology integration efforts.

The label 'digital libraries' has come to be used in several ways. Some use it to refer primarily to *collections* of digital information; others use it to refer primarily to the information *technologies* managing them. The most appropriate meaning encompasses both of these; digital libraries are large-scale, organized collections of multimedia data with information management tools and methods capable of presenting data as useful information and knowledge to people in a variety of social and organizational contexts.[1] This sense of the term implies, correctly, that digital libraries both reveal and require new models for information access and use by increasingly diverse, numerous and populous user 'communities' in the broadest sense of the term.

One of the primary goals of digital libraries research and development is to produce research paradigms and products which serve diverse communities of users with a broad range of information needs – and increasingly elevated levels of expectation. To achieve this goal researchers must look beyond technology into domain, social, legal, economic contexts and be informed by user and usage studies at each stage of the technologies design and development cycle. 'Digital libraries' has emerged as a natural topical ground for constructive interaction between researchers from many disciplinary domains and other stakeholders in the development and use of networked knowledge repositories.

Conceptually, digital libraries mirror collections and library services in the physical world. A digital library is analogous to a 'traditional' library in terms of the diversity and complexity of its collection. Its contents, although residing on electronic media, are stored in familiar forms (as journals, reports, photos, maps, recordings, etc.) and referred to using familiar terminologies. Digital libraries draw on many of the same methods of organizing, indexing and cataloging information as traditional libraries, with software systems automating some of the services performed by librarians in indexing and interpreting users' requests for information. Many users experience a sense of cognitive familiarity when exploring and navigating through a digital library.

Although analogizing digital libraries to traditional libraries is apt, comparing the two as competing forms is not. Digital libraries technologies will complement library functions and services; librarians will continue to inform the technologies development toward this end. Digital libraries technologies will be drawn into and transform many institutional forms including libraries, universities, laboratories, schools and businesses. The rate and extent to which this occurs will depend upon numerous factors including:

- externalities at the societal level, such as
  - resolution of legal issues surrounding intellectual property
  - investment in national communications infrastructure
- local institutional and organizational constraints, such as
  - availability of resources
  - user demands
  - leadership of individuals who manage organizations
- technology breakthroughs capable of transforming social and occupational practices on a very large scale.

A primary example of the latter is the World Wide Web which has grown from about 50 registered sites in 1993 to 1200 by early 1995, to more than 15 million at present and which continues to expand at a breathtaking pace. Phenomena like the growth of the Internet and World Wide Web point to undiscovered, unanticipated information needs and proclivities of societies.

Research in digital libraries explores critical technological and social issues in the development and use of large-scale networked knowledge repositories. The technology goals, simply put, are to efficiently and effectively create, capture, store, search and retrieve information from electronic collections of text, images, maps, audio recordings, video and film clips and combinations of these (multimedia). For researchers, the key issues centre on how best to do this. Integration of component technologies into usable systems and studies at each stage of the information lifecycle is essential to producing high-quality, enduring information resources and infrastructure. Attempts to address these issues draw into play and drive some of the most advanced research in high performance computing and communications technologies.

Because of the richness of content and wide variation in information types stored in digital libraries, users are inclined to demand high functionality from these systems. Historically, information search and retrieval research has focused on relatively simple models in which a well-defined 'user' comes to a static system with a well-defined problem, which translates into a query, which maps into an explicit information request, which may or may not be filled by the system. Systems based on these models often *program users* into constrained, recursive processes of problem definition, task consideration, source identification, query formulation, search and retrieval, evaluation of results and iterative cycles within these. Digital libraries offer a richer, less constraining environment for information discovery, search and retrieval – dynamic environments which invite creativity. Users without well-defined problems can browse, filter, select, associate, obtain references and links, tabulate, evaluate, compare and analyse as well as simply search and retrieve information.

Human-centered systems (HCS) is a relatively new perspective which provides a larger analytical framework for thinking about information systems. From the HCS perspective, humans are part of the system being studied from the beginning. Success is measured by the ability of the technologies to adapt to human needs. In the case of digital libraries, technologies are still being designed and developed by those who will not be the primary users of them, but the cross-cultural distances are shrinking. Helping to understand the relationships between digital libraries technologies, content, use and users is central. Over time, digital libraries research will make major contributions in the transition to information-centered institutional forms and practices in many dimensions of society.

Digital libraries and libraries

For centuries knowledge has been gathered, recorded, organized and stored in repositories of various kinds. The most common of these is the traditional library. This model has limitations associated with storage and access to information, because most of the knowledge collected by libraries has been recorded on physical media. Within the past decade the number and kinds of digital information resources have proliferated. Computing system advances and the networking revolution has resulted in a remarkable expansion in abilities to generate and disseminate information in digital formats on electronic media. These technology-based developments have led to speculation on new concepts of the nature, role and use of data archives and libraries. New forms of knowledge repositories have become feasible, both technologically and economically.[2]

Digital libraries are like traditional libraries in that they involve large collections of diverse information and there are common issues concerning organization, retrieval, access, storage, archiving and preservation of the information. However, digital libraries are different in that the properties of physical location and storage of local copies for individual use no longer need apply. This decoupling of storage, organization and access along with the ease of authoring, annotation, and support for collaborative work groups offers significant advantages.[3]

As a result of new technologies, libraries as institutions are confronted with new challenges and new opportunities. The University of Michigan Digital

Libraries Initiative project information material states: 'Combining traditional notions of libraries with contemporary technological capabilities (such as the WWW) is a meeting of dissimilars. Libraries have traditionally stressed service, organization, and centralization. The WWW has embodied flexibility, rapid evolution, and decentralization. Digital libraries somehow need to bring these together.'[4] And it goes on:

> Much of the early work on digital libraries took the centralized, structured view of a library as given. The goal was to provide access though electronic means to libraries' increasingly large volume of digital resources. This approach did not fully appreciate the opportunities for decentralization, rapid evolution and openness that are part of networking . . . Many observers did not trust that the traditional values of service, organization, access, and preservation inherent in libraries as institutions could be maintained in an environment like the World Wide Web.

The concern that libraries as we have known them may disappear from physical space to be reconstituted in cyberspace is not warranted. Libraries are also institutions, where people go to work and learn, to provide services and to receive them. They are valued, in part, not only by virtue of the richness of their collections but because of the richness of their physical environment – a 'place' with 'things' where people interact directly. Taken together, libraries constitute one of the most powerful and enduring intellectual institutions in our culture. And, like many other institutions, they have meaning and value that cannot be calculated by simply summing the values of component functions and services. Digital libraries technologies will as likely enhance the value of libraries as institutions as diminish it. The key challenge is merging the separate perspectives. As noted in a recent workshop on distributed knowledge environments, one valuable aspect of digital libraries is their ability to preserve discourse, to provide a better context in which to communicate about and understand information. Understanding how to preserve the central features of the library is an important part of this (see Figure 5.1).[5]

Issues for libraries

The issues confronting libraries can be grouped into several categories:

- technological issues: what to do about acquisition and conversion of digital media, obsolescence, stable long-term access, etc.;
- organizational issues: how can/should the organization respond to changing roles and responsibilities thrust upon it;
- economic issues: who will bear the costs and will there be economies of scale;
- legal and regulatory issues: resolving intellectual property issues associated with acquiring and making digital collections available.

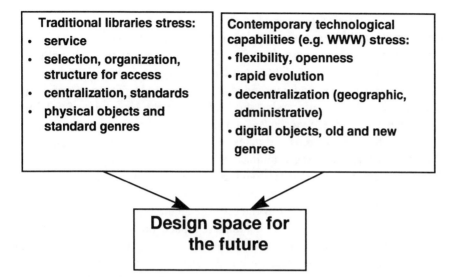

Fig. 5.1   *Merging perspectives*
(Courtesy of the University of Michigan Digital Libraries Initiative Project)

Some of these can be addressed at the local level; others require national or global attention and cooperation. Resolving problems at each level will benefit from increased coordination of efforts between organizations.

The technological issues may well prove to be the most tractable. The growing body of experience associated with retrospective conversion of physical media, acquisition of native digital documents in forms that can be used and preservation and archiving of digital materials, indicates that this is achievable on a large-scale. However, it is also generally true that the effort required exceeds prior expectations in terms of human labour and cost.

Archiving digital material has proved to be as painstaking and arduous as printed material. Electronic media, like physical media, become obsolete and degrades. New software may not be able to use data prepared for different software or even earlier versions of the same. Storage devices and device types become obsolete and the physical media on which data is stored degrades. Selecting proper strategies for long-term preservation and use of complex digital objects is essential before undertaking the actual tasks.*

---

* One vivid example where lack of foresight and attention to the issues of obsolescence has proven to be very costly is the year 2000 problem. Hardware and software systems around the world using two-digit date codes may fail when the clock strikes midnight on 31 December 1999.

Scanning and indexing physical artefacts has also proven to be human labour-intensive. To create new resources that meet quality and completeness standards for researchers wishing to use these frequently requires meticulous handling and documentation of artefacts. The requirements vary for each type of media and digital object according to the intended use. For example, to scan an aerial photo transparency for initial processing and loading into the University of California, Santa Barbara's (UCSB) Alexandria Digital Libraries project testbed requires more than 12 separate steps and takes 15–20 minutes. It requires manipulating the photographic image, the scanning equipment and the software. Then indexes for the image must be digitized and geo-referencing completed. Finally, the image file (30MB at 600dpi) must be incorporated properly into the logical space of the digital library as defined by the software architecture. There are numerous potential benefits from research to automate aspects of the process.

Conversion of textual materials is equally exacting. One exemplary effort demonstrating large scale conversion and dissemination of textual materials is the JSTOR Project. <http://www.jstor.org>. JSTOR (Journal STORage) is a non-profit organization founded by the Andrew W. Mellon Foundation. Its goals are to develop a reliable and comprehensive digital archive of important journal literature and to make this available to libraries in an economic way, via licensing agreements. Initially ten journals in history and economics were selected for retrospective conversion into digital formats. This has now expanded in terms of subject area and number of journals. Back issues from the journals are scanned at 600 dpi, converted into ASCII text and indexed to allow rapid search and retrieval.

Current research

As noted earlier, current research in digital libraries explores issues in the development and use of large scale networked information stores with the aim of efficiently and effectively handling and manipulating knowledge from multimedia collections.

Topical research areas seen as fundamental to the further development of digital libraries include:

- creating, capturing and describing (metadata) large volumes of information in numerous formats;
- indexing, categorizing, organizing and combining heterogeneous, distributed information
- developing software and algorithms for information exploration and manipulation (browsing, searching, filtering, abstracting, summarizing);
- developing tools, protocols and procedures for advancing the utilization of net-

worked information stores distributed around the nation and around the world;

- studying the impact of these technologies on individuals, communities, organizations, sectors, and society at large.[6]

To move beyond research prototype systems to operational systems of value another level of research is required as well. Research at this level explores alternatives for combining technologies and content to create new knowledge infrastructure for a wide variety of intellectual and social ends. To achieve this, elements of the entire digital libraries lifecycle must be considered, including:

- core technologies and system components (functional attributes and the component technologies upon which these depend);
- system architectures and technology integration (architectures for the integration of individual resources and technologies into useful systems);
- the nature of information artefacts, collections and services in rapidly changing technology environments (new and emerging forms of data, documents, rights management, network billing, economic models, etc.);
- contexts of deployment and use (the influence of intellectual, social, organizational, cultural, international and other contexts on the development, use and impact of digital libraries);
- infrastructure (enduring resources and the communities they are meant to benefit).

A useful categorization of digital libraries research can be based on grouping the major issues into systems-centered, artefact-centered, and human-centered research. These areas are interdependent, but together provide a useful framework for discussion.[7]

- Systems-centered research focuses on issues of architecture design, scaling, interoperability, reliability and adaptivity.
- Collection-centered research focuses on issues of building, maintaining, preserving, and providing access (including intellectual property and fair use ramifications).
- Human-centered research focuses on user and community needs, practices, and expectations and matching technologies to these.

The NSF/DARPA/NASA Digital Libraries Initiative (DLI)

In 1994 six research projects aimed at developing new technologies for digital libraries were funded through a joint initiative of the National Science Foundation, the Department of Defense Advanced Research Projects Agency, and the National Aeronautics and Space Administration. The DLI grew out of increasing demand for network-based systems and services capable of providing diverse communities of users with coherent access to large, distributed repositories of knowledge. Base Federal funding is $24.4 million over a four year period. The six projects were selected from the 75 proposals received.

Each of the six DLI projects brings together multidisciplinary teams of researchers and users from a lead university with those from other organizations. More than 75 separate organizations have formed partnering relationships with the projects. The organizations represent diverse interests in digital libraries technologies and include major US computer and communications companies, academic institutions at all levels, libraries, publishers, government and state agencies, professional associations, and other organizations with a stake in large-scale knowledge repositories and information management.

The six projects function and are managed as a collaborative effort with the common goal to dramatically advance the means to collect, store, organize and use widely distributed knowledge resources containing diverse types of information and content stored in a variety of electronic forms.

The projects have become highly visible and influential efforts, playing a leader role in the digital libraries research community. The range of activities encompassed by the projects includes not only research and development of technologies but, equally important, investigation of issues in librarianship, user-based design and evaluation, sociological issues, network economics and billing, and management of terms and conditions of the use of intellectual property in digital media. All of these areas contain obstacles which might hinder the establishment of widespread and generally useful digital libraries.

The most up-to-date and comprehensive information on the projects' activities can be obtained from their individual World Wide Web (WWW) sites. Each project's WWW site contains the original proposal submitted to the NSF, research and testbed highlights, progress reports, technical papers, seminar and conference schedules and attendance lists and in most cases, limited access to a working prototype of the testbed (see Figure 5.2).

University of California, Berkeley <http://elib.cs.berkeley.edu/>

This UCB project is producing a prototype multimedia digital library with a focus on environmental information. The effort is aimed at achieving 'work-centered' digital libraries. Work groups require more sophisticated digital library services and collaborative task support than individuals to effectively utilize massive distributed repositories of multimedia information. The research agenda includes an ambitious list of topics related to user-oriented access to large distributed collections of diverse data types.[8] Current research topics include:

Project	Research focus	WWW URL
Carnegie Mellon University and Partners	interactive digital video	http:// informedia.cs.cmu.edu
Univ of California, Berkeley and Partners	database approaches to media integration & access	http:// elib.cs.berkeley.edu/
Univ of Illinois and Partners	SGML, semantic search and retrieval	http://www.grainger.uiuc.edu/dli
Stanford University and Partners	interoperability, interfaces	http://www-diglib.stanford.edu
Univ of California, Santa Barbara and Partners	spatial-referencing of geographic information	http://alexandria.sdc.ucsb.edu
University of Michigan and Partners	intelligent agents for distributed collections	http://www.sils.umich.edu/ UMDL/HomePage.html

Fig. 5.2   *Digital Libraries Initiative Project Information Snapshot*

- **Multivalent documents**: multivalent documents offer one model for textual documents in a networked environment. In this concept a document is construed as multiple, distributed layers of closely related information. Layers interact via 'behaviours' and dynamically compose to produce increasingly useful products.
- **Intelligent access to text**: the goal of current language research is automatic topic assignment to unlabelled text. The method employs statistical disambiguation and category assignment techniques.
- **Intelligent access to images**: image research is concerned with access to testbed content by exploiting the shape, colour, texture and other visual information found in the images. Through this, it is possible to establish and recognize classes of objects and build more extended retrieval techniques.
- **User-oriented design studies**: in-depth interviews and observations of users of the testbed has resulted in accurate user needs assessment and interface design feedback.

The testbed incorporates Illustra relational DBMS technologies, a Dienst document server and a variety of research software for accessing the digital corpora. Public access to the testbed is provided via the WWW. Interoperability has been achieved with other repositories including the UCSB testbed. Current testbed holdings exceed 500GB, including approximately 40,000 images in the form of maps, photographs and drawings, and nearly 50,000 pages of documents representing environmental impact reports, technical papers and journal articles. The project aims to put online over 3.5TB of data by the end of the current funding cycle. Recently, the IBM Corporation donated a 6–18TB tape storage jukebox to the project (see Figure 5.3).

Type	Examples	Dec 96	
Documents	articles, EIRs, water reports	96,600 pp	48GB
Images	DWR wildflowers Corel Habitats Total	15,506 7,437 28,101 158 52,000	306GB
Aerial photos	Suisun March Sac-SJ Delta	500 img	3.4GB
Sensor Data	Delta fish flow	30days	.02MB
GIS Data	dams, fish, watersheds, etc.	various	52MB
DOQs	SF Bay Area	102 Img	5GB
Digital Line	SF Bay		100MB
Graphs	North Coast		100MB
Total			**363GB**

Fig. 5.3 *UCB testbed collections*
(Courtesy of the University of California, Berkeley, Digital Libraries Initiative Project)

University of California, Santa Barbara <*http://alexandria.sdc.ucsb.edu/*>

Project Alexandria is developing a digital library providing easy access to large and diverse collections of maps, images and other forms of spatially indexed information. The project has produced a CD-ROM and Rapid Prototype System based on commercial geographic information system (GIS) technology. Current efforts are aimed at implementing content-based searches of maps and images based on the use of gazetteers for named features in maps and texture matching in images. Current research topics include:

- Metadata: current research includes semantic interoperability for metadata and development of a 'top-down' framework for metadata modelling.
- Indexing and search: research focuses on content-based indexing and browsing of maps and images via texture features, similarity search, learning, geographically referenced documents and spatial proximity search. Multidimensional indexing for spatially indexed information and characterization of items in terms

of complex and fuzzy 'spatial footprints' is also being pursued.

- Storage: content-based data placement storage hierarchy and developing compact image storage schemes for wavelet-based, multi-resolution, subregion retrieval are important topics being addressed.
- Wavelets: research on various wavelet issues includes colour multispectral wavelets, quantization, transmission over noisy networks, characterization of lossiness and processing in wavelet domain.

The Alexandria Digital Library (ADL) testbed is based on traditional map library approaches and services and is housed in the Map and Imagery Laboratory (MIL) in the Davidson Library at UCSB. It currently supports a number of commercial database management systems, geographic information systems, and, partially, the CORBA/ILU (Common Object Request Broker Architecture/Inter-language Unification) distributed object system, which is managed by the Object Management Group. Current holdings include 6.5 million gazetteer records (metadata) and 8000 maps and images. This is expected to grow in the next year to 1½ million map and image records. Work is progressing on implementation of an Alexandria atlas containing domestic and international datasets. It is anticipated that this testbed will evolve into an operational resource for a large user community (see Figure 5.4).

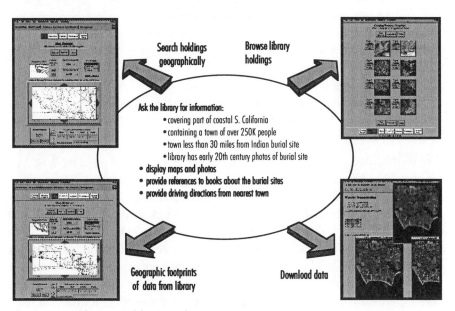

Fig. 5.4 *Web Accessible GIS Library*
(Courtesy of the University of California, Santa Barbara, Digital Libraries
Initiative Project)

University of Illinois <http://www.grainger.uiuc.edu/dli>

This project is based on the new Grainger Engineering Library Information Center at the University of Illinois in Urbana-Champaign and is centered around journals and magazines in the engineering and science literature. There are two focuses of the testbed: the first on processing, indexing, searching, and displaying an SGML-based document collection, and the second on WWW infrastructure which can be used to support semantic search. An important aspect of the project is constructing an applications environment for information analysis as a demonstration of what information technology will be possible in the 21st century. Current research topics include:

- Semantic federation across repositories: an on-going experiment involving concept space generation for journal abstracts across technical fields. A recently begun collaboration with the Santa Barbara DLl project extends the approach to geographic metadata.
- Internet interface: the research goal is a multiple view user interface for Internet resources.
- Stateful gateways: the research addresses transparent connection to distributed repositories. This involves extensive protocol translation across multiple repositories and the saving of the search state.
- Social science and user evaluation research: sociological investigations and usability studies relate both to the testbed and more generally to the changing nature of information infrastructure and its affect on 'communities' in the broad sense of the term.
- Image processing research: this research aims to link image databases to the SGML engineering journal testbed. The initial test suite is a subset of images from the Getty Museum sponsored image databases of paintings and photographs of artefacts.

The testbed documents are received directly from publishing partners in SGML format. Fifty journals from five publishers are now in production. The testbed team explores processing, indexing, search, retrieval and display of the full-text SGML articles. Extensive efforts have been directed at analysis and normalization of publisher SGML text and accompanying DTDs (Document Type Definitions). Handling mathematical formulas within SGML documents is also a research challenge. In May 1996 a successful workshop was organized to address some of these issues.[9] The project is cooperating with Carnegie Mellon to explore implementations of the Netbill system for providing network 'for-pay' services.

University of Michigan
<http://www.sils.umich.edu/UMDL/HomePage.html>

The broad goal of the project is to create and evaluate an agent-based architecture for digital libraries, one capable of supporting information access and brokering in large-scale, heterogeneous, dynamic organizations of hybrid (digital and print-on-paper) collections and services. Software agents represent collections and services. A basic premise is that an agent architecture is inherently more extensible than traditional client-server systems. The testbed will support research in earth and space science domains as well as provide learning resources for high school science classes. Current research topics include:

- Agent architectures: the effort focuses on agents in three categories: interface agents, collection agents, and a variety of mediator agents. The research challenge is to support scaling (size, complexity, and functionality) and interoperability in digital library collections and services.
- Economic modelling: this research concentrates on frameworks and architectures to manage intellectual properties and to provide sound methods for coordinating and allocating the vast resources in digital libraries.
- Customizable user interfaces: interfaces are being developed to support various classes of users and approaches to exploring information spaces that combine browsing, search, social filtering, and management of display screens.
- User evaluation and educational applications: the project is using the testbed to conduct experiments into project-centered learning in high school science classes and general public understanding of earth and space science. Researchers also look to create components of future scholarly communication and learning environments for undergraduate and research institutions.

The testbed software library includes agents to provide access to a Broad System of Ordering and thesaurus. Other specific agents include task planners, registry agents, remora agent, indexers, and an early version of an auction server. There are tools for building agents and other useful software modules, including an enhanced Z39.50 client, the inquiry interface developed for use in teaching middle and high school science, and an FTL search engine. The project has established strategic relationships with numerous publishers. A major contributor is Elsevier Journals (see Figure 5.5).

Stanford University <http://wwwdiglib.stanford.edu/diglib/pub/>

The Stanford Integrated Digital Library Project is exploring interoperability technologies and approaches through distributed object technologies. The primary goal is to enable uniform, easy access to the large number of networked information sources and collections. Major progress has been made in the devel-

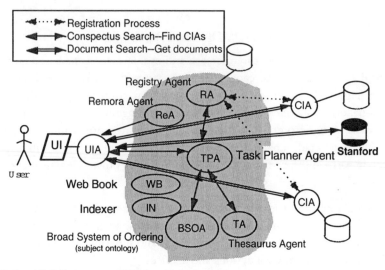

Fig 5.5 *UMDL Agents 1996*
(Courtesy of the University of Michigan Digital Libraries Inititive Project)

opment of protocols and proxies for the delivery of information and search services. Current research topics include:

- Interoperability: efforts concentrate on building the 'Infobus' architecture, proxies and testbed. A goal is to obtain interoperability among heterogeneous query, data and library services.
- User interface: visualization of search results and control of library-related tasks associated with services is a focus. Construction of drag-and-drop digital library desktop, and easy delivery of InfoBus access software will positively impact user-level interaction with the InfoBus.
- Effective information discovery and filtering.
- Task automation through agents.
- Economics and network billing: this work focuses on the economic issues in managing rights related to multiple digital libraries services and on shopping models for electronic commerce.

The testbed includes CORBA-distributed object technologies. Testbed service proxies developed are now operating with University of Michigan and University of Illinois testbeds. The testbed information content includes full-text and bibliographic data from Knight-Ridder Dialog Information Service and a variety of commercial search services, copy detection mechanisms, analysis tools and summarization tools. The project collaborates closely with the Networked Computer Science Technical Reports Library (NCSTRL) research group (see Figure 5.6).

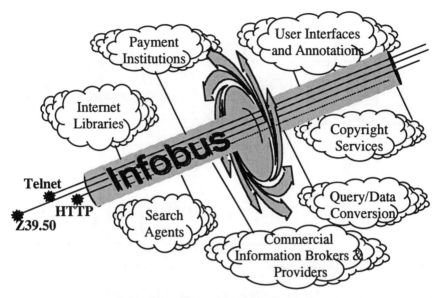

Fig. 5.6   *The Stanford Digital Library Project Infobus*
(Courtesy of the Stanford University Digital Libraries Initiative Project)

Carnegie Mellon University <http://informedia.cs.cmu.edu/>

The Informedia interactive online digital video library system is being created by Carnegie Mellon University (CMU) and the WQED/Pittsburgh public broadcasting system to enable users to access, explore and retrieve science and mathematics materials from video archives. The project has made significant strides in speech, image and language understanding for video library creation, including news-on-demand processing. The main research thrust is demonstrating that artificial intelligence approaches (natural language, video segmentation, image recognition, etc.) can be successfully integrated and applied to multimedia information to produce digital video libraries. Current research topics include:

- Speech understanding for automatically derived transcripts and spoken queries.
- Image understanding for video 'paragraphing' (segmentation) and content-based retrieval.
- Natural language processing for titling, summarization, and parsing of transcripts and queries.
- Human-system integration for video object display, navigation, browsing and reuse.
- Network authentication and billing for controlled access.
- Data architectures and network protocols for retrieval-on-demand and library interoperability.

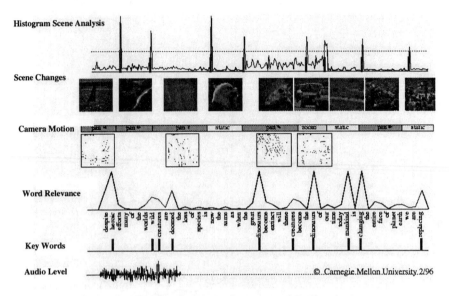

Fig. 5.7   *Informedia DVL Application of Integrated Technologies*
(Courtesy of the Carnegie Mellon University Digital Libraries Initiative
Project)

- User studies for validation and assessment.

The testbed comprises two video corpora, one in the domain of science documentaries and lectures ('Winchester Testbed') and the other broadcast news ('News-On-Demand'). Creation of content is fully automated, but requires manual correction in some cases. Queries are received in both typed and spoken forms. The current size of the Winchester Testbed is about 50 hours of video. The News-On-Demand corpora contains 150 hours (approximately 20,000 separate stories) and changes daily. The testbed goal is 1000 hours of digital video and audio selected from such sources as broadcast science programs developed by WQED and aired by PBS, video from documentary production, British Open University college level classes in the sciences, and the Fairfax County Schools, Va, Electronic Field Trip programs for elementary school students (see Figure 5.7).

Partnering

A key component to the success of the Digital Libraries Initiative projects and program has been the building of partnerships both on the sponsor side and the performer side. The DLI projects have been exceptionally successful in building meaningful partnerships with other organizations. These have resulted in technology exchange, transfer of knowledge and resources, collaborative research, and valuable personal interaction. Through partnerships, the DLI projects have been able to enlarge their topical scope, increase testbed contents and functionality and gain additional support for research. Several of the projects report cost-sharing of more than 200% of their base Federal funding. The projects reciprocate by involving partners in the day-to-day experiences of their research and testbed efforts. The partners are early users of new research products and offer opportunities for professional learning and growth.

Partner relationships differ in degree and in type, change over time and involve differing levels of interaction. While each project/partner relation is unique they can be viewed as falling into a number of general types.[10]

- Partners contribute funding. In return, they actively participate in project activities, offer technical and management feedback, and receive early insights and guidance into on-going research.
- Partners send researchers to work on-site at the university for brief or extended periods of time. These researchers in become, *de facto*, members of the project research or testbed development teams. Often the outside researchers bring projects (and ideas!) which are integrated into and become an integral part of the research.
- Partners contribute testbed content or related information services. Publishers and libraries generally fall into this class. They might provide vast holdings, library-related services such as information indexing and organization skills, or help prepare these holdings for use in the testbeds. One example of this is marking up existing digital materials in SGML.
- Partners provide advanced technologies or access to advanced technologies primarily in the form of software and hardware. Examples are Hewlett-Packard (systems), IBM (mass storage), Xerox PARC (distributed object software) and there are many others.
- Projects send personnel to the partner organization. Often these are faculty and students. It serves to enrich and stimulate research projects of common interest, and broaden the experience and exposure of research staff from both organizations.
- Projects transfer newly developed technologies to the partner. This serves a valuable purpose in testing and verification across the system development cycles. Important examples of this occurring is in areas of interoperability protocols, user interfaces, network billing schemes, etc.
- Regular dialogue is established between individuals from the projects and partner organizations. This leads to new ideas and creative approaches to existing problems.

Some of the partnerships for each project are listed overleaf.

Project partnerships

Stanford University
Stanford University academic departments and libraries
WAIS Inc.
Xerox PARC
Association for Computing Machinery
Bell Communications Research
Knight-Ridder Information (Dialog)
Enterprise Integration Technologies
Hewlett-Packard Labs
Hitachi Corp.
Hughes Research Laboratory
Interconnect Technologies
Corporation Interval Research Corporation
MIT Press
O'Reilly and Associates
NASA Ames Advanced Interaction Media Group
NASA Ames Library
Naval Command, Control and Ocean Surveillance Center (NCCOSC)

Web site: <http://Walrus.Stanford.EDU/diglib/>

University of California, Berkeley
University of California, Berkeley academic departments and libraries
University of California, Office of the President
Hewlett Packard Corporation
Illustra
IBM Almaden
Philips Research
The Plumas Corporation
Ricoh California Research
Sun Microsystems
Xerox PARC
State of California:
   Department of Water Resources
   Department of Fish and Game
   Environment Resources Evaluation System
   Resources Agency
California State Library
Sonoma County Library
San Diego Association of Governments

Web site: <http://elib.cs.berkeley.edu/>

University of California, Santa Barbara
University of California, Santa Barbara academic departments and libraries
University of Tulsa, American Geological Institute
San Diego Supercomputer Center

University of Colorado, Boulder
University of Maine, Orono
Utah State University, Mojave Database Cooperative
University of New Mexico, Earth Data Analysis Center
Excalibur Technologies
Digital Equipment Corp.
ERDAS Inc.
Environmental Systems Research Institute Inc.
Hughes Inc.
Informix
Microsoft
Oracle Inc.
O2 Inc.
SPOT Image
Xerox Corporation
Library of Congress
NASA
U.S. Geological Survey
United States Navy (NAVO, Stennis)
United States Navy (NRaD, San Diego)
National Imagery and Mapping Agency St. Louis Public Library

Web site: <http://alexandria.sdc.ucsb.edu/>

University of Illinois
University of Illinois academic departments and libraries
Academic Press, Inc.
American Association for the Advancement of Science (AAAS)
American Astronomical Society (AAS)
American Chemical Society (ACS)
American Institute of Aeronautics and Astronautics (AIAA)
American Institute of Physics (AIP)
American Physical Society (APS)
American Society of Agricultural Engineers (ASAE)
American Society of Civil Engineers (ASCE)
American Society of Mechanical Engineers (ASME)
Institution of Electrical Engineers (IEE)
Institute of Electrical and Electronics Engineers (IEEE)
IEEE Computer Society
John Wiley & Sons
OpenText (Search Engine)
SoftQuad (Panorama, an SGML viewer)
Hewlett-Packard
Microsoft
NETBILL (Electronic Payment Scheme)

Web site: <http://www.grainger.uiuc.edu/dli/>

Carnegie Mellon University
Carnegie Mellon University academic departments and libraries
QED Communications, Pittsburgh, PA
Bell Atlantic
Digital Equipment Corporation
Fairfax County Schools, VA
Intel Corporation
Microsoft Corporation
Motorola
Telecom Italia
The Open University, UK
Vira I. Heinz Endowment
The Winchester Thurston School, Pittsburgh, PA

Web site: <http://www.informedia.cs.cmu.edu/>

University of Michigan
University of Michigan academic departments and libraries
Apple Computer
Eastman-Kodak
Hewlett-Packard
IBM
Sybase
American Mathematical Society
McGraw-Hill
Elsevier
University Microfilm International (UMI)
Encyclopedia Britannica
Ann Arbor Public Library
New York Public Library
Local public high schools

Web site: <http://www.si.umich.edu/UMDL/>

Recent international developments

Beginning in the summer of 1997 five international working groups focusing on cooperative digital libraries research and development are being formed. Jointly funded by the European Union and the National Science Foundation, the groups will foster international cooperation by generating joint research agendas. Each group will meet twice over a two-year period and examine topics related to multilingual issues, interoperability, metadata, search and retrieval, and intellectual property and economics. This effort is being organized jointly by the European Research Consortium for Informatics and Mathematics (ERCIM) and the University of Michigan School of Information on behalf of the Digital Libraries Initiative.

Future directions in digital libraries research

Based on experiences of the first two years of the DLI projects and related efforts, a number of research areas have emerged as particularly important. These include:

- processes of human understanding of information;
- new information objects and content;
- technologies integration at the component and system level;
- domain-specific repositories and intellectual infrastructure;
- intelligent agents on networks;
- interoperability;
- metadata;
- terms and conditions of intellectual properties;
- elements enabling electronic commerce;
- digital libraries as means and media for enabling collaboration;
- human-centered systems and social informatics;
- information-based computing.

To this list must be added, importantly, foreign language query and search, OCR, navigation and multilingual translation tools for effective and timely access to global knowledge bases. Science is international and increasingly relies upon international collaboration and research resources. Scientific research by citizens of many countries increasingly takes place outside their native countries. Access to foreign texts and data bases is critical in the sciences and humanities.

Of the large set of research topics denoted above, some are of more direct importance to traditional librarians than others. The section will discuss in more detail research on new document forms, metadata, interoperability, infrastructure, and human-centered information systems.

New forms of documents

The fundamental units of computing have traditionally been characters and numbers. This promises to change. One clue to future conceptual units is to be found in the expanding notion of a 'document'. A physical document can take many forms but is characterized by the basic attributes of *content*, and *structure* – how the content is presented. Structure enhances the meaning by supplying contextual information. Documents also can be characterized by type or genre. Documents existing in digital form acquire another propery: *digital format*. The digital format selected for a document has the potential to constrain (positively and negatively) its functionality and use. Digital documents can be searched, reorganized, annotated, linked to others, shared, etc. The content, structure and formats of documents can be treated independently to greatly expand functionality. In large collections, this adds new dimensions of usability.

For example, in the world of digital libraries, documents are viewed not only as items for individual reading, but as a means for group interaction and collaboration. 'Malleable' is one term applied to electronic documents that have the property of openness (others can edit, annotate, incorporate new sections, mark-up, etc.). Documents can present different views for different audiences. A simple version of a document meant for browsing by general audiences might be expanded on-demand to provide enough additional detail, background and context to satisfy serious researchers in the field. A single document might contain text, images, video clips, maps, lexicons, and additions and annotations provided by new 'authors' contributing to the work.

Mutlivalent documents

The University of California, Berkeley's multivalent document research demonstrates the potential of adding functionalities to digital documents. The multivalent document offers one model of documents for the networked digital world. This model construes documents as multiple, distributed layers of intimately related information. Layers combine in a variety of ways to produce increasingly useful behaviours. New layers can be added at any time by anyone who has been given permission to do so. Different layers can 'live' on systems distributed over the globe. The multivalent document can behave as an image of a page, as text or tables which can be manipulated, searched or sorted, depending upon the needs of a user.

In the spring of 1996, the Berkeley project made significant contributions to California's flood recovery efforts by making valuable data available as multivalent documents. One such data set contained authoritative information about all dams under the jurisdiction of the State of California. The project also developed Web-based form and map interfaces to these data, providing recovery efforts with the ability to quickly obtain answers to dam-related queries which were previously not easily obtainable by any means. This data set was supplemented by geo-referenced aerial photographs of the hard-hit areas and United States Geological Survey 'quad sheets', which are detailed area maps (see Figure 5.8).

SGML

Standard Generalized Mark-up Language (SGML) is a set of codes that allows one to subdivide a document into components (titles, formulas, paragraphs, diagrams, etc.). Marking up the structure means not only that documents from many different sources can be described structurally in a consistent fashion, but also affords new processing of them as documents. SGML documents can be stored more efficiently and retrieved by individual components. Most importantly,

Multivalent Documents:
Example

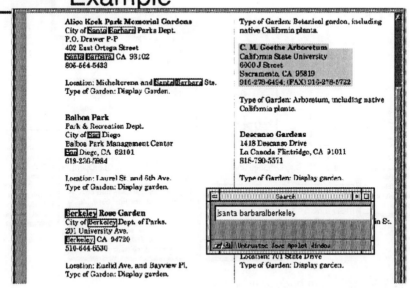

Fig. 5.8   *Multivalent documents: example*
(Courtesy of the University of California, Berkeley, Digital Libraries
Initiative Project)

SGML preserves the image of the document, allowing it to be displayed on a
video screen in the same way that the author or publisher intended it to look
when printed on paper. The University of Illinois DLI project is constructing an
SGML testbed to explore these issues in depth (see Figure 5.9).

Digital video libraries

Video combines audio and images and offers another type of complex document.
The CMU Informedia project derives useful functionalities from 'unbundling'
raw video, automatically converting the speech to text transcripts, which are
stored separately. Video media can be taken apart and interpreted separately
using different tools for different components, and then reassembled. Some of
the research at Carnegie Mellon is devoted to automatic speech recognition, converting speech to text so that the text can be searched using conventional tools.
Audio and image segments are searched using others. Storing and searching different media presents significant research challenges.[11]

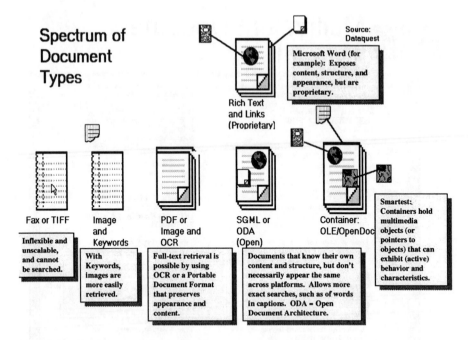

Fig. 5.9   *Spectrum of document types*
(Courtesy of the University of Illinois Digital Libraries Initiative Project)

Metadata

Metadata describes other data. One of the distinguishing features of a digital library is the attention placed on metadata collection and management. Metadata describes content, structure, context, and other aspects of a digital object and is critical to resource discovery (documents and images) in digital libraries. Easily as important as the data it describes in many applications, the maintenance and storage requirements for metadata can exceed that of the content it describes. Metadata can be stored, accessed and retrieved separately in networked environments and this greatly reduces the load on networks and systems.

A challenge for the digital libraries community is to define simple metadata elements that sufficiently describe a wide range of electronic information. The Online Computer Library Center (OCLC) and others have convened a valuable series of workshops ('The Dublin Core' workshop series) to address this issue which have resulted in a number of seminal papers.[12]

Interoperability

Heterogeneity of information resources and communication systems is a natural and unavoidable consequence of development in a competitive and creative technologies environment. Different approaches produce different systems and practices. Two of the important questions driving interoperability research are:

- How can users work across *existing* heterogeneous collections and systems with a minimum of difficulty?
- How can we develop future systems capable of adapting to an environment of rapid (and unpredictable) technological change, increasing variety and growing application needs?

The IITA (Information Infrastructure Technology and Applications) Report states:

> It should be noted that, at this relatively early stage in the evolution of digital library technology, it is of vital importance that projects strive for approaches that incorporate high functionality and extensibility. A high level of functionality in the standards and protocols used, even if not fully exploited initially, will postpone the time when the inertia of the installed base begins to confine research opportunities. Careful design of extensibility in digital library systems will facilitate continued research progress and understanding of the impact of new approaches on the user community without the need to attempt to displace an installed base.[13]

Achieving interoperability leads to apparent uniformity and transparency of diverse, distributed information repositories. A very complex, multicomponent system will appear to a user as a single simple one. The goals should not be limited to *systems* interoperability. Interoperability must also be achieved in other dimensions such as:

- time (interoperability from old systems to new systems);
- language (multilingual interoperability);
- syntax (distributed search across heterogeneous repositories and services);
- semantics (users can access classes of digital objects similar in *meaning* to those that they have literally requested).

The DLI projects are taking different approaches to address some of the interoperability issues. Researchers at Stanford are devising different sets of protocols for translating requests from different systems (see Figure 5.10).

Researchers at the University of Michigan are taking another approach, the use of 'agents'. Agents are essentially bits of software that, like protocols, exist and operate behind the scenes, not intruding into a user's awareness.

Researchers at the University of Illinois project are exploring automatic indexing of concepts by generating concept spaces based on term frequencies and co-occurrence. This research will be useful for term suggestion in such activities as interactive search. Merging individual community concept spaces supports vocabulary switching – utilizing the terminology of one subject to search for sim-

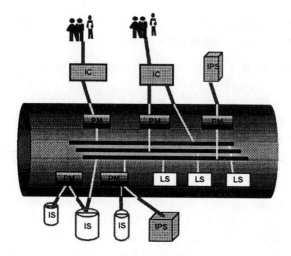

PM: Protocol Machine
LS: Library Service
IC: Interface Client
IS: Information Source
IPS: Information
      Processing Service

Fig. 5.10   *The Information Bus*
(Courtesy of the Stanford University Digital Libraries Initative Project)

ilar concepts in another. This capability is an essential aspect of semantic inter-operability. Vocabulary-switching experiments are very computationally intensive. A large-scale simulation carried out at the National Center for Supercomputing Applications generating concept spaces for 10,000,000 journal abstracts across 1000 subject areas in engineering and science required a week of dedicated computer time on a 64-node parallel supercomputing system.

Digital library capabilities must be projected to achieve interoperability and the inevitably increasing service requirements demanded by users. An illustrative case in point is the current demand to expand Internet services. Existing Internet protocols (such as http, the basis of the World Wide Web) are generally perceived as inadequate and research must move beyond the current base of deployed protocols and systems without threatening ubiquity of access.

Digital libraries as intellectual infrastructure

Beyond interoperability is infrastructure. Many experts contend that it is now timely and proper for nationally sponsored efforts to move digital libraries activities beyond fundamental research and testbeds to building operational systems. This is an important step. Operational systems containing collections of value to domain scholars become part of that communities' intellectual infrastructure – resources upon which advancement of their knowledge depends. This affords new opportunities, not only for domain researchers, but also for emerging inter-disciplinary research focusing on the integration and impact of computerization and networked information in domain, social, organizational and institutional contexts. This is especially important as computerization moves beyond the confines of organizations into new situations of personal and public use – an expansive phenomenon of the 1990s.[14]

Digital libraries as infrastructure will acquire many of the qualities defined by Star and Ruhleder:[15]

- *Embeddedness*. Infrastructure is 'sunk' into, or inside of other structures, social arrangements and technologies;
- *Transparency*. Infrastructure is transparent to use, in the sense that it does not have to be reinvented each time or assembled for each task, but invisibly supports those tasks;
- *Reach or scope*. This may be either spatial or temporal – infrastructure has reach beyond a one-off event or one-site practice;
- *Learned as part of membership*. The taken-for-grantedness of things and tools. Infrastructure is a *sine qua non* of membership in a community of practice.[15a] Strangers and outsiders encounter infrastructure as new participants acquire a naturalized familiarity with its objects in order to become members, leading directly to the following:
- *Links with conventions of practice*. Infrastructure both shapes and is shaped by the conventions of a community of practice.[15b]
- *Embodiment of standards*. Modified by scope and often by conflicting conventions, infrastructure takes on transparency by plugging into other infrastructures and tools in a standardized fashion.

  Builds on an installed base. Infrastructure does not grow *de novo*; it wrestles with the 'inertia of the installed base', and inherits strengths and limitations from that base. Optical fibers run along old railroad lines; new systems are back-compatible with previous ones; and failing to account for these constraints may be fatal or distorting to new development processes.[15c]
- *Becomes visible upon breakdown*. The normally invisible quality of working infrastructure becomes visible when it breaks: the server is down, the bridge washes out, there is a power blackout. Even when there are back-up mechanisms or procedures, their existence further highlights the now-visible infrastructure.

Human-centered information systems

In the last several years there has been a growing recognition of the importance of understanding the ways in which humans interact with and relate to information systems. Digital libraries are one form of HCS systems. While there are impressive predictions for faster computers communicating over faster networks there are yet few organized R&D programmes focusing on how individuals, groups, and communities will interact with information systems in social, organizational and institutional settings to extract useful information for decision making and for general knowledge expansion. Insight into the adaptive processes in play is critical to achieving the high levels of service and functionality from systems, leading to acceptance and broad deployment of new information services.[16]

Thus, improvements in computing and communications technologies *per se* are only a part of what is needed to extract the full potential of information systems. Key issues will increasingly include questions of information presentation, manipulation and interaction, knowledge processing and human cognition, knowledge repositories, and information agents and environments.

HCS research serves the further understanding of the dynamic and reflexive interactions between human beings, the social and organizational constructs they create and information technologies by:

- exploring the roles of information technologies in many dimensions of life;
- motivating and framing the technical issues from the human perspective of individual and community needs;
- supporting heterogeneous, multilingual and multicultural communities as a set of research issues in and of themselves;
- understanding enough about human activities in creating, seeking, and using information to design systems that make people more effective and efficient;
- revealing new models, techniques and practices for design.

Implications for library managers

Library managers are in the middle of a technology flux which is being compared in scope and consequence to the invention and use of the printing press. The emergence of the Internet, World Wide Web and new information technologies for creating and managing distributed information repositories has cast traditional organizational and managerial functions in a new light, forcing new responsibilities on library staff at all levels of the organization.

Decision making regarding implementation of digital libraries technologies will be easier in those areas where the infrastructure is stable and technology trajectories are more predictable. Decisions in the human dimension of library services will be more challenging. Overall, issues associated with content (creation, acquisition and conversion of digital materials) will be more straightforward than issues of access (levels of access and services, intellectual properties, rights management, etc.), which will be more straightforward than issues of use and users of materials (what will be used by what users). This is not to say that associated costs will break out accordingly.

The following is a shortlist of suggestions for library mangers caught in the midst of this rapid and uncertain period of technological and institutional change:

Learn new vocabularies

To understand technology and technologists more fully, managers must become literate in the concepts and vocabularies that frame technological discourse. This will include learning unfamiliar terms (e.g. interoperability, semantic retrieval, federation) as well as new meanings applied to familiar terms (author, document) in the digital environment. This is not always easy, but is the first and most important step toward understanding and assessing the potential of digital resources.

Encourage interaction among staff

As more functions of the library merge traditional librarianship with technology, it is important that the technical and non-technical staff understand each other's values and work well together. A highly collaborative work environment is more likely to produce a smooth introduction of digital technologies into library operations and services.

Carefully match technologies and users

Managers of information systems in organizations have traditionally struggled in this area. For libraries it will be even more difficult because of the variety of services and users. One step in achieving this is to make users an integral part of the systems requirements and design processes.

Reach out and educate

Steps should be taken to orient users (and employees!) to make them aware of new library technology environments and services. If users are not introduced to and do not learn to benefit from new services, these will be underutilized.

Prepare for loss of control

Accompanying the transformation from management of physical to electronic media in libraries will be decentralization coupled with direct, unmediated use of a libraries' resources by many clients.

Connect and communicate

Active participation in local, national and international professional events and workgroups can reduce the risks associated with moving into the digital age. Professional library associations provide valuable leadership in establishing forums for assessing new technologies in the context of existing work practices. Conferences and workshops are important venues for learning and sharing.

Conclusions

Digital libraries services have emerged as a consequence of advances in computing, information, and communications technologies dating from the 1960s. Capabilities have advanced, slowly at first, from bibliographic to full-text search to multimedia browsing via the Internet and the World Wide Web; multimedia search capabilities are quickly being developed (see Figure 5.11).

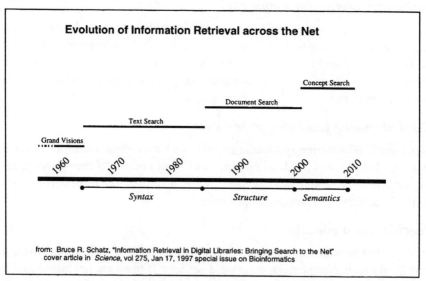

Fig. 5.11   *Evolution of information retrieval across the Net*
(Courtesy of the University of Illinois Digital Libraries Initiative Project)

New digital libraries capabilities suggest new uses and point to high future demand for new services throughout the world. Network-based knowledge repositories promise to revolutionize research and education. The social and economic impact of digital libraries research is likely to be unprecedented because of the scale involved. Creation, conversion, storage and use of digital information will not only stimulate national and global economies – it will change the way cultures emerge and conduct their affairs (Figure 5.12).

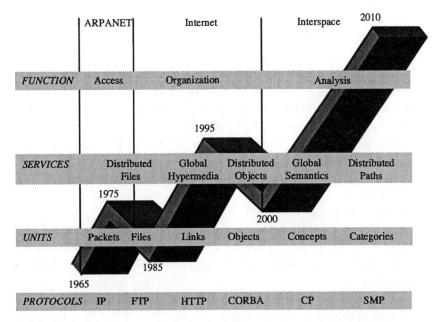

Fig. 5.12   *The third wave of Net evolution*
(Courtesy of the University of Illinois Digital Libraries Initiative Project)

References

1 Lynch, C. and Garcia-Molina, H., 'Interoperability, scaling, and the digital library research agenda', a report on the 18–19 May, 1995 Information Infrastucture Technology and Applications (IITA) Digital Libraries Workshop. <http://www.hpcc.gov/reports/reports-nco/iita-dlw/main.html>

2 Griffin, S., 'The NSF/DARPA/NASA Digital Libraries Initiative: a mid-term report', Proceedings of International Conference on Digital Libraries and Information Services for the 21st Century, Seoul, The Korean Library and Information Science Society, 1996, 228–41.

3 Wilensky, R., University of California, Berkeley Digital Libraries Initiative Project information materials, 1997.

4 Atkins, D., University of Michigan Digital Libraries Project information material(s), 1997.

5 Atkins, D. and Duguid, P. (manuscript), Report of the Santa Fe Planning Workshop on Distributed Knowledge Work Environments, 9–11 March 1997.

6 National Science Foundation, 'Research on Digital Libraries', NSF Program Announcement 93–141, Ballston, Va, 1993.

7 Atkins, D. and Duguid, P. (manuscript), Report of the Santa Fe Planning

Workshop on Distributed Knowledge Work Environments, 9–11 March 1997.

8 Wilensky, R., University of California, Berkeley Digital Libraries Initiative Project information materials, 1997.

9 Digital Libraries Initiative SGML Mathematics Workshop.
   <http://www.grainger.uiuc.edu/dli/dliwork.htm>

10 Griffin, S., 'The NSF/DARPA/NASA Digital Libraries Initiative: mid-term perspectives', *ERCIM news*, **27**, 1996, 15–16.

11 Friedlander, Amy, Accompanying text to the NSF Digital Libraries Initiatives Exhibit, 1997.

12 Weibel, Stuart, 'Metadata: the foundations of resource description', D-lib magazine.
   <http://www.dlib.org/dlib/July95/07weibel.html>

13 Lynch, C. and Garcia-Molina, H, Interoperability, scaling, and the digital library research agenda', a report on the 18–19 May, 1995 Information Infrastucture Technology and Applications (IITA) Digital Libraries Workshop.
   <http://www.hpcc.gov/reports/reports-nco/iita-dlw/main.html>

14 The Social Informatics Home Page.
   <http://www.slis.indiana.edu/SI>

15 Star, L. and Ruhleder, K., 'Steps toward an ecology of infrastructure: design and access for large information spaces', *Information systems research*, **7**, January 1996, 111–34.

15a Lave, J. and Wenger, E., *Situated learning: legitimate peripheral participation*, Cambridge, Cambridge University Press, 1992.

15b Becker, H. S., *Art worlds*, Berkeley, University of California Press, 1982.

15c Monteiro, E., Hanseth, O. and Hatling, M., 'Developing information infrastructure: standardization vs. flexibility.' (Working Paper No. 18) Science, Technology and Society. Norway: University of Trondheim, 1994.

16 Strong, G., Chien, Y.T., Hestenes, J. and Griffin, S., 'Human-centered information systems', *ERCIM news*, **26**, 12–13.

Additional references

Digital Libraries Initiative National Synchronization Home Page.
   <http://dli.grainger.uiuc.edu/national.htm>

Agre, P. E., 'Designing genres for new media: social, economic and political contexts', *The network observer*, **2** (11), 1995.
   <http://communication.ucsd.edu/pagre/tno/november-1995.html#designing>

Borgman, C., *From Gutenberg to the global information infrastructure: information access in a networked world*, Cambridge, MIT Press, 1997.

Chen, S., *Digital libraries: pushing the frontiers of cyberspace*, Cambridge, MIT Press, 1997.

Lesk, M., *Books, bytes and bucks: practical digital libraries*, in press.

Bishop, A. and Star S., 'Social informatics of digital library use and infrastructure', *Annual review of information science and technology*, New Jersey, Information Today, **31**, 1996, 301–401.

Committee on Information and Communications, National Science and Technology Council, Strategic Implementation Plan: America in the Age of Information. Washington, NSTC, March 1995.

Computer Science and Telecommunications Board, National Research Council, Evolving the High Performance Computing and Communication Initiative to Support the Nation's Information Infrastructure, Washington, National Academy Press, 1995.

Computer Science and Telecommunications Board, National Research Council, Realizing the Information Future: The Internet and Beyond, Washington, National Academy Press, 1994.

Schatz, B., Chen, H., et.al., 'Building large-scale digital libraries', Theme issue, *IEEE computer*, **29** (5), 1996, 22–76.

Fox, E., Akscyn, R., Furuta, R., Leggett, J. *et. al.*, 'Digital libraries', Theme issue, *Communications of the ACM*, **38** (4), 1995, 22–96.

6

MANAGING CHANGE IN DIGITAL STRUCTURES

Colin Steele

UNIVERSITY LIBRARIAN, AUSTRALIAN NATIONAL UNIVERSITY

Introduction

David Gerrold, a science fiction writer, has said 'the hardest lesson to learn is that learning is a continual process'. In the 21st century this will become a truism as lifelong learning and skills maintenance will be essential. According to the American Society for Training and Development, by the year 2000, 75% of the current workforce will have to be retrained just to keep up with the needs of a changing society.[1]

In terms of such change librarians and information workers need to know what types of structures they will be working in in the early 21st century. If universities are delivering information in a virtual university/distance learning setting then the whole concept of organization will change. Some of the factors to be taken into consideration are:

- virtual delivery of information to the desktop;
- reduced budgets in higher education and lower unit costs per student for mass education;
- lifelong learning requirements;
- global monopolization by commercial suppliers from Murdoch to Microsoft;
- outsourcing;
- job uncertainties;
- telecommuting work teams on the Net;
- 'dumbing down' of education.

In the above environment the need for leadership, personal involvement and rapid but reasoned decision making will be essential. The role of 'cybercoach' will be a complex, difficult and challenging one.

Background

The AUCC (Association of Universities and Colleges of Canada)/CARL Report

The changing world of scholarly communication: challenges and choices for Canada provides a useful current overview of issues and trends. It indicates the changes in scholarly communication that will affect the whole education spectrum. It recognizes:

> financial considerations have prevented some universities from investing in information technology to the same degree as have others. There is a very real danger that the wealth of opportunities afforded by electronic communication may not be available equally across the university system. Indeed, even within institutions, some faculties have far greater access than others to these technologies.
>
> In short, the current evolution of the scholarly communication system is affected by a series of complex issues, including questions relating to copyright, the basis for recognizing and rewarding scholars, the inability of university libraries to keep pace with the growing body of knowledge, and the daunting task of digitizing the enormous volume of knowledge that now resides largely in paper form if, indeed, that is a desired option. There are concerns, too, about the cost of investing in the infrastructure of information technology and telecommunications facilities.
>
> We are at a crossroads: there are critical questions to be considered, choices to be made, challenges to be met. We have a unique opportunity to offer our own contributions to influence the development of the scholarly communication system, and to advance solutions that reflect Canadian realities, goals and values. At the same time, we must recognize that changes in scholarly communication are taking place around the world, and that some of our choices will be limited by what occurs internationally.[2]

Human relations organization needs to be seen in the context of decentralized team operations. Classification and industrial guidelines need to be flexible and interactive rather than stratified and rigid. Carla Stoffle, the Dean of Libraries at the University of Arizona, summed up many of the staffing challenges in her 1996 Follett Lecture delivered at the University of Wales – 'The Emergence of Education and Knowledge Management as Major Functions of the Digital Library'.[3] She addresses the need to change large public sector institutions, which often contain many staff educated in a traditional librarianship environment and often in the same job for decades, to become as Stoffle puts it 'a customer focussed, continuous learning, constantly improving, flexible, quality-based library'.

In Australia reviews of university libraries are far more common than in the UK and USA. A whole 'grey' literature exists as in the reports of review teams which have ranged from one person at the University of Queensland to 11 at the Australian National University Library. The Chair of the 1982 ANU Library Review, Professor I.G. Ross, compared the reviewing of a library to reviewing a hotel! The question is whether the hotel is of the Hyatt or Sheraton variety or that of Fawlty Towers. This author sometimes wonders!

ANU Library Review

Certainly if one compared the 1982 Review of ANU Library with that of 1995 chaired by Professor Mairead Browne, the physical fabric of the hotel/library had become shabbier, the staff were overworked but had extended their range of services quite dramatically. The 1995 ANU Library Review which submitted its Report (URL: **http://ELISA/elisa/anulib/libreview.html**) had three librarians among its members – John Shipp (then Chair of the Council of Australian University Libraries and Librarian of the University of Wollongong), Helen Hayes (Chair of the Australian Council of Library and Information Services and Librarian of the University of Melbourne) and Dr Peter Lyman, Librarian of the University of California at Berkeley.

One review paragraph indicated that the library problems faced at ANU were not atypical. While ANU is one of a kind, the Committee was struck, nonetheless, by the universality of many of the Library's problems. It indicated:

> Large libraries in Australia and elsewhere are experiencing similar problems of underlying structural inadequacies and the problems which flow from these in areas of staff morale, commitment to changing models of service provision and so on. In addition, there are common environmental factors which are placing enormous pressure on the Library such as the growing mismatch of funding and real costs, and the consequences of shifts in academic and research priorities. This is not to suggest that these problems are not serious and do not have to be tackled. It is intended, rather, to point out that a number of the problems at the ANU Library are not unique but reflect a general trend.

At ANU most of the senior staff have been in position for over 15 years, some for more than 25 years. They were thus appointed early in their careers but were in some cases conditioned by the 1960's philosophies of collection development rather than collection management or prioritized client service. A move to a largely non-hierarchical networked organization which takes risks and is action focused was not particularly welcomed by some. Of the staff at ANU, 80% are female and the average age is the early fifties. The ANU staff numbers were 206 FTEs in 1976 but only 154 FTEs in 1997, despite the University having doubled in size in the period as well as the demands and challenges of the Net, the convergence of functions on campus, etc. The proportion of the ANU budget spent on staff in 1997 was 46%, while the proportion spent on information (including books and serials) was 44%.

The ANU, a predominantly research institution, has one of the lowest staffing ratios of major research libraries in the world. The scene was set for local change which serves as a microcosm of the global scene. From the ANU Library Review the Library management, staff and unions agreed to move to a flatter, team-based subject and functional 'cluster' model, with almost totally devolved budgets, so that there could be flexibility between the various budget votes including staff, book and serial, maintenance, equipment votes etc.

The ANU Library Steering Committee included elected staff representatives, a TQM consultant, a senior official of the National Tertiary Education Union, the librarian and the industrial officer. It met frequently during 1996 and the first half of 1997 and provided a useful preliminary sounding board for the major issues that had to come out of the process. One of the side debates in the ANU restructure process was the belief held by many of the library staff of the inviolability and exclusivity of library qualifications. But what does it mean in 1997 that a staff member has a sole library degree (BLib) or a postgraduate library qualification gained in the 1960s or 1970s if continued updating of the wider environment has not occurred? Libraries need a broad range of skills which cannot be tied exclusively to degrees which when obtained may have contained little or no leadership, management or people skills or lacked a wider vision of the information universe.

The education industry will be challenged from large IT firms such as Microsoft. The library is no longer sacrosanct as the 'heart of the university' if indeed it ever was. What will be the library's role in the total knowledge management environment? When the user is the information focal point at the desktop level, what is the role of the librarian and information worker? Flexibility, responsiveness, team-based projects and quality benchmarking will need to be ubiquitous.

The ANU currently has a variety of classification grades (e.g. librarian, computing, administrative). These qualification debates are false divisions in an interchangeable support structure. I won't even enter the debate on academic/general staff dichotomies. This author lectured on the Electronic Library at the University of Tasmania last year:

> The 'general staff' have as much to offer as academic staff in the access to and transmission of knowledge. The students will be in 'interactive ' mode in learning, while researchers will decide from their desktop where they will access information . . . We cannot allow local internal 'turf wars' between various parts of campuses at a time when overall resources are declining. The library profession or increasingly as I would prefer to put it those who work in libraries will need to decide their role in this future.[4]

IT skills will be an important element of such clusters. The cluster or group management structures reflected in the ANU and University of Queensland Library reorganizations sees, and will continue to see, development of a mix of skills. At above core support level the use of Information Technology Library Officers (ITLO) in the University of Queensland environment has provided new skills for staff in the software installation and maintenance at an HEW3/4 level in subject groupings in areas previously guarded by centralized network support groups. The best mix may be one of effective decentralization with agreed overall standards of service support. ANU's Audit Office looked at ANU Library's IT strategies and achievements in 1996 and, while praising certain aspects, found weaknesses in the lack of the integration of IT into the overall strategic planning process and clear priority settings. Customer satisfaction, and the need to benchmark and continually evaluate obviously takes resources on a regular basis. Let's ignore those who say they are too busy to evaluate their operations, for otherwise how do they effectively judge their operations – historical models are no longer relevant. The users who never enter the Library, for example, are just as relevant as those who do!

Changes in access to information

The economic downturn, in Australia exacerbated by the Howard Government's decision in 1996 to make universities meet pay rises out of recurrent funding, will lead to a greater need for marketing, entrepreneuralism and accountability. Issues such as outsourcing need to be carefully evaluated. Griffith University Library in Brisbane has reduced its technical services staff from 42 to 27 in the period 1996–7 by outsourcing a major part of its technical services staffing to suppliers like Blackwells. These sort of economies to allow for the provision of new services will be as closely examined as those in the USA such at Lehigh although a consortium of Western Australian University libraries has not been able to replicate the cost savings of Griffith in their analyses of technical services costs.

At the time of writing Stanford University Library is quoting interlibrary loan delivery costs within a 24 hour period, which is cheaper than many Australian university libraries can provide and certainly cheaper than UnCover costs. There is probably a much cheaper labour component which Stanford can utilize relative to Australian costs but as an early indication of the globalization of access and delivery it could reflect the future labour distribution costs of, say, the clothing and programming industries.

Whither such global libraries and what does this mean for staffing and management? Somehow more funds despite this economic downturn, have to be given to continuous learning and training for staff. Some staff may not be able to 'regrow' but the vast majority of staff will be motivated to continuity of creativity. As Stoffle has indicated, we need to look not at the present but the future in meeting the evolving needs of our client groups. Change may be fast but requires cultural changes in attitudes of staff. Libraries are often disadvantaged by their inability to measure their service output: this is much easier in industries where there is a readily defined product.

Virtual universities

Outside the individual sections within an organizational structure there is now an increasing overlapping of functions, embodied ultimately in the virtual university concept. What will be the backdrop for libraries and IT centres in this educational framework? The virtual university concept is one, if not the major, scenario for the 21st century. There are a number of models in this context (e.g. niche and mega-university concepts) as Daniel has argued.[5] Two significant seminars in the second half of 1996, one in Singapore sponsored by the British Council and IDP Australia and the other at Melbourne University, which produced some fascinating future scenarios and models.[6] In this area of development, the traditional university may cease to exist and therefore IT centres and libraries will mutate organizationally within each concept, perhaps as virtual libraries on the one hand and local support organizations with specialized assistance on the other.

The Western Governors University

<http://www.westgov.org/smart/vu/vuOd13~1.htm>

is another model. It has as its aims:

- Removal of the obstacles of both time and place to post secondary education opportunities for individual and corporate citizens of the west.
- A means for learners to obtain formal recognition of the skills and knowledge obtained outside a traditional higher education (campus) context and/or from multiple providers through the assessment and certification of competency.
- Joint development of new learning and assessment materials among states and with private entities
- Technology standards that will ensure connectivity.

The WGU is focusing its initial efforts on:

- linking employers and academic institutions in setting skills standards
- linking individuals seeking assessment of their competencies with assessment providers
- linking individuals seeking to enhance their level of competence in one or more of these areas with providers of educational programs/courses/modules who can meet the learners' requirements regarding time, place, and content of services delivered
- providing support services needed to help ensure that students receive appropriate guidance and that barriers to access to education offerings are minimized or removed entirely
- providing credentials to individuals (academic degrees and industry-recognized certificates) based on assessment of competencies.

The other issue which arises is the diversity of approaches required by teams. At ANU Library the teams have been encouraged to choose the model best suited to meet their client needs. The essential point of the future is that users will not care who delivers the information providing it best meets their needs in content, delivery and is economically priced. If 'nomadic computing', as Professor Len Kleinrock of UCLA predicts, becomes the norm then the wired individual becomes the information universe rather than the large library.

Peter Lyman, in one of his perceptive overviews, has outlined the sea changes in access to information encapsulated in the term 'digital library'.[7] We have to move from the imitation of print electronically to the creation of new knowledge access patterns and useage. Clifford Lynch also picked up this point at the 1996 ASIS Annual Meeting in Baltimore with the emergence of a set of new genres of communication as we move away from the 'tyranny of text',[8] We will also need to move to personalized systems developments in terms of information organization.

Convergence of structures

What are the steps in the development of such a scenario and core centralization to achieve decentralization? In some cases it is convergence of structures on campus, in others cooperation. In the UK convergence of IT, libraries and teaching/learning facilities is very much more common than in Australia. Fifty of the 98 UK universities have some form of convergence, ranging from total staffing integration at Hull and Birmingham Universities, to Leeds and Sussex Universities where sharing cooperatively is in place but the Librarian is Dean or Director of Information Services/Planning and is responsible for overall strategic planning. Four-fifths of the converged areas resulted in the person responsible for overall coordination being the 'former' or actual university librarian.

At Arizona State University a large computer cluster linked to the Library has recently been opened with $20m US funding. A new position of Associate Vice-President of Academic Affairs has been created. At the University of Southern California the Leavey 'teaching' Library was opened in 1995 for total round-the-clock access in a high-tech environment. In 1997 the Leavey Information Commons is a centre for librarians, navigation assistants and computer consultants to deliver information to users at homes, offices and computer user clusters. At USC the newly created post of Chief Information Officer has in its portfolio to create a consolidated managerial environment for administrative information systems, university computing services, university telecommunications, university libraries, and other information providers and facilitators on campus. This position will chair the university's new Information Council, which will be composed of representatives from each of USC's primary information providers and facilitators. The council's initial mandate is to devise and recommend, by no later than July 1997, a strategic plan – complete with comprehensive, long range objectives – for the university's information systems.

Dartmouth College have initiated planning for an 80,000 square foot extension to the library building which will accommodate Academic Computing to form 'computarian' alliances. The University of North Carolina at Charlotte has been planning for an expanded and renovated library facility for several years. As a part of the planning process, a library 'Vision for Today, A Building for Tomorrow' has been developed which includes a significant number of concepts and principles. It states *inter alia* that:

> As information technologies change, faculty and students no longer need to come to the facility because there are alternate means of finding, accessing, and delivering information. Therefore, if Library and Information Services both as an organization and a building which houses its functions are to be relevant to the University, contact with customers must be the emphasis. No service can or will exist without the customer. Client service is thus the key.

The Paul Hamlyn Learning Resource Centre at Thames Valley University has a Head of Development who is quoted:

> People are looking for information in different formats now – not just book and booklists. We are trying to create the old scholar-librarian type of model by employing cyberlibrarians, who can pull together information that is published on the Net, on CD-ROM, in databases. They will bring it into electronic libraries on the intranet, and then make it learning material by adding comments and linking it to specific courses.[9]

We are therefore seeing more physical concentration of facilities as well as remote Net use. As for libraries, if research library material is relatively little used then we don't need extensive opening hours (expensive in Australian terms) to cater for needs but instead have lengthy borrowing periods. Libraries can then concentrate on what is being used and make material available electronically outside the physical library confines (e.g. for course material, electronic textbooks and document supply).

How do staff interact in this process of convergence which has as its aim the better provision of teaching and research locally, nationally and globally? As the Cornell University FABIT (Faculty Advisory Board on Information Technology) Report stated: 'We have done a good job of distributing technology, but we have not done as good a job of distributing the support infrastructure. Central staff and faculty work well together, but we haven't achieved a level of organization that is efficient; too often we practice in the same area, sometimes creating duplication while leaving other areas unaddressed'.[10] To achieve this synergy, we may be better served by a vocabulary that does away with terms like 'librarian' which are rooted in historical missions and goals. Staff values can be fixed to historical routines when new paradigms are required. Library schools in America now have become schools of information with courses such as the Implementation of distributed information systems.

Technologies and innovation

The CAUSE (College and University Systems Exchange) Current Issues Committee (1996) has produced a thought-provoking set of questions concerning the integration of technology in teaching and learning. It argues: 'As the necessary technology and support become more readily available, faculty will integrate World Wide Web, multimedia, desktop video, and other new technologies into the teaching and learning process to serve students on campus, within commuting distance, and at great distances from the institution. Other providers will enter and compete for educational services business'.[11] CAUSE identified the issues that need to be addressed:

- What is the role of information technology in the transition from teacher-centred to learner-centred instruction?
- What is the information resources organization's role in this transformation – leader, supporter, participant in the creative process?
- How do we help our institutions to approach this in a way that effectively plans for and leverages the investments that will be necessary in technology, process, and pedagogy?
- Is there a model for effectively supporting faculty in using technology in their teaching and incorporating it into the learning experience of their students?
- How do we address the policy issues and challenges raised by distance education?

Catherine Lilly and Gloria Thiele have identified the following aspects as necessary in re-engineering in a university environment. Firstly, to develop customer-focused and marketing concepts that enable information technology staff to become more customer driven and secondly, to link process innovation into total quality programmes, strategic data planning and continuous improvement. Leadership is required more then ever in the management portfolio.[12] We probably need a visionary leadership, albeit one not too divorced from reality.

Structures and staffing

We need to evaluate services overall so that the total vision is apparent. Sheila Creth in her 1996 October Follett Lecture titled her talk 'The Electronic Library – Slouching Toward the Future or Creating a New Information Environment'!

The term 'slouching' may be a relevant one for some in the library profession? The organization by division of knowledge will be the key to coping with the change process. The IT environment is usually more associated with change than has been the case with libraries. The 1996 Council of Australian University Librarians (CAUL) seminar on 'Convergence in Universities' held at Adelaide University heard comments that, generally speaking, IT professionals were insensitive to users but were able to introduce rapid change, whereas the reverse was true for the library environment – it is slow to change but good with users who come into a library!

At the CAUSE '96 Conference in San Francisco Patricia Battin and Brian Hawkins provided the following influences on 'The Changing Role of the Information Resources Professional':

- traditional roles will need to change, a radical change may not be in individuals' best interests in the short term;
- future education will be customized rather than centralized;
- change may be discontinuous and transformational;
- need for budget flexibility, access will be ownership;
- need for contribution from scholars, librarians and information technologists;
- perception of information technologists as 'anarchist' and librarians as 'control freaks';
- need to establish a baseline of service.

Our ultimate work will be measured in outcomes and needs to be based on evolving and flexible competencies and skill. Gilliland and Tynan have stated an immense amount of time in an organization is given to 'terrorists' who complain, refuse to offer solutions and participate in eventual ones. They believe leaders must focus time on those individuals and the teams that are committed to their project and being part of the solution. Hierarchies exist throughout institutions and need to be addressed at all levels if a true team-based solution is to emerge.[13]

New technologies have to be incorporated into complex and often inflexible structures. Dr Peter Taylor, coauthor of a recent report 'Flexibility, Technology and Academics' Practices: Tantalizing Tales and Muddy Maps' found 'formidable barriers to change – mainly funding work against the introduction of flexible delivery technologies and that universities concentrated on helping staff acquire technical skills rather than thinking about new teaching patterns'.[14] We need to integrate ideas management with the managing of user needs. John Kao brings up the jazz metaphor by the synthesis of individual effort into a collective form.[15] Others might prefer the Wagnerian style of leadership but in a distributed learning environment, particularly when telecommuting is common, this is hardly likely to succeed.

The Institute of Data Processing Management has predicted (*The Times* Internet 23/10/96) that, as companies move from different office networks to intranets and simpler networks based on Internet standards the need for large numbers of network specialists and systems integrators will be removed. The report concluded 'prepare for retirement or retrain preferably out of IT'. Grim words indeed. Yet in contrast Richard Day, Director of Black Horse Relocation, in the same issue, argues knowledge of IT is vital for future employment. One suspects here it is how IT is defined. In addition, according to more than 700 chief executives, chairmen and managing directors of UK companies, the most important skill a job applicant can cultivate is the ability to work in a team.

Deborah Allmayer and Phyllis Davidson, respectively Human Resources Administrator and Director, University Computing Services of Indiana University, in their paper 'The Employee and Organization of the Future' to the CAUSE '96 Conference argued that the traditional principles of employment are 'dead'. Their organization of the future:

> Could only support continued employment for those jobs that contribute to the stated goals of the organization, placing immediate demands on incumbents to become employees of the future – committed to those goals, adapting to change with multiple skills . . . For our partnership to be credible, management had to accept its obligations as well. Communicating organizational direction and engaging in dialogue, facilitating a professional growth plan and providing opportunities to achieve those development objectives for staff members became essential elements of the manager's tasks.[16]

Teamwork

'Power teams' has been a jargon phrase in the business community, with teams establishing their own goals within an overall strategic framework. Does it really matter how a team achieves the goal as long as it does so within the agreed financial, strategic and physical parameters. Power teams can exist in both the long term or short term. The mix of skills in short-term projects provide results and a sense of achievement when a task is finished. Reward and satisfaction mechanisms need to be in place for both operational situations. Library manager 'burn out' may still occur even in the decentralized structures. One response in public sector positions might be for more contract positions with higher rewards being the norm and mobility to assist freshness and hard decision making. This would be analogous to the private sector managerial situation.

The CAUSE pamphlet *Reflections on leadership* (CAUSE Professional Papers #15) identified leadership as 'contextual'. More than one of the writers like Kao used the example of taking sequential solo leads in a jazz group in contrast to the conducting of an orchestra, a metaphor much favoured by the Vice-Chancellor of the University of Southern Cross. The need for new leadership images is constant. Thus Thomas West, Vice-Chancellor of the State University of California, has canvassed the transition of the CIO 'from Butch Cassidy to City Slicker', i.e. from greenhorns in the IT area to accomplished practitioners in the widest sense.[17] West stresses only the most broadly based and adaptable IT personnel will be able to function at the highest level, i.e. they should not only have the vision but also be able to manage the change process. There clearly needs to be a team-based approach and input at the top of organizations as no one can encompass all the future IT environment in its total context. Indeed IT will be seamless in many operations.

The stresses and strains on library structures will be profound in the period up to the end of the decade given the important government policies, budget reductions and the impact of both divergent and emerging technologies on information infrastructure. Do we need new forms of leadership and structures to enable the effective operation of staffing delivery? Accountability in an era of unpredictability will be essential. Time frame horizons of change are lessening, yet our traditional strategic plans have usually had a three to five year horizon. Certainly in technology implementation a three-year horizon is probably about as far as one can predict at the moment. As Thomas Shaughnessy of Minnesota has said 'the most important reason for restructuring, however, is also the most abstract, namely, that libraries must be organized to deal with the extraordinary changes that are occurring in the environment'.[18]

The issue then is team difficulty in appreciating the complexity of the total picture and interpreting this in their local context of client needs. The tension between central core standards and the necessary decentralization will occur. What is the projected role of librarians? Are they the Internet facilitators, the analysers of Web indexes, the creators of Web content, the integral element of the teaching and research process? Search tools will continue to advance with relevancy rankings, file format interchangeability, document operability etc. Nonetheless the specialization and subdivision of information will require specialists with rankings devoted to academic needs. Some of the current developments in the Asian Virtual Library scene at ANU will emerge in this context as research goals, methods and interpretation differ a great deal from popular Net sites indexing.

Distributed work environments

Michael Lesk of Bellcore has indicated that by 2010 scholars will use text libraries as currently they use manuscript collections. Most of the new information produced by 2010 will be in digital form and only the material that has economic or major academic value will be retrospectively scanned and digitized unless costs begin to reduce significantly. Professor Carol Tenopir, in analysing the end user searching trends, notes that for 25 years the end-user markets had been difficult and relatively static because:

- not many end-users knew what online searching was;
- not many end-users had the equipment to go online;
- not many end-users were willing to learn how to search;
- and, not many end-users were willing to pay for online information.[19]

Currently these have changed because of the Net and five major end-user trends have emerged: Web versions, end-user systems through the library, integration of information sources, the rethinking of proprietary software solutions, and specialized focus/customized products. As we bring systems to users we will see increasingly sophisticated Web enhancements. In terms of content, developments such as Biomed Net and Engineering Information Village set examples of intellectual conglomeration.

As the technical developments divide into predicability and basic operations (e.g. one-stop boxes for TV, information and entertainment provision) then network infrastructures, which currently take up a lot of discussion, may become only a question of price and performance. Mobile computing and wireless/networks high bandwidth will lead to distributed work environments, including libraries, which will demand a new paradigm of responsiblity, accountability and service provision.

The first market for them will be the Digital Upscale Believers (DUBS). Paul Mockapetris of the company @Home talking at the December CNI Conference in San Francisco spoke of his company's role – @Home's strategy makes use of:

- caching and data replication
- proactive network management
- added value at every level of the network.

Gore Vidal identifies stages of civilization which include theocratic, democratic and dictatorial, all of which are essentially cyclical. As the individual user in the 21st century becomes one-to-one with the information provider, he or she will be as the seventh-century monk in the scriptoria and a cyclical pattern will occur. In the IT environment West identifies the academic, bureaucratic, technocratic and network-centric processes – the latter to include individual empowerment on the one hand and the facilitation process at the managerial levels.

The Benton Foundation Report 'Buildings, Books and Bytes' found that in America the age group 18–24 was the least enthusiastic of any age group about the importance of libraries in a digital future.[20] This presumably was because of the flow of the TV and Nintendo generations into the Net 'nerds' environment. This study said that if this age group wanted to enhance their computer skills it would be from 'someone they know' rather then from a local library. In the Benton Report public libraries were perceived in the USA to be reactive and to be 'behind the technology curve'. Interestingly, the 'super-bookstores' like the Web-based Borders bookshop were seen as competitors with discount offers and presumably cybercafés. Libraries in the academic area in Australia are probably in less danger, unless the user becomes the focal point of information access. Physical and temporal walls will change for libraries in the 21st century. Twenty-four hour reference services will be available both publicly and privately.

The challenges identified by the University of California in its 1996 Digital Library Framework are extremely relevant for most Australian libraries.[21] They aim from an organizational perspective to provide a set of human, financial, and technological systems which enable knowledge generation, access, and use, with four primary roles:

- information preservation, storage, and retrieval;
- information access and delivery via electronic communications;
- the online publishing of the scholarly and scientific knowledge base, or knowledge management;
- information management consultation and training.

It is important to note that these roles are viable only in the context of new business models which are scaleable with an exponential growth in digital information.

Working collaboratively at a distance will come as a significant achievement as hierarchical structures evolve into regular team-based work groups and then into individual joined together from home bases in university content creation and knowledge provision. Dr Clifford Lynch from the University of California System-wide Automation indicated at the January 1997 Online Conference in Sydney that the World Wide Web is not a library. There will be a need for organizational overlays but that organization may well not reside in libraries but rather in software houses!

Future trends

The Polish writer Stanislaw Lem once said 'Thoughts, like fleas, jump from man to man. But they don't bite everybody.' In the 21st century structures to provide access to information will have as many variants as cybernetic fleas. The one constant will be the direct access of information and entertainment by the user at his or her desktop in the office or home. What are some of the technologies that will 'enable' this future? Will it be a 'wireless future', with college and university libraries unplugged, as Clifton Dale Foster argued at the December 1996 CAUSE Conference? Northrop Frye, the Canadian author, has said 'our real crystal ball is a rear view mirror'. One way out of this is not to say what are the standards or the physical pieces of equipment that will provide desktop access but rather what is the concept and what will be the results. The video is ubiquitous, but not with Beta standards. Digital audio tapes and digital assistants hit a time warp but the concept of the latter is increasingly valid. George Gilder believes the Java 'tele-puter' will overtake the PC and will be as portable as a cellular phone.

The question will also then occur of 'who pays' – already we are seeing gaps in access between university libraries on the one hand and public and small special libraries on the other. If Pay-TV increasingly charges by sequential 'slots', as it does already with the rounds of boxing, then the greed of the media moguls will know no bounds in the information arena. We do need to monitor and retain the intellectual property of the creators in the academic arena.

The move to intranets either within a single organization or within a group, the new Optus AARNet in Australia or the US Internet Two concept dedicated to academic traffic, will continue. Voice and video will also become norms in the future with digital slimline TVs interactive for shopping, banking, information, and entertainment. This trend will need to be associated with cable modem and similarly high-speed delivery mechanisms associated with digital compression devices. Users will have to figure real costs into the operations unless subsidized. The economists Hal Vanon from University of California at Berkeley and Jeff Mackie-Mason of Michigan University are just two of the commentators who believe use-based pricing is essential to encourage the rational allocation of scarce transmission capacity.

Just think of the current legal problems of America Online with its offer of unlimited use monthly subscription. The leasing of international lines which benefits the US may be overcome by the Graves/Gates satellite provision. Cost could also be segregated by type of access, e.g. currently higher costs for video and substantially less for e-mail or basic text. Through the protocol of RSVP people will be able to specify the quality of the service they need and be theoretically billed for it. Many of the IT provisions of the 21st century will be 'invisible'. How many TV repairmen are there now? My TV has lasted 20 years without needing repair, yet in the 1950s and 1960s TV repairmen were ubiquitous. The Net provider support firms are currently mushrooming but once delivery mechanisms and software become standard they too might disappear.

The Internet as depicted in David Brin's *Earth* is simply taken for granted by the characters of the novel. Brin wrote:

And to think, some idiots predicted that we'd someday found our economy on information. That we'd base money on it! On information? The problem isn't scarcity. There's too damned much of it. The problem usually wasn't getting access to information. It was to stave off drowning in it. People bought personalized filter programs to skim a few droplets from that sea and keep the rest out. For some, subjective reality became the selected entertainments and special-interest zones passed through by those tailored shells. Here a man watches nothing but detective films from the days of cops and robbers – a limitless supply of formula fiction. Next door a woman hears and reads only opinions that match her own, because other points of view are culled by her loyal guardian software.[22]

Bruce Schatz has shown how the immediate access to scientific literature is now possible, whereas once it was just the dream of writers like H. G. Wells (The World Brain concept) or information science analysts like J. C. R. Licklider in his book *Libraries of the future*.[23] Now large-scale simulations on the HP Convex Exemplar supercomputer at the National Center for Supercomputer Applications have resulted in generating concept spaces for 10 million journals abstracts across 1000 subject areas covering all engineering and science disciplines – the largest vocabulary-switching computation ever achieved in information science. Future developments will require automatic indexing with scaleable semantics to coordinate searches among the one billion repositories likely in the next century.

Schatz concludes that the 'first major revolution of the Net millennium will come when the information infrastructure supports routine vocabulary switching. Then scientists will be able to break the bondage of their narrow specialities and effectively utilize the whole of scientific information in their research'.

Every technological change of a major nature leads to the debate as to whether technology drives the development or whether it enhances an agreed mission such as the educational process. That process clearly will be an encompassing multimedia one rather than the centuries-old print-on-paper environment as the TV generations of 'microserfs' come through. What we will need to blend is the increasing decentralization and individual access with the need for centralized coordination and facilitation.

Mirror sites, caching, competitive price structures, consortia deals are all part of the organizational infrastructure which have to meld with content provision, software gateways, intelligent agents etc. Structures will need to accommodate the now intertwined strands ranging from course content and development to network infrastructure to library proactive organizational skills. Virtual firms will mirror virtual universities and mass skills will be bought where they are cheapest, e.g. programmers in India. The virtual stock market is not far off in terms of home linkages to brokers and the world. The *New York Times* said of the 1939 World Fair 'television will never be a serious competitor for radio because people must sit and keep their eyes glued on a screen; the average American family hasn't got time for it'. What we currently don't have time for is to take in the myriad flow of information which encompasses print, TV and now Net access.

We're faced with a deluge of data, a hailstorm of hype, a depression of data, and an inundation of information! Information anxiety has been termed as the black hole between data and knowledge. Librarians and IT personnel will face future anxieties but someone has to be the interpreters – it's really whether the institutional frameworks we sit in are the right ones to allow the necessary growth. This is not the fashionable 'endengenous growth', cited by Victor Keegan, which leads to economics selectively booming from a knowledge or skills base.[24] Keegan further stated:

> Nearly 20 million words of technical information are being recorded every day – so a quick reader covering 1,000 words every three minutes for eight hours a day would need nearly five months to get through one day's output. Around 1,000 books are published every day; and one celebrated copy of the New York Times contained 1,612 pages and 12 million words – more data than a man in Bacon's time would have encountered in his lifetime.

Cybernetic sifting agents will thus be increasingly providing 'push' information supports which in science fiction terms will be neural links – the android Data in 'Star Trek' being the ultimate logical outcome.

Professor Donald Dennett of Tufts University at the Sydney Writers Festival in January 1997 illustrated his work on bringing philosophy and biological research together. Dennett sees the human mind as a conglomeration of 'robotic items' with consciousness as the software run by the brain computer. There is no reason, he argues, why machines cannot be conscious, because we ourselves are machines. Arthur C. Clarke in his recent novel *3001* invents 'braincaps', which allow small libraries of 'instant knowledge' to be transmitted, stored and interpreted in the human brain. It also incidentally brings social re-engineering in terms of criminal tendencies.

Implications for library managers

The current and future conditions which will prevail on library managers have been likened to whitewater rafting. Another comparison might be with 'cybersurfing', in which managers ride the crest of multiple changes or risk being 'dumped' by uncontrollable forces. The head librarian or information officer may well need to become more of a Chief Executive Officer (CEO), with the responsibilities and vision allied to more devolved structures.

The strategic plans and long-term horizons will have to be modified into rapid decision making and short-term political responses. Thus as IT and distance education converge the universities themselves will need to realign and strike national and global alliances. Radical changes to jobs will occur as telecommuting becomes possible in the satellite Internet delivery era with combined PC/TV set-boxes at home.

Input will then be measured on a piece or agreed contract basis with much more flexibility for the individual to determine when he or she wishes to make a contribution to the library or IT centres activity. In April 1997 I was privileged to be invited to attend the Mellon Foundation Seminar on 'Scholarly Communication and Technology' at Emory University in Atlanta. To observe the amount of wasted time in commuting by the inhabitants of Atlanta (let alone London, Sydney or Los Angeles) shows how much value-added leisure or business time can be liberated by telecommuting.

Client focus has to be the key. More effort will be needed to gauge the effectiveness of services, particularly when hard decisions are to be made because of reduced budgets and increased demands. Perhaps e-mail polling of users on a selective basis will be one performance measure.

Managers will have to juggle both fear and expectations. They will have to be coaches, mentors *and* hard decision makers at the end of the process. Knowledge managers themselves will need to be constantly aware of issues and trends so that with their teams they can be constantly flexible and realize stated goals with an ever-broadening environment of delivery. This won't be easy, but then the whole world will be changing in the 21st century in virtually all professions. Library managers will have more in common with their counterparts in other professions than ever before. Digital management will be both dynamic and demanding.

Conclusions

Sadly, perhaps, the entertainment industry also provides a model for the future. The world is dominated firstly by American media and secondly by the English language. Burgeoning local industries (e.g. Australian and British film industries) have risen and fallen, given US dominance of finance and distribution chains. Similarly, global libraries and global laboratories are not impossible in the future. The University of Illinios is working to create a worldwide facility which can be utilized anywhere in the world.

The same could be said societally. With the car and the move to suburbs, the ring-road hypermarkets in the UK and USA sprang up and inner-city corner shops died. By the 21st century, with online supermarket shopping and home delivery direct through timed deliveries or cool-store secure devices, the growth of 'isolationism' will continue for basic services. Social commuting will occur deliberately rather than randomly. If people today will pay $40 a week for ironing services in the cash-flush/time-poor environment, then the Internet is just one step away in service provision. Home shopping in the UK will get a boost in 1998 when B-Sky-B launches its digital satellites. These, B-Sky-B says, will have the computing power of an average PC and a very fast modem. B-Sky-B is negotiating with possible partners such as British Telecom (BT), in the hope that they will give initial subsidies for the decoders to kick-start the market. In return, they will be allowed to run home shopping and banking services on the system. As Hague has indicated, anyone with a satellite dish and a decoder could then go on shopping trips that cut out shops.[25]

Bill Gates also picked up the supermarket analogy in his address to the 1995 Food Business Forum when he congratulated supermarket executives in getting shoppers to do most of the work – drive to shopping conglomerates, buy food, load and unload trolleys and drive home. This is unproductive time. Information will be the same. Users will want their information accessible to them when they want it. Driving to a library, which may not be open, hoping to find the information wanted, is not the future model. The 24-hour reference library and IT service will supersede the check out circulation clerk. Can we manage the decentralized access with centralized overlays. Achievement by more focused and agreed results may be the only benchmark of the cottage cyberlibrary?

The future can be Utopian or Orwellian in cybernetic visions. Do we have Murdoch's dominance, the decline of the BBC and ABC, or do we have a myriad of individual Net accesses – a plurality of cyber villages but with most users ghettoized in their dedicated information and entertainment channels. Will digital harmonization increase the risks because of the growth of monopolies? The future will pose many digital dilemmas for library managers. Change, adaptability and vision will be needed more than ever. The super league of the information age will provide challenges as well as rewards as never before.

References

1 Oblinger, D. G. and Maruyama, M. K., *Distributed learning*, Boulder, CAUSE, 1996.
2 Association of Universities and Colleges of Canada and the Canadian Association of Research Libraries, The changing world of scholarly communication.
   <http://www.aucc.ca/english/sites/auccarl.htm>
3 Stoffle, Carla, 'The emergence of education and knowledge management as major functions of the digital library', Follett Lecture. University of Wales, Cardiff, 13 November 1996.
   <http://www.ukoln.ac.uk/follett/stoffle/paper.html>

4   Steele, C. R., 'Dinosaur or phoenix: the profession of librarianship', *Info*, University of Tasmania, 1996, 2–3.

5   Daniel, J., *Megauniversities and mega knowledge*, London, Kogan Paul, 1996.

6   Hart, Graeme and Mason, Jon (eds.), *The virtual university*, Symposium proceedings and case studies. Parkville, University of Melbourne, 1996.

7   Lyman, P., 'What is a digital library', *Daedulus*, **125** (4), December 1996, 1–33.

8   Lynch, C., 'Reflection on our future', *Bulletin of the American Society for Information Science*, **23** (2), December 1996–January 1997, 21–22.

9   *Independent*, 7 October 1996, Section Two, 15.

10 Cornell University. 'Campus profile', *Cause/Effect*, **19** (2), Summer 1996, 28–31.

11 CAUSE, Current Issues Committee, 'Current issues for higher education information resources management', *Cause/Effect*, **19** (2) Summer 1996, 5–7.

12 Lilly, C. and Thiele, G., *Reengineering in a university setting: pathways and pitfalls*, Educom/CAUSE, 1996.

13 Gilliland, M. W. and Tynan M. and Smith K. L., 'Leadership and transformation in an environment of unpredictability', 1996 CAUSE Conference. (see Allmayer below for URL)

14 Taylor, P., Lopez, L. and Quadrelli, C., *Flexibility, technology and academics' practices*, Canberra, DEETYA, 1996.

15 Kao, J., *The art and discipline of business creativity*, Harper, 1996.
    <http://www.jamming.com/jamming.html>

16 Allmayer, D. and Davidson, Phyllis H., 'The employee and organization of the future: a partnership at all levels', Proceedings of the 1996 CAUSE Conference.
    <http://www.cause.org/information-resources/ir-library/text/cnc9642.txt>

17 West, Thomas W., 'More lessons from the CIO trail'. (CAUSE Professional Paper Series #15), Boulder, CAUSE, 1–4.

18 Shaughnessy, T. W., 'Lessons from restructuring the library', *Journal of academic librarianship*, **22** (4), July 1996, 251–6.

19 Tenopir, C., 'Trend In end user searching', *Library journal*, **121** (20), December 1996, 35.

20 Benton Foundation, *Building, books and bytes: libraries and communities in the digital age*, Kellogg Foundation, 1996.
    <http://www.benton.org/Library/Kellogg/buildings.html>

21 The University of California Digital Library. Executive Workshop Group, *A framework for planning and strategic initiatives report*. Available at:
    <http://sunsite.berkeley.edu/UCDL/toc.html>

22 Brin, D., *Earth*, New York, Bantam, 1991, 284–5.

23 Schatz, B. R., 'Information retrieval in digital libraries: bringing search to the Net', *Science*, **275**, 17 January 1997, 327–33.
24 *Guardian*, 5 November 1996, 2–3.
25 Hague, Helen, 'Beyond shopping', *Independent on Sunday*, Supplement, 6 October 1996, 14.

7

Strategic management of the electronic library in the UK higher education sector: implications of eLib's IMPEL2 project at the University of Northumbria at Newcastle

Graham Walton and Catherine Edwards

University of Northumbria, England

Introduction

This chapter will investigate how selected academic library and information services (LIS) in the UK have strategically managed their services in times of great change. The results of IMPEL2 (IMpact on People of Electronic Libraries) longitudinal qualitative case studies at five university libraries will be used to illustrate how LIS have reacted to the multiplicity of management and resource issues they are facing.

An environmental analysis of UK LIS is provided using a Sociological, Technological, Economic, Political (STEP) analysis, Porter's five forces model[1] and Ansoff's matrix.[2] This is followed by background on the IMPEL2 project and its methodology. There will then be an analysis of the lessons to be learned from IMPEL2 and the implications for managers. Emphasis will be placed on strategies needed in times of rapid and major change.

External and internal environmental analysis of academic library and information services

The academic LIS sector has faced change in many areas of its activities. As far back as 1968, Ansoff indicated that no business can assume perpetuity of demand for services; the environment should be appraised on an on-going basis and strategy should be subject to regular review.

Planning of future LIS is concerned with the long-term effect of current decisions. In order to strategically develop services for the future, risk can be reduced by improving the quality of information available to decision-makers. The external environment must be appraised in order to establish the implications for planned services. A danger is that the external environment is cast into a set of permanently developed truths. For effective strategy formulation a realistic and informative review of both the external and internal environments is crucial. In the commercial sector this can be achieved using STEP analysis, Porter's five forces model and Ansoff's matrix. An attempt to apply these three models to the LIS academic sector is made later in the chapter.

Michael E. Porter is Professor at Harvard Business School and is the world's leading authority in the field of competitive strategy. He is also a director and strategic consultant to many US and international companies. He is arguably the single most influential writer on business strategy. He has seen strategy as a principle that can be applied not just to individual companies but to entire sectors. By analysing the strategic requirements of sectors, Porter developed the five forces model. These five forces are: threat of new entry; power of users; power of suppliers; substitute products and services; and jockeying for position. They are explained further below.

In the five forces Porter argues that the five forces can vary from industry to industry but together they determine the long-term industry profitability:

- prices firms charge, costs they accept and level of investment required are affected;
- market share and therefore profitability are limited by the threat of new entrants;
- margins will be eroded by powerful buyers or suppliers;
- volume will be eroded by the presence of substitutes.

The industry structure will dictate the strength of each of the five forces. Porter has developed two other powerful tools for the analysis of competition and determination of strategy: value chains and generic strategies. These can also be applied to the LIS sector but that will have to be on another day. In combination these three tools developed by Porter allow the LIS strategic manager to understand together economic forces and strategic pressures.

Professor H. Igor Ansoff has been Distinguished Professor of Strategic Management at United States International University, California since 1983. He has written over 120 articles relating to strategic management. He produced his product/mission matrix in 1965 and it is still as relevant in the 1990s. The underlying assumption of Ansoff's model is that there are two different types of competitive advantage:

- advantages in accessing given consumer groups
- advantages in particular products or product types.

It is also worth highlighting that this matrix has to be applied to both the output and input ends of the organization. A strategy may be appropriate for service delivery but inappropriate for resource acquisition.

Even though both Porter's and Ansoff's models were developed for the commercial environment, their robustness can be seen in their wider applications, including the LIS sector. They both allow LIS managers to look at the external and internal environments and align the position of the library to achieve good results. A key factor in libraries' strategic success is how the external environment is analysed and interpreted. If an accurate picture is gained then the LIS can develop new services or phase out services or re-engineer the organization with a realistic level of certainty that these are appropriate strategies.

STEP Analysis of UK LIS external environment

The STEP factors in the UK LIS external environment are detailed below. These are external environmental factors of relevance to LIS strategy making in the early 1990s.

Sociological

- Acceptance of trend towards life-long learning, with people studying throughout their working lives and through different modes (e.g. part-time, distance learning).[3–10]
- Increasing number of women in the work force.[11]
- Growth of the mass higher education (HE) system with increasing numbers of non-standard entrants.[12–16]
- In the 'information age', recognition of information as an important commodity. Rate of change in all areas makes access to current information crucial.[17–20]

Technological

- Digitization is enabling information to be transferred from paper to electronic format as well as being produced electronically.[21]
- Local-area networks (LANs) and wide-area networks (WANs) are making access to electronic information easier.[22–3]
- Electronic communication via e-mail, video conference, bulletin boards, discussion lists is becoming increasingly acceptable.[24]
- The ability to store information electronically (via CD-ROM, floppy disk, file-server) gives major advantages in terms of storage and access.[25–7]

Economic

- Books and journals are increasing in price over and above the UK rate of inflation.[28]
- Funding levels for HE from UK central government are being reduced.[29–30]
- HE costs are increasingly needing to be borne by students.[31]

Political

- Most significantly, central government is increasingly involving itself in HE policy.[32–4]

The factors identified in the STEP analysis will inform the strategic development of academic LIS. If they are ignored and not considered in strategy formulation, there is a danger that LIS will provide academic staff and students with services that are inappropriate to their altered needs. The main purpose of the STEP analysis is to increase the information stock and reduce the level of uncertainty about the environment. Its main advantage is that it is a simple tool and easily implemented.

Porter's five forces (Figure 7.1)

Porter's argument is that the key to strategic formulation lies in understanding the underlying competitive forces that determine the profitability of an organization. If the word 'success' is substituted for 'profitability', the theory may be

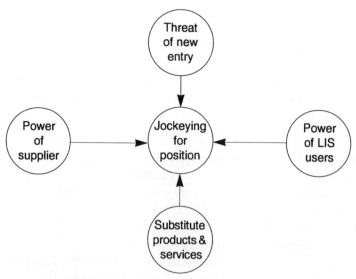

Fig. 7.1   *Porter's five forces*

applied to the non-commercial sector. The argument is that the groundwork for strategic action is an understanding of the sources of competitive pressure. Porter has proposed five basic forces which influence strategy in any sector. These are listed below.

Threat of new entry

The HE sector has become very competitive. Institutions are continually developing new courses and modes of delivery. It is possible to undertake degree courses where physical location of the university is not important. In some areas, courses (e.g. nursing) are being delivered on a competitive, contractual basis. There are also commercial services which challenge existing university LIS.

Power of users of LIS

Users can demand higher-quality service and play off different providers against each other. In the age of customer-driven services, users are becoming powerful in most areas. Demands for LIS are high so the users can have a major influence on services. Conversely, they have full access only to their own institution's LIS, which diminishes their power.

Power of suppliers

Suppliers' power is decreased when no company dominates, and the product is unique. LIS can use a range of book suppliers, periodical subscription agents and software suppliers. This enables LIS to force down prices, demand higher quality and increase competition between suppliers.

Substitute products and services

This force is central to the development of LIS in the 1990s and beyond. Electronic journals, Internet, World Wide Web, easy access for end-users to electronic databases will become increasingly important. LIS will be shaped by how they move to the electronic environment.

Jockeying for position

This refers to how services are altered and developed in the light of the above forces in comparison to other LIS. Even though academic LIS are not in competition with each other, this force is still applicable. In order to support their university's aims for excellence, new services will be developed, new collaborations and affiliations made. Electronic services will continue to be central to this.

Porter's ideas can be developed for LIS as they seek to maximize their own competencies in relation to the five forces. By anticipating the force factors influencing the LIS environment, it is possible to exploit changes. Once the forces have been analysed, their aggregate impact on individual libraries must be assessed. This analysis will then contribute towards establishing individual LIS strategy.

Ansoff's matrix

In the sections above, the STEP models and Porter's five forces were used to try to highlight the factors that are shaping HE LIS as we approach the end of the 1990s. In a later section (Lessons Learned), details will be given about how different IMPEL2 LIS have coped with the external environment. Once the external environment has been scanned, it may be appropriate to consider another management model which may support strategic development: Ansoff's matrix (Table 7.1). Even though the matrix was developed for the commercial sector, it does help LIS strategic managers establish how services can be developed. LIS managers must shape services so that there is a reasonable expectation that they will meet the university's objectives. Strategic ideas should be practical and implementable within the resource constraints.

Table 7.1   *Ansoff's matrix applied to higher education LIS*

	Existing range of LIS	New range of LIS
Existing users of LIS	Market penetration	Service development
New users of LIS	Market development	Diversification

Market penetration occurs when an LIS strategy is based on increasing the level of use by an institution's existing academic staff and students. It is a very safe strategy as it is based on delivering familiar services to users whose characteristics are well known. In two of the five IMPEL2 sites studied longitudinally, this strategic development approach was taken, though there were indications that this would change at one of these.

The student profiles of UK universities throughout the 1990s have been altering considerably. LIS cannot control their market; they must supply services, usually to the staff and students belonging to their institution. Franchized courses, part-time courses, distance learning courses and modular courses are examples of the variety represented across the IMPEL2 sites. If a university develops its market, the LIS must have a **market development** strategy. Again in IMPEL2 sites, services were being developed which were flexible to cope with the new user profile. There was a stable culture in those IMPEL2 sites which did not for the time being have to move to market development.

Service development occurs when LIS strategic managers have an awareness of both users' requirements and gaps in the existing range of LIS. Very often users of LIS will supply the pressure for new services to be run as part of the normal range of LIS. Referring back to Porter's five forces, the threat of new products are forcing all LIS to develop electronic services. In certain sites the service development strategy had taken place prior to the IMPEL1 study. If the library fails in supplying these new services, this will be an opportunity lost and users will increasingly go elsewhere.

Another key issue in service development is the need to be able to produce new LIS rapidly in response to users' requirements. If LIS can have a rapid turnaround in service development, service planning and service launching, there will be an enhanced perception of the library within the university. The focus must not be on the features of the new service, but on the benefits to the user.

The strategy with the greatest risk is **diversification**. Here the LIS develops new services to new users at the same time. A key difference between a commercial organization and LIS is that the decision to diversify or not is out of the LIS control. If a university develops its market, the LIS must also strategically alter its services accordingly. The rapid development of electronically based services forces LIS into a diversification strategy. In the commercial sector, diversification occurs where there is heavy competition. With the emphasis in HE on performance tables and quality ratings, this competitive culture is becoming more and more apparent. This is a good representation of the dilemma facing LIS: supplying new services to increased numbers of users with a falling unit of resource. Evidence of organizational upheaval and uncertainty were present in IMPEL2 sites where this diversification strategy was present.

IMPEL2 Project: background

Following the Funding Councils' Review of HE libraries[35] funding was directed to the Electronic Libraries Programme (eLib) over three years, with the aim of accelerating electronic library developments in the academic sector. IMPEL2 was funded under eLib's Supporting Studies segment to monitor organizational and cultural change associated with increasingly electronic LIS environments. The rationale underpinning the project was that while a great deal of technology-based activity such as digitization of text, development of networked resources and document delivery was underway, too little attention was being paid to the human and social implications of change in LIS: 'A major problem is that those who develop and implement new information technologies have not focused enough on human factors of the change process.'[36]

The Department of Information and Library Management and the Information Services Department at the University of Northumbria at Newcastle had been working jointly on a project, IMPEL1, focusing on the changing role of qualified librarians in the HE sector. IMPEL1 (1993–5) consisted of qualitative case studies in six university LIS across the UK, which were selected using a purposive sampling technique as being at the more developed end of the electronic library development spectrum. The purposive sample ensured a richer set of data than would a purely random sample. The case study methodology was based on a triangulation of:

- In-depth, semi-structured interviews with 82 library and related support staff including computer staff and also institutional managers or chairs of relevant committees.
- Questionnaires delivered to all levels of LIS staff.
- Scrutiny of documentation – institutional strategies, information or IT strategies, LIS staffing structure diagrams, staff training programmes etc.

Confidential case study reports were prepared for each of the six sites, and their findings discussed and validated at a participants' workshop. Workshop participants were in accord over the key issues identified by IMPEL1 as being significant in terms of their working experience. These issues related to:

- institutional factors (relating to an institution's history, politics, structure, commitment and vision);
- strategic factors (IT or information strategy, decision-making processes);
- LIS management structures (hierarchies, teams, communications channels);
- technological factors (capacity, reliability, support);
- LIS relations with computer centres (convergence, territoriality, definition of roles, shared goals, communications, culture differences);
- users (subject specialism, end-user instruction, relations with academic departments);
- LIS staff (workloads, IT skills, attitudes, awareness of issues, constraints on service provision, training and development);
- management of change (policies, practices).

IMPEL2 took both the methodology and these basic premises as a foundation for a broader and deeper study. It has four strands:

- Strand A staff study: a longitudinal LIS staff study in five of the six original IMPEL1 sites plus an HE college library and a Consortium of University Research Libraries (CURL).
- Strand B user study: study of student and academic staff users of electronic information systems and services in IMPEL2 sites.
- Strand C resource-based learning study: study of the impacts on LIS of institutional resource-based learning policies.

- Strand D staff training and development study: study of needs and practice for the electronic library.

A fifth strand (Strand E evaluation project), a formal evaluation of eLib's Netskills and EduLib Projects, was added later.

As in IMPEL1, work was based on case studies, although for IMPEL2 the number rose from six to 24, with a total of around 300 interviews or focus groups, giving the project team a wide view of activity across the country and also a headache in terms of data management. The approach taken to dealing with the large volume of material was to coordinate the data collection, the data processing and the data analysis. Each project officer would:

- Adopt a common approach to case studies, concentrating on previously agreed key themes plus his or her own particular focus.
- Process the data according to prescribed systems.
- Index the data using computer software for qualitative data analysis according to an agreed indexing structure.
- Compile case study reports based on a common format while not disguising particular features of any case.

In this way, validity and comparability of findings across the four project strands is increased. The coordinated approach brings rigour and control to the study while maintaining the degree of flexibility essential in qualitative work. Two major reviews of the literature[37–8] compiled by the IMPEL team describe fully the background and issues surrounding the work.

IMPEL2 Project: longitudinal study of five academic libraries 1994–5 and 1996–7: lessons learned

The key issues implicated in the management of the evolving electronic LIS identified in the IMPEL1 study have already been established (see previous section). These issues are used to shape the following discussion which has a longitudinal perspective. Five HE institutions that were the subject of the IMPEL1 study in 1994–5 were revisited for the IMPEL2 Strand A Staff Study in 1996–7; many of the same individuals were re-interviewed after the two-year interval in order to assess change and development in these particular institutions through their diverse characteristics. They may be seen to represent the HE sector fairly comprehensively, although in this sample no HE colleges were studied. The five institutions were a 1960s university, a small inner-city technologically-based university, a large inner city former polytechnic, an old civic university and a postgraduate university. The extent of change observable over two years varied between sites from a certain degree of stagnation, through incremental development and consolidation to major organizational restructuring.

Institutional issues

LIS are becoming increasingly central to the core business of HE institutions,[39] which is teaching and research activities. This is particularly the case as academic departments are subject to rigorous quality assessment of these activities, which are themselves underpinned by LIS and computing centres. In these times of financial stringency, the role and effectiveness of central services comes under close scrutiny and they must be seen to be delivering responsive and cost-efficient services. Given that all HE institutions have been subject to reduced per capita funding, three IMPEL2 sites had, to some extent, been spared the worst impacts of this, although forthcoming cuts were anticipated. Two had been severely affected with profound consequences for their LIS. In one case, two rounds of budget restrictions had necessitated a 25% reduction in LIS staff and a consequent staffing restructuring in order to maintain an optimum service to users. In another, LIS managers were forced to reconsider fundamentally its level of service and to abandon activities previously considered desirable or even essential. In the former case, there had been warning of forthcoming cuts, which enabled the LIS to reposition itself appropriately in order to remain proactive. In the latter, the danger of becoming a passive, reactive service was evident; additional factors in this case were an increase in student numbers over the two years of 3000 (increasing the current total to around 20,000) and a growth in the number of remote sites and franchised and partner colleges. This site had experienced the largest growth in the student body among the sample, the other four gaining modest numbers compatible with the national trend. The combination of a large increase in student numbers and severe funding cuts poses serious problems for LIS. The 'electronic solution' is also constrained by shortage of funds and staff.

All the LIS in question had an acute understanding of the vital function of their services for their institutions, not least in the light of the growth of student-centred and resource based learning. Students are turning increasingly to LIS and computing centres for support which may be unavailable in hard-pressed academic departments. More questionable was the level of understanding by senior institutional management of this vital function. Universities, unlike most corporate businesses, traditionally cling to the devolved power base structure; this was certainly the case in the IMPEL2 sites. There was no evidence over the two years of any shift in this position. The retention of funding and decision-making within faculties, departments or schools may represent a continued effort to sustain autonomy and academic freedom, particularly in a climate of increased central governmental control and influence. This tradition, however, creates a tension for central services which seek to raise their profile as equals with teaching departments that continue to regard them as secondary support services.

Where funding cuts had been most acute, these had been directed at central services, despite institutional strategic documentation which confirmed commitment to information technology (IT) and availability of information for the whole community. There appeared to be a mis-match between this expressed commitment and actual decisions taken. Where central services had been badly cut – in one site, for instance, the Computing Centre staff had been cut by 50% – staff expressed profound frustration over institutional failure to recognize the potential damage that they felt would inevitably occur to the teaching and research efforts of the institution. There was no direct evidence, however, that institutional managers viewed increasingly electronic services as being cheaper and therefore worthy of reduced funding.

The universal complaint of LIS staff and managers was of lack of central initiative and direction for IT and information on campus. Very little progress was evident here over the five sites. Indeed in one site all initiatives appeared to have been on hold and impetus lost in the run up to the appointment of a new vice-chancellor; this was demotivating and demoralizing for LIS staff who were well aware of the danger of losing ground to other institutions while they were 'treading water.' In two sites, the LIS had had lengthy periods under the direction of an acting head; these interregnums were somewhat static as an acting head is less likely to take important decisions affecting the future of his or her service. Here, clarity of direction and vision at departmental level had been to some extent lost.

Although the devolved power base structure persisted, efforts had been made in at least four sites to rationalize the institutional management or committee structure to reflect the changing role of information on campuses. This may indicate some recognition of the need for central direction in these matters although any impacts were slow to reveal themselves. On one site, although the library and computer committees had merged, this was not yet reflected in the working relations between the two services. Despite management restructuring, LIS and computing centres typically reported to different line managers. There was room for some optimism that institutions were streamlining their efforts, although the picture was still somewhat confused, not least by the element of institutional politics which characterizes HE. The most stability was observed in sites where funding had remained comparatively consistent, where student numbers had not exploded and where either the institutional management and/or LIS management had remained unchanged. Where this was the case, change over the two-year period tended to be incremental, with consolidation of previous efforts and direction.

Strategic issues

The five sites had not responded uniformly to the Higher Education Funding

Councils' requirement that information strategies be produced. The five responses may be briefly summed up:

- Information strategy not yet written, the exercise considered to be time-consuming and of little use.
- Information strategy in the implementation phase.
- Information strategy in place (two sites).
- Information strategy not yet written, likely to be forthcoming now new vice-chancellor appointed.

The sites where an information strategy was in place were possibly those with the greatest degree of central institutional direction, although the impacts of the strategy differed. In one, compiling the strategy appeared to be largely a paper exercise, a further expression of institutional commitment to IT, borne out to a lesser extent on the ground. In the other, the document had been accepted at the highest levels and had been a catalyst in forcing a merger between library and computing support services; in this way, the strategy document was considered to be politically motivated rather than user-driven.

The site where an information strategy had been rejected or postponed was a highly devolved institution. The institutional managers considered that the existing information systems strategy was in effect an information strategy when viewed in conjunction with the corporate plan. The librarian, frustrated by lack of central initiative, would have liked to have seen a shorter, integrated document, not schools-based as was the existing information systems strategy. A campus-wide strategy would inevitably have forced a more central view of information services and possibly raised the profile of the LIS.

Where the information strategy was in the hands of a new vice-chancellor and his team, it is possible to speculate that recent severe cutbacks in the computing centre would have been reduced or managed more appropriately, had such a strategy been in place earlier. Its absence may also be implicated in the perceived failure to capitalize on and fully exploit the early IT developments on that site, which had been fully networked since the late 1980s. Some concern was expressed that administrative information would receive greater attention in a future strategy than computing and library information

In the site where the information strategy was in the implementation stage, some dissatisfaction was expressed about the balance of its content, being heavily based on existing library plans. The ideal balance of input from LIS, computing and administration was lacking, and library plans appeared to have been seized upon as providing the solution. It must be questioned whether this is the proper way to address the question of institution-wide policy making. In the end the LIS may not be strengthened by such an approach. The proposed plan did not address the question of administrative information, which was a source of concern. A senior institutional manager confessed himself suspicious of those who claim to have a 'vision' for future developments in IT. Whether this view reflected the difficulty of sustaining any kind of vision in a fast changing environment, or unwillingness to pin colours to the mast or simple political expediency, is far from certain.

The status of information strategies within IMPEL2's five sites is likely to mirror the nationwide picture, where in some institutions there is no strategy, in some it is under development, in some it is viewed largely as a paper exercise, in some it has important political and strategic significance. The project's experience would suggest that the status of information strategies within individual institutions may be symbolic of the culture of the institution. A true campus-wide strategy implies a cohesive institutional approach to IT and information; IMPEL2's experience suggests that not all senior managers fully grasp that fact or that they may even fear it. LIS managers seek direction and commitment from their institutional managers; an Information Strategy may symbolize this to a greater or lesser extent, but absence of a strategy acts as a definite constraint upon LIS managers.

Library planning exercises were particularly prominent in two sites, reflecting the culture of staff involvement in those sites. In one, the exercise followed the appointment of a new LIS director and sought to involve and inform all levels of staff. In another, a lengthy two-stage exercise had involved a SWOT analysis and study of the external environment; it too involved all levels of staff. Barriers to staff involvement in library planning were staff shortages, split sites, lack of staff commitment and heavy workloads.

In all five sites, LIS directors were increasingly involved in strategic issues, necessitating the delegation of operational matters as far as possible. Such is the role of the LIS director within HE institutions at this time. In the site where an acting head had been in place for a lengthy period, there was concern, not that the LIS would fail to operate on a day-to-day basis, but that as a department it could be out-manoeuvred at a political level.

LIS management structures

Over the two-year period there had been both stasis and change in the staffing structures of the five LIS:

- Two non-converged services remained unchanged, retaining long-standing directors and traditional hierarchies.
- One organizationally converged service remained static.
- One formerly non-converged LIS service converged with the user support sec-

tion of the computing centre.
- One radically restructured from a flattish hierarchy into a faculty team structure. It remained non-converged.

In 1994–5 only one of the five sites had a converged LIS and computing service; by 1997 two had converged services. In the early converged service, LIS and computing had been organizationally rather than operationally merged under one director, with quite distinct library and computing divisions, coming together on a project basis rather than on day-to-day operations. The structure had remained largely unchanged since the late 1980s. An acting director had been in place for almost a year in a holding rather than a development role. It was likely that an incoming director would soon look to see how appropriate the structure was in an increasingly electronic environment. Although diagrammatic links could be made between LIS subject staff and 'matching' computing advisory staff, these were tenuous in practice. This was a possible area for greater joint working, to the advantage of departments. Despite organizational convergence, a traditional LIS hierarchy remained unchanged.

In the recently converged service, the former computing user support service was converged with the LIS academic services section, under the direction of the former librarian, with the aim of providing a one-stop shop for any user query relating to IT or information. It was too early to make judgements as to the success of the converged structure. At the time of the study, although the theory of the move was appreciated by staff, the practical aspects were more difficult. A number of IT posts had been lost at the time of the merger, increasing the strain on existing staff. Tasks were being devolved downwards wherever possible so that middle-grade staff gained more management roles and library assistants' tasks were increased. Because of heavy workloads, there was no opportunity for assistants to gain higher level skills and the gulf between support staff and 'professional' staff appeared wider than ever. Cataloguing and classification was added to the task list of information staff, so that cataloguers could be deployed elsewhere. The convergence had not occurred upon the retirement of a head of service, or the appointment of a new one, but appeared to be politically motivated. Increasing overlap between LIS and computing was a more minor factor behind the change, but in this case IT could be seen as a pretext for organizational change than a genuine driver.

In two sites, the opportunity for convergence had presented itself but had been rejected; in one case it was the computing director who retired, in the other the LIS director moved elsewhere. Both were fully networked, compact sites with relatively small student numbers where convergence would have appeared a logical move. In one, the existing structure was stable and working reasonably well so that convergence may have introduced an unwelcome level of turbulence. By contrast, in the other, there was a great deal of instability and low regard for the computing centre which had been drastically cut – not an ideal climate for massive organizational change. Interestingly both institutions opted for the status quo for the time being, neither having the will to go down the convergence route. A 'watch and wait' policy was preferred.

The site that restructured its LIS into faculty teams did so in response to severe staffing cuts with the accompanying rationale that a team structure allied to faculties was a more appropriate structure in a changing environment, more responsive to the needs of its users. The team structure moved the focus away from function-based activity to information provision for departments. Each team contained information specialists, information assistants, a coordinator and clerical assistants. Processes such as acquisitions and cataloguing were done within the multiskilled teams. Cross-library responsibilities also remained, forming a horizontal matrix underlying the team structure. The main problems encountered had been acquiring the correct balance between teams, the training requirement for multiskilling, line management and reporting. The change had been greeted by staff with mixed feelings who felt that the theory of self-managed teams was not always matched by the practice. There was opportunity for assistants to be significantly upskilled but it was not possible to regrade or reward them accordingly.

Clearly it is more feasible to achieve a restructuring in a small site with a small staff than in a very large or distributed LIS system. One such site retained a traditional type of hierarchical structure in its distributed system, although this was no longer considered appropriate in all areas. Attempts to move towards a more team approach had fallen foul of entrenched attitudes and possibly some inbuilt sluggishness associated with large organizations. More professional staff had recently been recruited in preference to support staff because of the increasing complexity of LIS work managing electronic systems and sources alongside print. Senior clerical staff were undertaking a wider range of tasks, from management tasks to process tasks. Professional staff were also increasingly engaged in management roles.

There was wide variability between IMPEL2's five sites in the extent of organizational change they had experienced over two years. A detectable theme across all, however, was that of 'stratification' within staffing grades:

- Directors and senior managers drawn increasingly away into strategic roles, devolving operational roles downwards.
- Stratification of professional staff into more managerial roles.
- Stratification of information staff with stronger IT skills, interest and experi-

ence than their colleagues.
- Stratification at support levels, where very able staff may undertake more 'professional' tasks, leaving less skilled tasks to less skilled staff.

This factor is no doubt due to the increasing range and complexity of roles and tasks undertaken in LIS at the present time. It appears somewhat at odds with the 'multiskilling' approach sometimes promoted but less often achieved. The 'stratification factor' is a potential cause of tension in LIS which is unlikely to diminish as the rate and scale of change continues.

Technology

All five sites are relatively well advanced in terms of the provision of electronic information, managing electronic sources alongside print and other traditional media. In comparison to the 1994–5 study, technology itself was lower down the list of expressed concerns, having been accepted as part of everyday life. New CD-ROM databases had been purchased but LIS were often constrained in their acquisition of new sources or preferred sources by finance. Staff were frustrated by the need to mix and match sources, knowing that the 'best' source may be too expensive. They were also frustrated and constrained by publishers' pricing policies which prevented the networking of products or inhibited the replacement of hard copy with electronic versions even though users may have welcomed electronic versions. The range of different interfaces and search engines (numbered as 39 and 19 respectively in one site) continued to stretch the skills of LIS staff. One institution had rejected a bid for a new CD-ROM network on the grounds of cost; this decision, revealed a lack of understanding at the most senior levels of the value and level of use of networked CD-ROMs and severely inhibited information provision on this site. With the increase in PCs housed in libraries, staff sought ways to ensure that they were employed for serious use, by restricting access to electronic mail, for instance, or by physically patrolling PC clusters.

The major technological impact reported had been that of the Internet and the World Wide Web which had scarcely featured two years previously. Students were ready users of the Internet, often seeing it as the first and most important information source to investigate, to the worry of LIS staff who were inclined to discourage its use because of its chaotic and uncontrolled nature. Staff complained that shortage of time prevented them from spending time investigating Internet sources; interested individuals, however, were more inclined to exploit its potential.

Uncertainty about managing the Internet and the Web was pervasive: whether to integrate it fully into LIS services, and if so, how; or whether this was something that stood outside the range of sources managed by LIS – an optional add-on for which the user was ultimately responsible. Further uncertainty was detectable over whether Internet development was the responsibility of the LIS staff or computing staff, whose roles tended to overlap in this area. Tension was caused by differing approaches to the Internet, computing staff tending to stress technological aspects and marketing potential, LIS staff anxious to stress the value of its information content. A promising approach had been developed in one site where a joint Web team (LIS, computing and marketing input) was coordinating the university's Web pages, and evidently working successfully together. In another site, a network development officer had been appointed (although only part-time) to coordinate and integrate the Internet into the service and encourage a somewhat reluctant LIS staff to take it on board; the staff training implications had not yet been addressed. Subject staff in IMPEL2 sites were not uniformly engaged in Web page development, this occurring in pockets where enthusiastic staff were engaged in designing pages pointing to good Internet sites and sources in their subject areas. Inevitably certain subjects, such as aeronautics and chemistry, were more fruitful than others, such as business.

The picture was of patchy use and acceptance of the Internet by LIS staff, some embracing it readily, some fearing it as yet another layer of added work. Another source of uncertainty was the question of Internet training for users. What, if any, training should be offered and by whom? In one site the computing centre offered a well-developed set of Internet training courses, but this was the exception among the sample.

Signs of the power of electronic developments to significantly change the roles of LIS staff were becoming more evident:

- Powerful housekeeping systems enabled more tasks, including cataloguing, to be devolved down to more junior staff.
- A project substituting hard copy journals with an electronic current awareness and document delivery service. This project had been carefully prepared, the department selected because of an existing poor journal collection and its staff's receptive attitude. The change had been extremely well received, so much so that interlibrary loans increased by 162%. Extension to other departments was under consideration.
- A Web project to design forms (e.g. interlibrary loans, reservation requests) for remote use by end users.

The impacts of these projects and others such as eLib networked resources, digitization and collaborative projects, for the roles, deployment and training of LIS staff, are beginning to be felt. The strategic implications are evident and will become increasingly important in the next few years.

Basic technological support for LIS showed some improvement over two years, three sites having appointed more computer officers. Although the officers had more hardware to look after, it was more robust than previously, so the firefighting content of their jobs had somewhat reduced. LIS computer officers had extremely heavy workloads which prevented them doing the developmental work which they wished to do. LIS staff wanted their computer officers to be visible, readily available, and to have good interpersonal skills. In two sites (one converged, one non-converged) there was a problem with fault reporting arrangements, where the onus remained with LIS staff to chase up faults reported to computing staff. They complained of not being told when a fault would be mended and whether it had been mended or partially mended. Overall, however, by 1996–7, organizational and institutional issues appeared to cause more concern than technological issues.

Relations with computer centre

A disturbing observation enabled by the longitudinal study was that in none of the five sites had working relations between the LIS and computer centres significantly developed. Even in the long-standing converged service, collaborative working was limited to one-off projects. The so-called 'cultural' differences between LIS and computing staff were often problematic and at times a source of conflict. In the recently converged service, both IT and LIS staff were surprised at the depth of cultural difference that they perceived in each other; this was brutally exposed at the joint help desk, where differing approaches to user support was a cause of tension. However, this help desk had been running for only a short space of time, and these tensions were being addressed. LIS staff were accused of excessive 'handholding' of users, leaving the desk to accompany them to the shelves. IT staff were accused of not appreciating the subtleties of the reference enquiry process and their method of handing out leaflets and manuals or simply directing users to the OPAC. LIS staff had a culture of 'discuss and analyse', while IT staff had a culture of 'quick fixes.' IT staff were irked by the way LIS staff constantly stressed their 'professionalism'. These tensions and feelings of territoriality were bad for the service, users being the ultimate victims. Shortage of staff and heavy workloads were preventing the anticipated sharing of knowledge and experience, so that early goodwill was dissipated. There was an acute need for basic training for both groups of staff, which had not taken place before the help desk was set up. In the early-converged site, a proposed joint LIS and computing advisory desk had not come to fruition, again as a result of territorial feelings on both sides.

One large non-converged site was also experiencing territorial difficulties as areas of overlap between LIS and computing centre increased. Historical factors exacerbated the situation – computing had traditionally delivered training to research students and staff, while LIS had traditionally offered training to everyone including undergraduates. The computing centre viewed recent LIS initiatives in developing its provision of both basic IT and information skills as invading their patch and relations between the two services deteriorated. This question of user education, coupled with that of access to and support of PC workstations on campus was producing stalemate. Again unfortunately, the users were likely to suffer as two vital central services failed to coordinate their effort.

Good relations between LIS and computing centres did not appear to relate to whether they were converged or non-converged. Comparison with other IMPEL2 sites not involved in the longitudinal study indicated that more significant factors were:

- The institutional ethos surrounding the coordination of support for users – user- driven is more constructive than politics-driven.
- The balance of personalities at senior levels in LIS and computing centres.
- The balance of power and stability between LIS and computing centres.
- Respect for each other's skills and expertise.
- Adequate staffing levels in both services.

End-user instruction

Recent library literature and electronic discussion lists indicate that end-user instruction is at the front of people's minds at the present time. While many LIS accept the concept of the 'self-explanatory library', most agree that users also need support from staff. However, there is uncertainty about what level of support it is feasible to provide given the differing circumstances of individual LIS, and about who should provide it. The issue was certainly more acute in 1996–7 than in 1994–5.

Two IMPEL2 sites illustrate the disparity of end-user support activity which can now be found in academic LIS. The basis for the disparity was largely financial. In both sites the situation in 1996–7 was vastly different from that in 1994–5. In the first site, stringent financial cuts, coupled with increases to an already large student body, had forced the LIS to scrutinize its service to see which desirable and even essential services could be eliminated. Of necessity, previous efforts to embed IT and information skills into the curriculum had been abandoned. Teaching of these skills was now the responsibility of academic departments, although LIS staff questioned the consistency and adequacy of such an approach. The LIS was to deliver basic library induction only, to the dismay of its subject staff. The institutional policy to cut central rather than teaching departments was at odds with the view that IT and information skills, too, were essential to the university's mission. LIS staff anticipated that the policy would rebound on their service as students disadvantaged by lack of basic skills would resort to the LIS for help.

In the second site – which at the time of the study had not been subject to stringent financial cuts, and indeed had recently obtained additional funding for stock and grants for hardware purchase – the picture was different. The LIS had been extremely proactive in developing its teaching provision for its community, spurred on by quality assessment requirements for academic departments which scrutinize IT and information skills provision. The LIS was defining its role within the university as the department that was skilled in electronic information. Where space allowed, teaching suites had been built – the physical symbol of the policy. A Skills Teaching Task Group had compiled an information skills teaching manual to assist staff in lesson materials, structure, content and delivery, teaching aids and evaluation. In addition, all LIS staff engaged in teaching were now required to attend the in-house teaching skills course.

The second site described is an example of the Follett ideal of a partnership between LIS and teaching departments, the so-called 'para-academic' role, which the first site was unable to adopt. A future study would indicate the implications of two such different policies in the longer term.

Staff in other sites continued to examine the relevance and quality of their user education, for example, making sessions more active for attendees, with a greater element of critical thinking. While LIS felt sure that 'information' skills lay within their province, responsibility for basic IT tended to be less certain. Undergraduate students again were the ones to suffer from policies or historical practices of computer centres to support only research and teaching staff. This problem requires effective collaboration between LIS and computing staff for its solution.

LIS staff issues

LIS staff who took part in IMPEL2 did not feel that the impact of the developing electronic library on their work was significantly different from two years ago, with the exception of the impact of the Internet. Electronic systems and sources were very much part of their lives. There was a strong sense that LIS were poised to develop electronic services further but that they were constrained by:

- the requirement to do more with less financial resource and fewer staff;
- heavy workloads;
- time constraints on training;
- shortage of hardware and inadequate networking capacity;
- entrenched attitudes among academic staff;
- patchy links with teaching departments;

- publishers' pricing policies;
- inconsistent approaches to IT skills teaching;
- the variety of software and computing platforms in teaching departments;
- slow responses from computing staff (e.g. delays in mounting up-to-date editions of CD-ROM databases);
- lack of central direction for the development of electronic information;
- time taken adjusting to organizational changes.

Joint training with computing staff had not developed in the two year period. Attempts to develop more systematic training programmes for LIS staff were evident, particularly at library assistant levels. Two useful examples of this were found: in one site a list of competencies for assistants had been compiled so that training needs were identified; in another, the multiskilling requirements for team working were monitored using a skills matrix whereby assistants assessed their own expertise across a range of tasks, which was then compared with an expert's assessment. Simple methods such as these seem beneficial in that a problem defined may be a problem already partly solved. By contrast, due to heavy workloads and the impossibility of 'keeping up', some assistants on one site were reported to have 'given up'.

Professional staff were receiving more management training, reflecting the trend for management roles to be devolved downward when possible. The need for database training continued unabated. A senior manager identified a training problem for middle-grade staff among whom there was a wide range of ability and also a wide range of tasks.

High stress levels and low morale were associated with major organizational changes. A senior manager admitted spending increasing amounts of time 'counselling' staff, but was untrained in counselling skills. Apart from the one example of professional staff who were required to attend in-house teaching skills sessions, most were undertaking teaching without this kind of support. Some expressed interest in the EduLib Project, an eLib project that delivers teaching skills to LIS staff.

Clearly, the training needs for staff working in an electronic environment were not only IT-based. The need for teaching skills, interpersonal skills and management skills was recognized by large numbers of staff as they endeavoured to cope with and manage change.

Change management

LIS that had been involved in the 1994–5 study were well aware of the management demands of the rapidly changing scene. One lesson learned from IMPEL2 was that the enemy of good change management is shortage of time to follow textbook procedures such as good communications and involvement of all levels of staff. Staff freely admitted that they resented changes that they perceived to have been imposed on them.

The luxury of time had not been afforded to the LIS which was involved, by institutional decision, in amalgamating its user support with that of the computing centre. Had it been able to conduct help desk training *prior* to its inception, it may have been possible to minimize problems. In this case, as in the case of organizational restructuring in the face of severe budget cuts, there was both low morale and dogged optimism among staff; the fear of ultimately losing one's job underlay all other feelings.

Preparation of up-to-date documentation by LIS was a sign that change was being managed as effectively as possible. LIS that continued to study the external as well as the internal environment were well placed to make a case for additional funding and to seize initiative. Library planning procedures were more evident than two years previously and did involve all levels of staff. In one site, a library planning process had begun upon the appointment of a new director. This involved a thorough environmental analysis before scrutiny of the vision statement, mission, strategic objectives, followed by analysis of strategic processes and critical success factors. The ultimate plan would incorporate TQM. A planning and resources officer had a key role in supporting the director in the planning process. Cost attribution matrices had been constructed. These identify in a detailed way all the standard LIS services and the tailored services which individual departments might receive. This makes clear the departments and TQA assessors exactly what the LIS does for departments and provides a basis for service level agreements. In this site also, a new library system had been effectively planned and installed with the particular involvement of those who would be using it most. A range of systems had been assessed in order to single out those that would best meet the requirements of that LIS which was particularly short-staffed; the choice hinged on the system's ability to move quickly between functions and to eventually accommodate all housekeeping functions, so freeing up staff to support users and information specialists. Here the link between electronic systems and the demands on LIS was clear, enabling staff to focus increasingly on users rather than processes.

In another site, library planning was into a second stage, with the aim of clarifying the future direction for the LIS. A pre-planning exercise involved four working groups looking into faults measurement, academic background factors, changes in IT and a SWOT analysis. The outcome of these investigations was three planning groups focusing on the development of new services, marketing the service and human resources. This intensive programme reflected a less reactive, more user-centred approach to service, a period of consolidation of past achievements and consideration of future development.

Library planning and systematic management of change had a lower profile during periods when the appointment of LIS directors was pending and when organizational changes were in their most active phase.

STEP analysis, Porter's five forces and Ansoff's matrix applied to LIS

It is important that the reader can make explicit links between the management models and the key issues identified by IMPEL2 in the previous section. Table 7.2 represents the authors' concerns to relate these together. This is a limited and subjective exercise designed to help readers develop a greater understanding of the relationship between these three models and LIS practice.

Table 7.2 *STEP Analysis, Porter's five forces and Ansoff's matrix applied to LIS*

Key issues	Related factors	Theoretical model
Institutional issues	Reduction in budgets	STEP
	Lack of institutional strategic direction	Porter
	Internal and governmental politics	STEP/Porter
Strategic issues	Information strategies	STEP
	Strategic planning	Porter/Ansoff
LIS management structures	Convergence	STEP
	LIS organizational structures	Ansoff
Technology	Impact on LIS staff roles/uncertainty	Porter/STEP
	Constraints on development	Porter/STEP
	Impact of single technology (Internet)	Porter/STEP
LIS relations with computer centre	Cultural differences	Porter
	Territoriality	Porter
	Significance/insignificance of convergence issue	Ansoff
End-user instruction	Differences in approach	Porter/Ansoff
	Delivery of core IT skills	Porter/Ansoff
LIS staff issues	Reduced threat of IT	STEP
	Staff training and development	Ansoff
	Stress of organizational change	Porter
Change management	Time shortage/theory v practice	STEP
	Impact of loss of authoritative leader	Ansoff

The **STEP** model is relevant to the reduction in budgets and the governmental politics. These are all significant factors that are outside the control of LIS. Similarly the production of institutional information strategies is a requirement of an external authority. Organizational pressure to converge the library and computer units is a global phenomenon as the differences in paper-based and electronic textual information become blurred. In the intervening period between the two longitudinal case studies information technology continued to be pervasive and accepted as part of everyday life. The rate at which change has to be implemented continued to accelerate beyond the direct control of people affected by the change.

Table 7.2 also shows the significance of **Porter's five forces** model. LIS strategic planning and emerging internal LIS are represented by the 'jockeying for position'. This force also relates to cultural differences and changing roles of library and IT staff. Developing new commercial document delivery services and new electronic information sources can be likened to the 'threat of new entry' and 'substitute products' respectively. Individual universities and their LIS users will expect some level of electronic service delivery and development. They will demonstrate their potential 'power' in a variety of ways to which the LIS may respond. All five forces have relevance to LIS organizational change and its associated stresses.

When an LIS establishes its strategy **Ansoff's** model becomes applicable. LIS can choose to supply existing services to the same user population. If this strategy is adopted the LIS risks being left behind by the electronic revolution. On the other hand, if an LIS decides to invest in the development of new electronic services and ignores traditional services totally, users will not be served. A safer approach will be to continue delivering traditional services to existing users while at the same time not ignoring electronic options. This option is not always possible as the profile of higher education students changes in terms of mode of attendance, geographical location and basic abilities/experience.

Managerial issues and implications
Discontinuous change

Change management and organizational development have become well-worn phrases in the 1990s. The importance of how LIS react to change and how they introduce changes is not diminishing. Indeed, Handy[40] has produced some ideas which show that the nature of change itself is developing. He describes the concept of discontinuous change where no clear patterns of change are identifiable and where the smallest changes can have the biggest impact. He identifies two major sources of discontinuity: economics and technology. The declining unit of resource was particularly evident in two IMPEL2 sites. Financial cuts had fundamentally altered the delivery of LIS. Information technology had also introduced basic changes to services. Handy[41] describes the mixture of technology and economics as a 'potent blend'.

Discontinuous change is not seen by Handy as a negative development. Indeed, he argues that it should be sought and embraced. It is questionable for how long the IMPEL2 sites that have remained relatively static and unaffected can protect themselves from the discontinuous changes faced in other IMPEL2 sites. When discontinuity is prevalent, staying still is not optional.

Flexibility

Services need to be developed at a quicker pace. LIS must respond to alterations in budget (either increases or decreases). Developments at an institutional level should be mirrored and furthered in the LIS itself. The key factor, if the above is to be achieved, is flexibility. There has to be a responsive management structure that will invariably become flatter.[42-3] This need for flexibility means that LIS managers have to take on new roles. They will become part of teams and responsible for coordinating resources. Responsibility will then need to be devolved to allow the LIS staff the necessary flexibility. If power is distributed then managers will be occupied with coordination and communication.

Creativity

There are various reasons why LIS need to be creative in ensuring the delivery of quality services. Work by Handy,[44] shows the rapid increases in change. Familiar LIS practices must be thought about in new ways so that creativity may be encouraged. Flatter organizations are more conducive to innovation than are bureaucracies. Sites have undergone structural reorganization in order to encourage creativity. It is still possible to encourage creativity in LIS that have retained a bureaucratic culture; subgroups may be set up and given freedom and flexibility to develop new services; matrix structures may be introduced to improve responsiveness or transform the climate and culture.

Majaro[45] has indicated three features that must be present in creative organizations. These features should exist harmoniously:

- a climate conducive to creative thinking
- an effective system for communicating ideas
- procedures for managing innovation

LIS staff need the opportunity to share ideas. They need also to be aware of changes outside the library. These needs are more easily fulfilled within a climate of informality and participation. LIS managers have important roles if universities are to posses creative library services. They must become involved in empowering their staff to produce good work. Individuals should be offered the opportunity to develop; promising ideas should be encouraged and nurtured.

Intuition

Intuitive judgements will become central as LIS managers decide the shape of future services. There is a temptation to see intuition as being an imperfect tool and one that could lead to flawed strategies. On the other hand, Agor[46] has proposed that intuition is invaluable to decision making in times of rapid change which are laden with crises. The situation at some of the IMPEL2 sites would reflect this description. The successful use of intuition depends on having a deep understanding of the subject. Good intuitive decisions are based on facts and experiences gained over a period of years. Agor does point out that intuitive judgements are impaired when egos are bound up in decision making. The political nature of computing and library relationships could make this difficult sometimes. His research also established the following as applicable for intuitive decisions:

- **High risk:** in the LIS sector, high risk is represented in the large investments needed for new electronic services. There is no absolute guarantee that this strategy will be successful.
- **Choice needed from various plausible options:** identical information is now available in a range of media (hard copy, CD-ROM, magnetic tape, Internet, floppy disk). They are all feasible options but the LIS manager has to decide which is appropriate for the user population.
- **No option favoured owing to incomplete information:** universities very often need responses from LIS quickly. In these circumstances there is often an inadequate stock of information for logical, structured decision making. Reliance on creativity, flexibility and innovation is not adequate in itself in LIS strategy formulation. It is also important that LIS have strong management information systems, effective communication channels and good internal cooperation. Where these are all in place there is no reason why LIS cannot make effective strategies to deliver electronic services to its user population.

Conclusions

It is always a difficult task to attempt to forecast how things will develop over a period of years. The rate of change is not making this any easier. An informed observer of the UK LIS higher education external environment could make the following predictions:

- the unit of resourcing will either stay the same or more likely continue to reduce

- central government involvement in higher education will not diminish
- existing technology will continue to develop at an ever increasing rate
- there will some as-yet unidentified technology that will have major implications for LIS
- users of university LIS will demand more flexibility, easier access and quicker development of new services.

IMPEL2 has been in the fortunate position to be able to monitor the LIS sector at a time of great turbulence. During the rest of 1997 the IMPEL2 team will be producing material that will help higher education LIS develop electronic services. Evidence supports the supposition made in IMPEL1 that the limiting factors to electronic LIS are human and organizational rather than technological. Some of the environmental factors have the potential to be threats to the service itself or opportunities for the LIS to become even more central in the higher education process. The three models described – STEP, Porter's five forces and Ansoff's matrix – assist the LIS strategic manager in deciding how an individual LIS reacts to this environment.

The intention will be for IMPEL2 to disseminate its findings in as many ways as possible during 1997 and 1998. The LIS professional has long been criticized for not making decisions that are based on evidence or research. IMPEL2 should produce information that will provide the data to help in the decision making. This data, along with an individual LIS manager's deep experience and perceptive intuition, will be crucial in ensuring LIS develop and provide valued services to academic staff and students in the new millennium.

References

1   Porter, M. E., 'How competition forces shape strategy', *Readings in strategic management*, , D. Asch and C. Bowman (eds.), Macmillan, 1989.

2   Ansoff, H. I., *Corporate strategy*, Harmondsworth, Penguin, 1968.

3   Cowell, R., 'The new model university for the millennium', *The Times higher education supplement*, **1190**, 25 August 1995, 12–13.

4   Hartley, D., 'Teaching and learning in an expanding higher education system (the MacFarlane Report): a technical fix?', *Studies in higher education*, **20** (2), 1995, 147–57.

5   Bleasdale, C., 'Information skills versus study skills', *Sconul newsletter*, **3**, Autumn 1994, 31–3.

6   Heery, M., 'Modularization: a library perspective', *Copol newsletter*, **56** (50), 1991, 46–50.

7   Ball, C., 'Learning organizations and lifelong learners – the shape of things to come in the learning society', *Scottish journal of adult and continuing education*, **1**

(2), Autumn 1994, 57–63, 65.

8   Smith, D., Scott, P. and Mackay, L., 'Mission impossible? Access and the dash to growth in British higher education', *Higher education quarterly*, **47** (4), Autumn 1993, 316–33.

9   Myhill, M., '2020 – a space oddity (or where do we go from here?)', *Education libraries journal*, **37** (2), 1994, 29–40.

10   Nicastro, M. L., 'Interactive learning in marketing classes', *Marketing news*, **23** (15), 1989, 16.

11   Abercrombie, N. and Warde, A., *Contemporary British society: a new introduction to sociology*, Cambridge, Polity Press, 1994, 217.

12   Goodwin, P., 'What's your problem?: the present day realities of higher education in libraries', *Sconul newsletter*, **4**, Spring 1995, 33–5.

13   Brophy, P., 'Performance measures in academic libraries; a polytechnic perspective', *British journal of academic librarianship*, **4** (2), 1989, 99–110.

14   Matthews, G., 'The main features of post-binary higher education: a preliminary assessment', *Reflections on higher education*, **5**, July 1993, 62–8.

15   Becher, T., 'The state and the university curriculum in Britain', *European journal of education*, **29** (3), 1994, 231–45.

16   Daniel, J., 'The challenge of mass higher education', *Studies in higher education*, **18** (2), 1993, 197–203.

17   Heseltine, R., 'The challenge of learning in cyberspace', *Library Association record*, **97** (8), 1995, 432–3.

18   Line, M., 'Service and self service: the electronic library from the user's point of view', *Opportunity 2000: understanding and serving users in an electronic library. 15th International Essen Symposium*, A. H. Helal and J. Weiss (eds.), Essen, Essen University Library, 1993, 284–94.

19   Report of the Joint Funding Councils' Libraries Review Group (Chairman: Prof. Sir Brian Follett), Bristol, HEFCE, 1993.

20   Line, M., 'Line's five laws of librarianship . . . and one all embracing law', *Library Association record*, **98** (3), March 1996, 144.

21   Dempsey, L., 'Libraries and networking', *Library & information briefings*, 37/38, December 1992.

22   De Gennaro, R., 'The impact of technology on libraries in the information society', *Proceedings of the 2nd Pacific conference on new information technology for library and information professionals, educational media specialists and technologists*, Singapore, 29–31 May 1989, Ching-Chih Chen and D. I. Raitt (eds.), West Newton, MicroUse Information, 1989, 81–9.

23   White, H. S., 'Information technology, users and intermediaries in the 21st century: some observations and predictions', *Opportunity 2000: understanding and serving users in an electronic library*, 15th International Essen Symposium,

A. H. Helal and J. Weiss (eds.), Essen, Essen University Library, 1993, 1–14.

24 Meadows, J., 'Is the future beginning to work: academics and networks', *Changing patterns of online information. Proceedings of the UKOLUG state of the art conference 1994*, C. J. Armstrong and R. J. Hartley (eds.), 63–71.

25 Corrall, S., 'Information specialists of the future: professional development and renewal', *Information superhighway: the role of librarians, information scientists and intermediaries*, 17th International Essen Symposium, Essen, Essen University Library, 1994, 1–6.

26 Royan, B., 'Gateway not storehouse: the academic library in an electronic age', *Computers in Libraries International 94*, Proceedings of the Eighth Annual Computers in Libraries International Conference, M. Auckland (Director), London, Mecklermedia, 1994, 71–6.

27 Osswald, A., 'Intelligent gateways: functions for the benefit of the electronic library', *Opportunity 2000: understanding and serving users in an electronic library*, 15th International Essen Symposium, A. H. Helal and J. Weiss (eds.), Essen, Essen University Library, 1993, 183–97.

28 Op. cit., (19).

29 Ashworth, J. M., 'Higher Education foundation lecture: universities in the 21st centuries – old wine in new bottles or new wine in old bottles?', *Reflections on higher education*, **5**, July 1993, 46–61.

30 Op. cit., (26).

31 Richards, H., 'Levy hangs in balance', *The Times higher education supplement*, **1213**, 2 February 1996, 1.

32 Pritchard, R. M. O., 'Government power in British higher education', *Studies in higher education*, **19** (3), 1994, 253–65.

33 Becher, T., 'The state and the university curriculum in Britain', *European Journal of Education*, **29** (3), 1994, 231–45.

34 Halsey, A. H. Higher education: donnish decline. *The Guardian*, 7 February 1995, 7.

35 Op. cit., (19).

36 'Acknowledgement of the past: the first step in changing the future', *Journal of academic librarianship*, **19** (4), (Editorial), Sept. 1993, 211.

37 Edwards, C., Day, J. M. and Walton, G., 'Key areas in the management of change in higher education libraries in the 1990s: relevance of the IMPEL project', *British journal of academic librarianship*, **8** (3), 1993, 139–77.

38 Day, J. M., Walton, G., Bent, M., Curry, S., Edwards, C. and Jackson, M., 'Higher education, teaching, learning and the electronic library: a review of the literature for the IMPEL2 project: monitoring organizational and cultural change', *The new review of academic librarianship*, **2**, 1996, 131–204.

39 Op. cit., (19).

40 Handy, C., 'The age of unreason', *Creative management*, J. Henry, London, Sage, 1991, 269–82.
41 Ibid., 275.
42 Von Wahlde, B. V., 'The impact of the virtual library on library management and organization', *Opportunity 2000: understanding and serving users in an electronic library*. 15th International Essen Symposium, A. H. Helal and J. Weiss (eds.), Essen, Essen University Library, 1993, 27–42.
43 Corrall, S., 'Middle managers – a defunct species?', *Library manager*, **1**, November 1994, 25.
44 Op. cit., (40).
45 Majaro, S., *The creative gap*, London, Longman, 1988.
46 Agor, W. H., 'The logic of intuition: how top executives make important decisions', *Creative management*, J. Henry, London, Sage, 1991, 163–77.

8

THE HEART AND BRAIN OF THE INFORMATION SOCIETY: PUBLIC LIBRARIES IN THE 21ST CENTURY

Chris Batt

BOROUGH LIBRARIES AND MUSEUM OFFICER, LONDON BOROUGH OF CROYDON, ENGLAND

Introduction

When starting to write this chapter, I inclined to a more quizzical title. Something like **More questions than answers** seemed to fit the mood of the moment. To make any attempt to predict the future we need some reference points – points of departure that can give us direction into the unknown or only partly known. The received opinion (promoted by me as frequently as by others, I hasten to add) is that the future of the public library will be intimately entwined with the information society. This is the premise underpinning much of the thinking and research now taking place within the public library sector, certainly across Europe. Two obvious examples are the EU libraries programme 'Public libraries and the information society study' (PLIS),[1] and the views expressed about the UK public library service in the Department of National Heritage's policy statement *Reading the future*.[2]

Yet, within my own work and the work of others I am left with a nagging feeling that we frequently make assumptions about the future that are general rather than specific. We believe in the importance of the information society; there are many documents telling us it is a revolution which will affect the lives of everyone. We want to believe those messages since, within the world of public libraries, we professionals can make quick and easy connections with the tenets of the information society. An alliance with something so important, so 'centre stage', guarantees longevity. That is how the logic goes.

Let me state immediately that I do believe my final choice of title is justifiable on more than just emotion and hope. What I will try to do in the next few pages is to make more concrete the connections between public libraries now and possible futures. Particularly, to make those connections within the context of individuals; to dig into the fine grain of life rather than remain at the macro/strategic level which is the world of politicians and planners.

There are two simple questions that emerged from my initial brooding over what I was going to say. First, what is a public library? And second, what is the information society? They seem easy enough questions to articulate, at least. They may, of course, be easier to ask than to answer! We begin with question one.

What is a public library?

The most obvious answer, and one that the majority of the users of our services might offer, is that the public library is a place, a building, which is visited to borrow books and to obtain information. There are other things that might be added by some users: a place to study, a place to rest or shelter from the rain, a place to meet people, or a place to display artistic talent. These are all significant activities which represent established outputs from the service. However in an analysis of where the public library service is now and where it could go, there needs to be a closer examination of not just what it does, but why the present financial and organizational frameworks should remain. To use an analogy from another sector, we lived for many years in the UK with a monopolistic telecommunications industry. Deregulation of that industry has certainly provided more choice for more people; some might say too much.

From the very beginning of the public library movement in the middle of the 19th century, the public library has been seen as a public good, a service funded from non-private funds for the benefit of the whole community, originally with charitable support, now from taxes, by and large free at point of use, and in theory equally available to each and every member of a particular community. A service that is considered essential to a community's well being and not, therefore, available only on the basis of ability to pay. Recent years have seen the management of many traditional public goods change as competition has been introduced, at least to the tendering of management contracts. Despite this move towards more competition within local government, the public library service has remained generally unaffected. In the UK, the 1995 report *Contracting out in public libraries* concluded that *'there is a strongly argued case for the provision of library services to remain essentially within the public sector'*[3] and although more recent UK reports from the Department of National Heritage (e.g. *Reading the future*) have suggested that 'contracting out' may still be on the agenda, the case is clearly not so obvious as it is for leisure centres, swimming pools, refuse collection and professional services.

I do not believe it is unreasonable to suggest that even though the public library service was almost invisible to national government for much of this century, in the minds of those citizens who are the service's users, it likely to be the most important public resource available to them. Yes, of course, education is essential, but for most of our lives we do not use directly schools or colleges. The public library is available to be wandered into whenever wanted and for whatever reason – assuming it is open.

Recently there have been a number of national studies in the UK that have attempted to bring more structure to our understanding about the nature of and roles for the public library service. There are three studies worthy of mention. 'Objectives for public libraries'[4] is a research project intended to produce a menu of key activities and service aims, allowing service managers to make more explicit the process of service delivery and evaluation. It suggested core activities such as community information, reference services, economic well-being, independent learning, reading and literacy, recreation and networking. *Borrowed time*[5] took a more sociological perspective, placing the role of the public library within the context of wider community life. The report suggested that the public library plays a key role in the processes of social well-being, education and information provision; for many the public library is the only community resource that they use consistently. Finally, the 'Review of public libraries in England and Wales' tried to give clarity to the perceptions of public libraries of both library staff and library users. It underlined the fact that the majority of citizens believe that the service should be controlled directly by the local authority. It defined 13 core functions and purposes including, 'creating a public library service that will be a community asset in which local people can take pride, and which others will respect – an asset that helps local people to identify with their community'.[6]

On the one hand we find that the UK public library service remains a core public good providing a wide range of services, with broad support, while on the other hand, due to funding restrictions, there are insufficient funds to maintain the existing stock of buildings or the traditional resources. This is a problem faced by public libraries in many places beyond the UK. The European Commission's 'Public libraries and the information society' study, referred to above, demonstrated clearly that overall European public libraries are under-funded for the services they should be providing now and for the challenges they will face in the future. That under-funding is at once money to deliver service and money to re-skill and enrich the human resource.

The PLIS study did more than just make a semi-political statement about the need for additional funding. It showed very clearly that there is a significant divide between the most advanced and forward-looking public library services and the rest of the pack. That is as true for the UK as it is across the rest of Europe. In this respect investment in information technology resources is a potent indicator. Within the public sector, public libraries were in the vanguard of IT implementation. By the latter half of the 1970s a number of public libraries had made significant investment in library management systems to manage circulation and basic cataloguing – perhaps with a computer-produced fiche catalogue. By the mid-1980s, 50% of UK public libraries had such systems for circulation and in 1993 the figure had risen to 80%.[1] There are other applications which some public libraries now treat as normal. CD-ROM and Internet access offer new routes to information while the PC has allowed the better management of many of the databases that public libraries have traditionally maintained – community information being the most obvious example.

However, while the best UK public library services lead Europe in the investment made and the demonstrable benefit that has been delivered to communities served, these developments remain patchy. This is a factor we will have to retain in mind when we consider the future of public libraries. Responding to change requires a number of components to be in place. Money, naturally, but also professional and managerial commitment to change, technical skills and most of all a shared vision of what the future will be like. This latter factor is of critical importance for, as we shall see, although public libraries have a long and honourable tradition of cooperation, the future will place cooperation and resource sharing, centre stage, at the heart of what they do.

I am aware that, having started with the question, 'what is a public library?', I have failed to go far past the view that a customer might have. A number of landmarks for the public library manager may have been highlighted, but a complete and robust definition has not be presented. This summarizes, perhaps, the problem that service managers face constantly. It is the elephant dilemma. Try to describe an elephant to a child who has never seen one, not even a picture – its size, its shape, the trunk – and they will find it very hard to grasp what you say. Yet once they have seen one, they (like the elephant itself) will never forget! So it is with the public library. Everyone has his or her own model of what it is for, what it is like, and description will always fail to get to that personal level. But, once you use the service, you know the value.

Next we need to consider briefly the nature of the information society in so far as it has implications for the future of the public library service.

What is the information society?

I do not intend to spend too long on this question, since the deeper you dig the harder it is to come up with some general concepts. It has been evident for as long as a people have cared to notice, that information is a vital component of our lives and our societies. Facts, information, intelligence, whatever you call them are fundamental to our behaviour patterns. Business, social interaction, government, everything you can think of depends on accurate information for its success. So, what is new? The popularization of computer technology and communications is the obvious answer to that question, and their convergence into a single entity. Called *computenications* some years ago by someone with no love of the English language, more recently the European Commission has used the word *telematics* and the phrase *information and communication technologies* (ICT), which at least sound less inelegant. Telematics is the linking of computer and communications technologies. To most people the information revolution, the information society, is the Internet. There have actually been significant developments. The first was the recognition that it would be possible to run a global network using industry standard communication technologies supported by a relatively simple common set of protocols. That has already happened and there are some 40 million happy Internet users running up phone bills with serious and not so serious business.

We are all aware of the effects of these factors. The Internet was for many years an esoteric domain inhabited by nerds, researchers, academics and the like. Now, within the space of a few years those pioneers have been joined by you, by me and by the supermarket down the road. I believe we should be cautious about the rate of diffusion of these changes within our communities. Globally, 40 million people is not that many! I do not suggest that we dismiss the implications of the information society as not relevant to us until 'it is there for all to see and use' since we will have missed any chances we may have had if we do that. We would also fail to take advantage of the wave of interest in public information and technological developments that the information society movement has engendered worldwide. Governments are developing policies and strategies and the European Commission has a number of projects and groups studying the implications of the impact of telematics on education, employment, culture and social behaviour patterns.

The second factor emerges from the first, having developed over a period of years and becoming an avalanche during the 1990s. This is the realization that, for the first time, it may be possible for the majority of citizens to have access to the electronic network and, more specifically, that everyone might benefit from the interchange of information that is now a minority activity. The European Commission has placed significant emphasis on exploring the implications of the popularization of telematics. The Information Society Forum of the European Commission has produced a number of documents addressing matters such as the impact on employment, social change, new education opportunities and so on. The message of these studies is that there is a real chance of making improvements to the lives of the people throughout Europe, making them better informed and better educated and building firmer democracies through greater inclusion and involvement, so long as the right actions and responses are put in place now. In 1996 in the UK, the House of Lords Select Committee on Science and Technology produced a report that reflected many of the views of the Information Society Forum, but placed a 'UK spin' on the subject. Indeed, all developed countries are now recognizing the importance of not being left behind in what could be a significant shift within society during the next few years.

There is now and will increasingly be competition within the aspects of information provision traditionally in the public service domain. So far that competition does not seem to have had significant impact on public information services, but if public library service managers believe that their tradition and/or services have unique value then they need to be making that clear to their political masters now. To that extent the popularization of the information society, despite its lack of clear definition or impact, is to be welcomed since it is a stimulus external to the local services.

To return to the question that heads this section – what is the information society? There is no one simple answer. The Information Society Forum in its First Annual Report suggests: 'We need to feel a sense of urgency, because the revolution is upon us. The Information Society is already part of many lives and at the heart of many economic activities. If we use fax/e-mail we have a toe in the Information Society. If we surf the World Wide Web we have a foot in the Information Society. If we work, learn and communicate with colleagues through a network we are in the Information Society.'[8]

The public library of the 21st century

Lest anyone approach this section in the belief that they will find here a simple, complete vision, I will stress now that will not be the case. How far general strategies for public libraries emerge remains to be seen, but should such strategies become apparent it will be years before they are adopted universally. At present the core services of public libraries across the land are very similar. The standards and availability of those services may differ, but their nature does not. The same is not true of information technology developments, which have evolved across a shorter timeframe and in a much less even way. While the rate of change may increase, as more managers of public library services see the imperative of exploiting IT to sustain and develop their services at the heart of the information society, new directions and new funding will be necessary. While it may never be possible to level the playing field completely, it is essential that all the players know what game is being played and where the field is! Here some of those landmarks will be described.

A note of caution. It seems to me highly likely that within a timeframe of, say, 20 years, most public libraries will not look greatly different from today. There are many public libraries in the UK today which do not look significantly different from the 1960s or earlier! Books will still be available to borrow and there will still be trained staff to provide guidance and access to information. It is likely that some of those people will be professionals from other disciplines, but more of that below. The point I am making here is that we should not be drawn into any uninformed assumptions that suddenly all public libraries large and small, urban and rural will undergo some sea change, emerging as something completely different.

It does seem certain that the most significant changes that will occur, indeed are occurring, in public libraries all involve the increasing use of networking. I do not dismiss the use of multimedia as a passing fad of no relevance, but the use of multimedia within the library building represents a move from one medium to another rather than a quantum shift in the nature of the service possibilities. Multimedia presents a whole host of new learning and information finding opportunities – rich databases, rapid searching and so on – but access to that within the library (or borrowed as a CD-ROM, for example) can be seen as the continuation of a service tradition that has been around for many, many years.

Certainly CD-ROM and other information technologies do bring changes to the pattern and segmentation of library use. CD-ROM, in some particular circumstances, is already a much more satisfactory medium of communication than the book. There can be few people who would rather search an untidy stack of newspapers in the forlorn hope of finding some item, than find all mentions of their topic at the touch of a button. Conversely can we envisage a time when people would rather read a CD-ROM novel than a printed one in bed? Service managers will need to understand these differences, segmenting customer demand to provide resources to their customers in the most suitable form. There are public libraries in the UK where service managers have already recognized this new dimension to the selection process but most have not.

At the risk of repetition, if we are to address the developments which will change the nature of the UK public library service, developments that could fundamentally re-engineer it, networking is the most potent force in our landscape. Of course, we cannot assume a technological imperative that will drive IT developments forward relentlessly. Other conditions will have to be right, and some of these were highlighted in the first section. Money, professional commitment, national policies for networking and for public information and, above all vision, will all have to be in place if we are to see significant enhancements to the roles of the public library. What follows here makes assumptions about these conditions to demonstrate possible new scenarios.

Earlier in the chapter a number of core activities were identified (lending books and information provision, for example), and it can be assumed that within any conceivable timeframe these activities will continue. For example, lending books is a role that public libraries seem likely to retain without significant challenge from other organizations or institutions. There will be a continuing need to make book-based resources accessible to citizens as a public good – the ultimate in recycling! Furthermore, there is strong evidence[5] to suggest that the public library fulfils a broad range of functions as a focus for community life. It seems certain that public libraries will remain physical places for many years to come. If they disappear, it will be owing to funding difficulties rather than through lack of community support. Far better to consider the implications and value of virtual public library *services* than to expect that physical presence will be replaced only by a building in cyberspace. What might those services be?

Community networking

Wherever people have formed themselves into communities there is a need for a resource that contains information about that community. Within developed societies communities are complex networks of groups and individuals interacting both at work and at play. Clubs and societies, social support organizations, health agencies and so on will all want to promote their services and every community will require some means of gathering and making available the resource. A typology of such community information might include:

- cultural resources and opportunities (arts groups, crafts, performing arts);
- educational resources (life-long learning, full-time education);
- citizens' rights and local democracy;
- economic activity/business development;
- welfare/health.

Within the UK and across Europe the public library has a long and honourable tradition as the focus for information of this type. Many public libraries have explored the possibility of using IT as the means of managing better these large datasets and making them more readily available to the service users. In considering how public libraries in the future will build on this history it is useful to examine the Freenet. The principle enshrined in the Freenet is very simple. Set up a server on the Net, fill it with all the community information you can find (either directly or with pointers to other relevant servers) and make access to it free to everyone. The result is a community resource that should fulfil all of the tasks that public libraries have traditionally undertaken with the management and delivery of community information and signposting. Add to the free access the ability to e-mail to other users of the Freenet and you begin to build a powerful tool for community development.

The first Freenet was launched in Cleveland, Ohio in 1986 and the Net search which I have just done suggests that, alongside the increasing number in North America, there are now Freenets popping up all over the world. Telnet into the Cleveland Freenet and you will find a menu listing a range of public buildings –

post office, library, university, court house and so on – known as the electronic town square. Choose an option and you get to see further options within the building. Newer Freenets offer Web-style hypertext connections.

The advantage of providing all the community information on such an open-access network is just that – accessibility. The system can be available 24 hours a day, seven days a week. However, assumptions cannot be made about the ability of local communities to gain access. Cleveland, Ohio is a go-getting industrial city on Lake Erie with a large university (Case Western Reserve, which runs the Cleveland Freenet) where we might expect to find a goodly proportion of the citizens with network access.

Freenets offer a very powerful model of what the future might be like. Start with community information, put it on to a Web server and promote it, and you will find people beating a path to your door for more. Today, most people may not be able to dial up the system from the privacy of their own homes, but schools and many businesses are getting net-connected. And why not put connections into branch libraries and voluntary services so that all the information is immediately available and searchable without the need for hundreds of paper copies? We have moved all our community information on to our Web Site (Croydon Online: **http://www.croydon.gov.uk**) and hope that within a very short time we can dispose of the 200 ring binders of information we send out to other agencies each year.

The kiosk movement that is gaining momentum is one manifestation of this approach to information access. The technology makes it possible to provide information kiosks in public places to give access to community and other information. That is step one, and it will become increasingly valuable as more and more people connect. However, the vision must go beyond just a community information network (CIN). We can and should be building the CIN, but should explore what new opportunities will emerge. In my view a community-computing network (CCN) includes the CIN, but in addition presents local communities with the means of doing totally new things. I will use the London Borough of Croydon as an example of how things might develop.

Croydon Online is already an active community resource, containing a selection of our more traditional data sets. We have started to put high-bandwidth connections into a number of schools and libraries. The schools will then have the chance to use the CIN if they wish, but they can also 'do their own thing'. They can build learning resources and share them with the other schools locally, indeed, with schools globally. The students can themselves create new ways of using the network. First off, they want to investigate the environment. We have a large quantity of data from Croydon's Agenda 21 team that can be mounted on Croydon Online for students studying the environment to use. They can explore it and add to it. The network has become a means of learning and sharing between different people and organizations. The same will be true of other groups: for example, mounting health data for the communities and professionals, encouraging local businesses to create new resources that can be shared locally and promoted globally. Then communities themselves could be encouraged to debate relevant topics, provide opinions for elected representatives and share between different communities – a new medium of local democracy.

There are two specific points arising from this. First, implicit in what I have said is that public libraries are ideally placed to take the lead. In the United States the universities started things moving; in Europe it should be public libraries. We can and should be the honest brokers who set the standards and enable things to happen. Second, we will not be able to retain over such a CCN the sort of control we like to maintain over the rest of our services. My point in the paragraph above is precisely that the CCN should be an enabler for communities, organizations and individuals to use as they think sensible and appropriate. We may maintain the canvas and the paints, even the economic and policing control systems, but the network must be of the people, for the people, etc. So 'tight/loose' will be the order of the day. The public library will be the agent, the enabler for its community and just occasionally, maybe, the information police. It could even manage the wider popularization of e-mail use as in Finland, where the government is considering the viability of providing an e-mail address for any citizen who wants one, using the public library service as the manager and main access route.

Community network connectivity will release a host of new opportunities for exchange and development – as yet, the public library currently has no rivals as the conductor of this orchestra of resources and organizations. The needs and values are already enshrined in the research that has been undertaken in examining the future of the information society. The public library has not been recognized within these studies as the main agent, but that situation has to change. Access to information should be a universal right, and public agencies will need to defend this right. Access to information will more and more in the future imply access to technological resources. What value networking for communities if the majority of citizens cannot gain access? Public libraries are already introducing Internet access. In the UK progress is steady but growing. Public libraries are also providing computer-assisted learning resources for citizen re-skilling and now with telecentres, where it is possible to use a wordprocessor, a spreadsheet or database, and gain access to the Internet. Despite the surge in interest in computers and networking, it will be many years before demand for such services declines due to universal home access. During the transition, the role as an access route into the community resources will be essential. These are all factors that underline the important role the public library has played and will play in the future, acting as the access safety net for those people who are unable to sustain their own means of access. Even when everyone has their own cyberniche at home, the public library will still be fulfilling a role at the heart of its community's computing network.

Lifelong learning

It has been suggested that the information society might equally be called the **lifelong learning** society,[8] since the need for lifelong learning will be vital for everyone within the information society. Currently, learning opportunities are of two types: those that are provided through the 'formal' network of primary, secondary and higher education, and those that are available more informally through community-based services. Adult education fulfils a key function as a means of enriching people's lives, but in recent years due to financial restrictions has tended to focus on popular subjects that can guarantee adequate numbers in each class.

Public libraries, of course, started their lives as the 'poor man's university' and have sustained this informal route into learning for well over a hundred years. Many people rely on the public library as the source to support their informal learning needs – hobby, employment, life skills, etc. Until recently the open learning activities of public libraries remained as invisible as all the other uses made of their services. Open learning has now become a political issue and the role of the public library recognized for what it had been for all those 'hidden' years – the ideal agent to give access to and support lifelong learning experiences. Public libraries are now creating alliances with educationalists to develop richer learning support services. There is in each community no public agency which is better suited, is more accepted or has the tradition to lead the open learning movement for that community.

Within this context of advice and guidance, the traditional role of the public library as an agent for lifelong learning could be transformed over the next 20 years. There are several factors required to justify this argument. First there will be the demand, within communities, for greater learning opportunities which will not be met through the traditional channels of learning. There are already many people who want to learn, but do not wish or are unable to attend university or college, or indeed cannot find an adult education class that is appropriate to their need. These people are frequently highly motivated within their own interest area and prepared to apply themselves if the opportunity becomes available. The model of the UK's Open University has demonstrated the effectiveness of remote learning.

The second significant factor is the shift that is taking place within universities to provide computer assisted learning resources for their students, to challenge the traditional didactic model of learning, allowing students to interact with computer-based courses at their own speed and to backtrack when necessary. Just as libraries have discovered the necessity to segment types of need and relate them to specific media for delivery, so universities are beginning to examine the situations when face-to-face contact with academic staff is needed and when a network-based learning resource will be most effective. The implications of such developments were touched upon in the Higher Education Funding Council (HEFC)'s Libraries Review[9] on electronic information resources within higher education, but the report did not make the obvious deduction from the evidence – that rather than take people to the learning experience it might be possible to do the reverse, delivering the experiences to the people.

There are many practical questions to be answered about the practicalities of offering wider access to sophisticated learning resources outside of a closed community of students. However, many of those questions relate to the status quo that exists now. Lack of quality in some of the resources, lack of suitable supporting material, lack of professional support remotely, lack of understanding about how those resources might be used. By whom and for what? The advantage of prognostication, of course, is that it is possible to set aside some of the detail and try to paint an outline future which others can fill in. Nevertheless, if one recognizes the growing need for lifelong learning (for business and pleasure) that is implied by the information society and one accepts that there will be an ever-increasing amount of networked-based learning resources, there must be obvious questions about the benefits of making connections between the two factors.

Imagine a citizen who is suddenly able to plug into high quality learning packages generated for use by university undergraduates rather than be limited to traditional library resources and some adult education opportunities. I am confident that, given the right mentoring, we could see a radical change in the way of personal development opportunities and in re-skilling. There are many people with the knowledge and experience to gain benefit from such resources, without the need for the standard issue of an advanced school learning certificate. They might need counselling locally to ensure that the packages they used were suitable; they would need access to human support and some would, of course, need access to the hardware. But what an opening out of the learning experience! At present some 27% of the population are able to enter higher education, which means that 73% are not able so to do. What a metamorphosis if 70%, or 80%, even 100% of learning resources were accessible to the local community and could be used by ordinary people with extraordinary interests. The woman who grows carnations or the man who breeds cats might find a course in genetics not beyond them and a means of enriching their practical skills. Moreover, it is possible that through e-mail and discussion lists they could become part of a global community of people with similar interests.

Are there other local institutions better suited to support such developments? My answer is a resounding no. There are other professionals with the necessary skills to support and develop this network learning, but the public library offers the ideal home for the organization and coordination of the resources and the professional skills. The community focus, the community resource centre. Networked-based learning will, of course, provide access at the chosen location – the home or the workplace perhaps – but there will be the need to manage the process for the community. The information society offers the chance to re-engineer higher education and at the same time make very visible the role of the public library in the lifelong learning process.

Network management

We have examined the implications of networking on the operation of long-standing services such as community information and open learning. We now turn to the role of managing access to information resources, which is fundamental to the public library – the community interface to the world of knowledge – which is set to be redefined with increasing network access. A pioneering study of the Internet in UK public libraries (Croydon Libraries Internet Project – CLIP)[10] had as one of its primary objectives to answer the question, 'can the Internet be used as a very large electronic reference book?'. This is not a trivial question for the public library service manager. It is evident to anyone who has taken time to surf the Net that there is a great deal of useful information to be found, if you know where to look and can be confident about the quality of that information.

CLIP demonstrated that, with careful management, it was possible to harvest information on the Net in anticipation of user needs. Also, training users in the use of the various search engines available could complement the traditional range of resources used by public libraries to answer the information needs of their users. The research project ran from 1994 until 1996 and during that period the nature of the Internet, the range of resources available and the means of locating those resources changed many times. It is obvious that the Internet does not resemble a public library in its organization and control. However, we can expect that during future years there will be significant change in the control systems that are available and the ease with which information searching may be done.

It is certain that for a considerable time into the future there will be a role for the intermediary, the person who can point in the right direction and can support the information hunter in his or her search. We must remember that being one of the information poor is not simply about lack of access to the necessary hardware:

it is equally about a lack of understanding and a lack of skills. One of the problems we librarians face in comprehending the limitations of our users is that we inhabit an information-rich world. It is natural for us to expect and to find information. Not so for the majority of people; their information world is limited by the television and maybe a newspaper, by a circle of friends to ask and, on occasion, a visit to the library.

Overcoming this information poverty will take time and effort. Public libraries will have a role providing access to and guidance around networked resources: a place for people to come to explore networks if they do not have the chance to do so elsewhere. More than this, those people will need help to learn how to deal with information, how to make judgements about what they want and how it is presented. This is an integral part of the role of the librarian in all types of libraries and, while some people argue that the Internet and global access will make traditional libraries and librarians fit only for a museum, such an argument ignores the reality of people's limited information horizons. It is worth making the point also that the public library as a signpost will remain an essential function. Bookmarking resources of local significance – business information, educational resources, topical sites, etc. – is a one-to-many activity that has always been central to the role of the public library.

The development of 'community signposting' might in the future extend to the concept of the 'personal virtual library' providing individual worlds for library users, all or partly in cyberspace. Individually packaged services have never really been feasible in the public library, apart from the book tucked under the counter for the favoured customer. Given the development of remote resource harvesting agents, e-mail and the listserv, it is worth speculating whether there will be a time in the future when the many and diverse users of public libraries could expect some form of SDI to support their business, their education or their leisure. How much it would cost and what value would be added remain questions for the future.

Finally, within this section dealing with the management of information resources across networks, it must be stressed that the landscape is not merely one of passive remote databases. There are people across the world who can be brought into the information network. Already there are cooperative networks of librarians who are prepared to help their colleagues to answer difficult reference questions. STUMPERS is a pioneering example. Using a listserv it allows a question to be posted to 800 reference librarians across the world in an instant. Any one of those librarians who thinks they can crack the question can e-mail the questioner. STUMPERS is not foolproof; you can receive several replies, each of which has a different answer, and there is no guarantee that any answer will appear. However the model of STUMPERS as a network of people is a development that would be impossible without the Internet. Such instant reaction does not work with snail mail and contacting 800 people around the world by telephone is not to be recommended!

Few public library users now realize that the service they see when they go to their local library is but the tip of an iceberg; that the smallest public library has access to the resources of the whole nation, and beyond. The interconnectivity of public libraries in the UK and further afield will create a much more proactive system that will allow resource sharing, if not in real time in something closer to it than has been possible in the past. There will be questions to ask about the economics of sharing skills across regions and international borders, but the opportunities for sharing created by the connectivity will have to be taken. They are too important to ignore.

Cooperative network publishing

It could be argued that this category is no more than an extension of managing networked information since it addresses the sharing of the resources held by public libraries. Nevertheless, I believe it is important to separate the class of activity out precisely because giving information 'back to the network' is fundamental to the re-engineering of our services. For better or for worse, the Internet has made everyone a publisher. If librarians have been willing to share in the past, then the future will launch us into a world of cyber-swapping.

There are two parts to this process. There will need to be infrastructure to allow cooperation to take place, and there will need to be adequate resources for network publication. In some activities this will not be a serious problem. We have already visited the area of community information. A public library that manages a community information database through a Web site is a network publisher; many are already doing just that. Stop and think of the benefits of finding ways of bringing those separate databases together so that a user might search for information beyond the boundaries of the local library service. Find out, for example, about activities and events for a holiday in another part of the country, or even abroad. The nature of the Internet means it is not a prerequisite that datasets are brought into one place. There are already studies examining the means of 'clumping' separate datasets into a region to allow searching across all of the databases at one time. There is also the possibility of using metadata structures to allow a search engine to harvest all the databases looking for keywords held in the data describing record content, just as a MARC record describes, in part, the content of a book.

There are even simpler strategies for exploiting network-based information sharing. One library could produce a networked service, perhaps business information, which all other libraries could use, rather than producing their own services. The money and time saved by avoiding the need to do the same thing as everyone else could be directed into new or enriched services that might, themselves, be shared with others. Such a model of organization goes right to the heart of the municipal independence that all local authorities have cherished. Of course, while cooperation has an established tradition, 'cooperative contracting out' may be harder to sell without reasonable guarantees to ensure continuity of service.

Having made that point, the UK still leads most of Europe in grass-roots cooperation. Project EARL (Electronic Access to Resources in Libraries: **http://www.earl.org.uk**) is a consortium of over 100 public libraries who are jointly developing Internet-based resources, some for their own locality, some for common use. There are task groups looking at a range of resource types – information for the Chinese, music, family history, community information are just a few examples – from over a dozen groups. EARL is a 'bottom-up' process since it is being driven by the needs of the library services themselves. While the project lacks the resources to fast track, the results of the cooperation are real service enhancements which enable resources from one library to be fully shared by other partners. Project EARL is but one strategy to exploit the Internet. Across Europe, public libraries are now becoming involved through local cooperation or national policy in building electronic networks linking public libraries together. Within Finland and Denmark the ministries of culture are investing in such strategies. The Ministry of Culture in the Flemish Communities (Belgium) is looking beyond just creating a physical network, to the sustaining infrastructure and organizations that will be necessary to enable separate public libraries to share and develop in cyberspace.

What are the common themes?

Clearly for the public library to retain a central position in community life in the coming decades there are a number of conditions that must be satisfied. Some of those conditions are within the control of service managers, others are not. In this section we will consider briefly those conditions and in the concluding section assess what actions can or should be taken to secure maximum community benefit.

Starting from the most obvious feature of the future that has been described, very little will be achieved without the physical connectivity necessary to make access to the Internet a reality for every public library in the country. In theory there are no technical barriers to those connections being made now. In some remote rural areas the cost of providing dedicated connections will be high, but in relation to percentage of population served by public libraries, there are no technical reasons why almost all should not be able to get easily to a public library with Internet connectivity. Were that connectivity in place, it could be argued that one important justification of the public library – as the information safety net – had been achieved. We must make a distinction between the theory and the practice.

To connect every public library together, while not a trivial task, is deliverable. There are two questions that emerge. The first relates to the use of the resulting network and the second relates to everything! The first question is, what services will there be on the network that are of use to citizens if such a 'people's net-work' could be created? The second question is, 'who pays?'. Second question first.

The marginal cost of adding a private, individual user to the network is extremely low. There are many IP (Information Provider) suppliers offering dial-up access for around £10 a month or lower. Adding 4000 public libraries does not represent a dramatic increase in network size, but there will be additional costs if those libraries are to have wide bandwidth and connections that are dedicated rather than dial-up. In November 1996 a bid was made by Information For All (set up by The Library Association and the Library and Information Commission) to the Millennium Commission for funding to install such a network (including hardware in libraries). It suggested a cost edging towards £100m, which is either a great deal of money, or not, depending on what you compare it with. More wor-rying perhaps are the estimated running costs of the network, which would place a large additional burden on public services already suffering from budget cuts. It is certain that to create the connectivity and infrastructure to sustain such a net-work will demand both extra capital and, maybe, additional revenue monies beyond those already provided. This will be a matter of national policy.

Turning to the first question – the services – cost must again be considered. The Internet at present is an arbitrary collection of services and information sources that are provided through altruism, fanaticism or as loss leaders. In the future there will be greatly increased commercial activity and more investment. The same will be true of the public service sector of networked information – investment to develop and sustain. Whether organized by public libraries work-ing together or coordinated by an agency bringing together all the official infor-mation resources of government, these information services will have to be funded to undertake their work, or at least they will need pump priming to get them stabilized. The government has already begun to explore the implications of electronic information resources in the recent discussion document 'govern-ment.direct'[11] which invited comment on the future rationalization of all public information resources and the means of interacting with government, both national and local.

The need for coordination cannot easily be denied and government.direct and other recent studies in both the UK and Europe suggest the need to develop national policies and strategies for coordination, cooperation and resource sharing. Project EARL has shown that it is possible to make considerable progress without major cost, but the future will require cooperation not only between enthusiastic public library service managers, but also between different organizations and professions. There will be financial and other vested interests in the new relationships that may need a more rigorous framework of strategy to be effective. Opening up access to networked-based learning resources is a good example of this. It is not unreasonable to assume that those agencies creating the resources will wish to have control over how they are used and may not look with favour on the idea of local communities being able to 'pick 'n' mix' from various resources from different organizations. Sorting out some equitable model for financial return is the easy bit here: dealing with cultural differences – learning through an institution rather than from within an institution – will be more difficult.

It is possible that new economic models will emerge that encourage the sharing of resources both nationally and internationally, and this may be most visible within the tertiary education sector as the traditional pattern of learning is broken up and broader, more competitive markets are created through networking. Certainly one of the most significant factors underlying all of the potential changes that have been described depend on new relationships and partnerships forming. The future public library will continue to be immersed in the informal cooperation that currently underlies much of what it does – sharing information with other agencies locally, lending resources regionally, and so on. However, new, more formal partnerships will be essential. As the agent for community resources there will have to be clearer lines of cooperation. As the local focus for lifelong learning other professionals will need to form part of the in-library resource; educators, advisers, even counsellors may be necessary. In my own central library we now house staff from the adult education service both to sell courses (the library is seen as the best outlet) and to run basic skills courses. Also, the careers service has its main public contact point in the library, again because the public library is seen as the key community information resource. These are small developments, but they represent a future trend that will be necessary to ensure that true collaboration and coordination is possible for the service of the citizens and their community.

What should happen?: implications and conclusions

It is worth remembering that the future benefits of the information society or, indeed, the future worth of the public library will not be solved just by getting the right people into a room and leaving them there until all the correct decisions, agreements and finances have been put in place. The move to an information society will be as much about social change and about the operation of national and international markets as about social and service engineering.

Public service developments will have to 'go with the flow' of technology and telecommunications developments rather than prescribe them, in just the same way as the success of universal networking will be about market pull rather than technology push. Citizens will have to see the worth of the services to be encouraged to actually use them. Those services will have to become as much a part of their lives as the telephone and the television – invisible as technologies, essential as tools for living. Of course, going with the flow suggests an outward-looking view of the future that has not always been apparent in the behaviour of public service managers. Sustaining services is important since public service is as much about providing continuity and reliability to people's lives as it is about doing new things.

Nevertheless, there are already opportunities to develop new services and plug in the traditional values of the public library to the roots of the information society. The Public Libraries and the Information Society Study suggested that despite some examples of innovation, generally across Europe there were barriers to development, lack of resources, lack of technical know-how, lack of vision and lack of commitment being the most significant. Some of these barriers will be easier to tackle than others.

Securing adequate resources to invest and develop or change professional motivation are not things that service managers will be able to secure without considerable effort. However, that effort would be helped if there were to be a clear vision of what the future role of the public library will be. A vision shared by the service managers and their staff that they feel confident to promote would do much to remind decision makers that the public library service exists. If those managing the services cannot sell the future to the people that matter, can we blame those people who can change things if they do not automatically look to the public library service? We need librarians with attitude; prepared to lobby and make clear to those people of influence what value the public library has to give to the quality of life for communities. There is a need for a manifesto that contains the vision and also demonstrates what actions and resources are needed to deliver that vision. DGXIII of the European Commission has recently launched a concerted action for public libraries, known as PubliCA, which is intended as a means of developing a human resources network of public library managers. PubliCA (**http://www.croydon.gov.uk/publica/index.htm**) will encourage the exchange of good practice, help to build a vision that will capture the importance of public libraries within the evolving information society and will act as a pressure group internationally.

If not everyone can be expected to be carried along by the vision, there will need to be a critical mass of opinion which shows just how important to social well-being the public library has been and will continue to be in the future. It has not been the tradition of librarians to be bullish, but now is the time to try. There is much to be gained by placing the public library service at the heart of the information society and too much to be lost if we do not.

References

1 European Union DGXIII, 'Public libraries and the information society study'. <http://www2.echo.lu/libraries/en/plis/homeplis.html>

2 Department of National Heritage, *Reading the future: Public Libraries Review*, London, DNH, 1997.

3 KPMG, *Department of National Heritage Study: Contracting-out in public libraries*, London, KPMG, June 1995.

4 Office of Arts And Libraries, *Setting objectives for public libraries*, Library and Information Series 19, London, HMSO, 1991.

5 Comedia, *Borrowed time: the future of public libraries in the UK*, Bournes Green, Comedia,1993.

6 Aslib, *Review of public libraries in England and Wales*, London, Aslib, 1995.

7 Batt, C., *Information technology in public libraries*, 5th edn, London, Library Association Publishing Ltd, 1994.

8 Information Society Forum, *First annual report*, June 1996. <http://www.ispo.cec.be/infoforum/pub/inrep1.html>

9 Higher Education Funding Council, *Libraries review*, (Follett Report), London, HEFC, 1993.

10 Batt, C. and Kirby, H., *CLIP – Croydon Libraries Internet Project*, British Library Research and Innovation Report 13, London, British Library, 1997.

11 government.direct: a prospectus for the electronic delivery of government services, Cmnd 3438, London, HMSO, 1996.

9

MARKET PROSPECTS FOR CONSUMER ONLINE SERVICES, AND IMPLICATIONS FOR LIBRARY AND INFORMATION SERVICES IN THE FUTURE*

Martin White

TFPL LTD, ENGLAND

Introduction

The Internet has now come to be such a part of our working lives as information professionals that we find it quite difficult at times to imagine how we managed without it. As a consultant I find it quite invaluable to have access to such a rich source of information at my desk, being able to look up information on companies while the prospective client is talking to me on the telephone. However a working life devoted to finding the information that others have not been able to has also made me very alert to what is missing from the WWW.

I am old enough to have started my career three decades ago working with 10,000-hole optical coincidence cards, and to have been mesmerized by the introduction of online searching, albeit at 300 baud using a Texas Silent 700 terminal with a thermal printer. Then came BRS providing access at 1200 baud, and the LEXIS service with full-text retrieval and document delivery, followed by CD-ROMs, and by the early 1990s it seemed that there was nothing much left for technology to offer!

However, across the Atlantic in the USA there were at least two interesting developments that seemed at the time to have little direct impact on information practitioners in Europe. The first of these was the Internet, developed in the 1960s to ensure that the US Government could continue to operate during a nuclear attack, and the second was the emergence in the late 1970s of online services for the consumer market, such as The Source, CompuServe and Prodigy.

---

* The views expressed in this paper are the personal views of the author, and not necessarily the views of TFPL Ltd or of any of the service providers mentioned in the paper.

Since the earliest days of the online industry there has been constant debate over the extent to which services tailored to the market environment in the USA would be adopted in Europe. The rapid growth over the last few years of online services designed to appeal to a mass market audience in the USA encouraged many of the companies operating these services to consider launching them in Europe. At the same time a number of European companies, observing the profits generated by these mass market services in the USA decided that the business model could be adapted to the European market, on either a national basis or a Europe-wide basis.

Much of this book is concerned with the emerging and future impact of the Internet on libraries and information professionals. In this chapter the focus will be on what have become known as mass market information services, and the role and impact that they will have on access to information by consumers and businesses in Europe. These services tend to be ignored in surveys and commentaries on electronic access to information, probably because their use by the information profession has been limited as they may be seen as little more than a source of games and entertainment. This view has been reinforced by the term 'consumer online services'. CompuServe in particular has always provided a range of services designed to meet the needs of the business community. A more accurate term is 'mass market online services' because the objective of the service operators is to have a subscriber based measured in millions rather than thousands. The characteristics of the services to be covered in this chapter are:

- they deliver a broad range of information, entertainment and transactional/e-mail services;
- they are targeted at individual users with no previous experience of using online services;
- they are often billed to a credit or charge card, on a monthly subscription basis;
- they offer access to the Internet and the WWW, usually with a standard browser;
- the service providers are in business to make profits, as are the suppliers of content to the services.

Although the services are primarily targeted at the consumer market, the small office-home office (SoHo) market is also an important sector, especially for CompuServe and Microsoft Network Service (MSN). Another important market is the manager working at home in the evenings and at weekends.

Service content

To understand the potential role of these services in expanding the resources of public libraries it might be useful to look in more detail at two services, America

Online (more often referred to as AOL) and CompuServe. AOL service has the largest base of subscribers of any of the other US services, as well as a growing subscriber base in Europe and Japan. The way in which both these services have developed over the last few years is described later in this chapter.

Unlike many other services, AOL uses proprietary software in terms of the screen display and the way that graphics and other features are handled by the computer. On the initial screen are icons for the following files, or channels as they are referred to by AOL: chat, computing, digital city, entertainment, finance, games, Internet, kids, learning, life, news, sport, travel, weather. The user interface is designed to be very easy to use, with a mixture of icons/graphics and drop-down lists. A considerable amount of editorial management goes into all these services, and AOL is no exception. The news channel shows this quite clearly because, although news is sourced from a variety of agencies and newspapers, the screen format can be changed on a minute by minute basis if appropriate to reflect the relative importance of news stories at that point in time.

Of particular interest in the context of this chapter is the Knowledge Network. AOL has given schools special discounts to promote the service, and the school itself. Through the service it is possible to link to the WWW sites of schools, but more important is the way in which the content has been developed with the input of teachers. For example, there is a file of commentaries on the books set for the GCSE examinations that are taken in UK schools at the age of 16, and in general the content has been developed especially for UK secondary schools, though from time to time the US origins of the service do become more evident. The Hutchison Encyclopedia is available, and for each term offers a range of associated terms to guide students.

In the library section of the learning channel a range of files and databases are categorized under the headings of arts and history, science and technology, language and literature, and general. The content of these files is carefully designed for each national market, and in the UK, as a result of the decision by AOL to target schools in their marketing campaign, there is a considerable amount of information linked closely with the requirements of the GCSE examinations.

Although this list might create the impression that the service is targeted specifically at children, in fact the service has been quite carefully constructed to be of broad general interest to all members of a family. Internet access is also possible from within AOL, but currently the service uses its own browser, and so the page appearance might not match that obtained with the Netscape and Microsoft browsers. In the USA AOL represents the largest single access point to the Internet.

Another important feature of AOL is the way in which the service can be used not only to send electronic mail, but also to enable real-time interactive messaging to take place. In this case two or more subscribers (up to at least ten!) can send text messages to each other in real time. The importance of these services in building subscriber loyalty cannot be overemphasized. The number of occasions in a week when there may be a need to use these services for information/reference purposes is quite small compared to the hours that are racked up in e-mail and interactive messaging. It is also possible to access the services that AOL offers in the USA, Canada, Germany, France and Japan, and this option enables students to practise their German and French language skills. There are, of course, no international call charges.

Initially AOL in the UK was seen very much as a service to be used by teenagers and students, but a survey carried out by the company in late 1996 shows that the profile of its subscribers was changing towards use by adults. The main characteristics of the AOL subscriber base are:

- 70% are aged between 35 and 64
- 89% are male
- the majority are professionals, managers or directors
- 58% earn over £25,000.

This migration is important in appreciating the potential role of the service, and the longer-term stability.

CompuServe has a larger European subscriber base than AOL, and has been providing services for a number of years. The content of the CompuServe service is more broadly based than that of AOL, and in particular has information of interest to the business community. The main categories are: business, communications, education and reference, entertainment, fun and games, home and leisure, magazines (mainly computer titles), news, shopping, sport, travel. The news section offers a wide range of titles, including a number of French and German titles, and Agence France Press. The business section is especially strong, and amongst the databases that can be accessed are: Duns Market Identifiers, Extel, Financial Times, ICC, Infocheck, Jordans, Kompass. This makes the service of particular value to a wide range of companies. Among the reference works is again the Hutchison Encyclopaedia. As with AOL there are extensive chat services, including a popular site for students.

On top of this content is a well-developed electronic mail service, and despite the attractions of using the Internet for e-mail, the CompuServe system is robust and widely used across the world, including Japan where CompuServe operates the Jifty-Serve service.

There is little to choose between the two services, and in addition the relaunched Microsoft Network also offers a mixture of content for consumers and for businesses.

Service development in the USA

The origins of the these services go back a very considerable way, with both CompuServe and The Source beginning operations in the mid-1980s. GEnie was launched by General Electric Information Services in 1985, and Prodigy was launched by IBM and Sears in 1988. The Source was acquired by CompuServe in 1984. America Online also dates back to 1985, as Quantum Computer Services. All these services were targeted at the bulletin board user in the USA, a large market that had grown up as a result of low-cost communications, a large installed base of PCs, a keyboard-literate user base, and the ability to communicate in English across a continent.

In the late 1980s the four majors – CompuServe, America Online, Prodigy and Genie – all grew at roughly the same rate. By the turn of the decade it was starting to look like a two horse race between CompuServe and Prodigy, with CompuServe having very good e-mail services, and Prodigy concentrating on the games market. Then Steve Case, who had worked his way up the marketing ladder in AOL, was appointed Chief Executive Officer of the company in 1992. Case then started to market the service in some highly effective ways, and by 1994 AOL had overtaken Prodigy to take second position to CompuServe.

During 1994 and 1995 two more services arrived on the scene. In late 1994 Apple launched eWorld and in mid-1995 Microsoft launched the Microsoft Network (MSN) as part of the Windows95 package. eWorld was developed in conjunction with America Online, and offered users a very innovative front-end. The main claim to fame of MSN was that it could be accessed directly through an icon on the Windows95 desktop, a facility that resulted in a complaint to the Department of Justice by many of Microsoft's competitors, although in the end no action was taken;.

The table below summarizes the rate of growth of subscribers to the leading services over the last five years, in thousands of subscribers.

Table 9.1 *Subscriber growth for the major online services (at year-end)*

	1990	1992	1994	1996
America Online	109	200	1500	5500
CompuServe	740	1130	1500	4700
Prodigy	440	1000	1200	1450
GEnie	70	100	100	55
eWorld			65	130
MSN				1000

Over the last few years there have been constant claims and counter-claims about subscriber levels, mainly because all the services have experienced very high levels of 'churn', with subscribers taking advantage of free access for a limited number if days, and then switching to another free offer from another service. This problem still exists, but at nowhere near the level of 1995 and 1996.

All the US services built their base of subscribers in a pre-Internet environment. Certainly the Internet was widely used in the USA from 1992 onwards, but the proprietary interfaces that the consumer services offered were much easier to use than Mosiac and the other browser applications available at that time. The introduction of the World Wide Web, and the Netscape Navigator browser changed the market dynamics in 1995. The question for the various services was whether they should embrace the Internet, or compete with it. After a number of dismissive statements from senior executives, the rush to adopt WWW standards gathered considerable momentum in late 1995 and 1996, with only America Online retaining its proprietary platform. The major losers were AT&T, who had bought the Interchange software from Ziff Davis, Microsoft, who totally underestimated the rate of growth of the WWW and subsequently had to relaunch the service, and Apple, who failed to capitalize on the very innovative features of eWorld.

Service development in Europe

During 1994 the attention of the US service providers switched to the European market. CompuServe had been quietly building up a strong subscriber base in Europe, mainly through the provision of a good e-mail service. Without going into the complex pre-launch histories, by the end of 1995 it was clear that there would be three competitors to CompuServe. America Online announced a deal with Bertelsmann (probably the world's largest media company) to set up AOL operations in Germany, France and the UK. Microsoft's ambitions for MSN were always global, and the company put quite a lot of effort into obtaining local content.

Europe Online was established by a diverse range of shareholders, brought together largely by Candace Johnson, who had been involved in the launch of the Astra satellite television service. The theory was that there would be publisher-shareholders in Germany, France and the UK, together with support from the Luxembourg financial community and AT&T, who were contributing their recently acquired Interchange software. Among the publishers involved with the service were the Pearson Group, publishers of the *Financial Times*, and Burda, one of the largest and most innovative of German publishing houses.

The first to launch was MSN, followed quickly by AOL/Bertelsmann in Germany, and then AOL in the UK. AOL France was launched at the MILIA exhibition in February 1996. In both Germany and the UK the AOL marketing machine has been very impressive, with (for example) deals being done to give schools low-cost access to AOL in the UK. The key marketing route for AOL in Europe, as in the USA, and also as mirrored by CompuServe, is to attach disks containing the registration software to magazines on display in newsagents, often referred to as cover-mounting.

By comparison Europe Online initially had a very low profile, a result of having to move from the Interchange platform to an Internet access route just before launch in December 1995, and apparently considerable differences of opinion between the shareholders about the direction of the business. The end result is that Europe Online crept out, rather than being launched.

The early part of 1996 saw an immense flurry of activity, with deals being done almost daily in an effort to build Internet capability and WWW browsing capabilities into the proprietary interfaces. Apple, beset by financial problems, closed down eWorld, and UK Online lost two senior staff. Prodigy was sold off to a venture fund, to the considerable relief of both IBM and Sears, and MSN was effectively relaunched as a WWW service, despite the considerable investment made by information providers developing content for the original proprietary platform. GEnie was also sold to a venture fund.

In June CompuServe announced a rapid migration to the WWW as H&R Block, its parent company, started the process to sell off CompuServe, as well as launching Wow! as a service targeted solely at the consumer marketplace in the USA. America Online also had its problems in June 1996 when it announced a pricing reduction, and this announcement, combined with fears about the future of AOL in the Internet world, resulted in a sharp drop in the share price. In July and August things started to get rather difficult, with CompuServe starting to see a decline in subscribers and a lacklustre start to Wow! The parent company then halted the sale of CompuServe. AOL had a 19-hour loss of service in early August and, despite breaking the $1bn revenue target, the share price was well below the 1996 peak.

In Europe all the services were struggling to maintain their ambitious growth targets. In June 1996 AOL reported that the service had 150,000 subscribers in Germany, with the announced target being 800,000 for the end of 1996. CompuServe had nearly 800,000 subscribers. Subscriber numbers for the UK services are difficult to establish, but by mid-year Tel-Me had 6000 subscribers, and UK Online, always intensely secretive about subscriber numbers, may have had even fewer. AOL reportedly had around 50,000 subscribers in the UK. Not exactly mass-market figures!

Then in August Europe Online ceased operation, having achieved a total of some 25,000 subscribers. At the heart of the problem was the fact that the various shareholders entered into the venture with rather different objectives and expectations. The move from the Interchange platform was not only a blow to AT&T but also delayed the launch and increased the development costs. By the middle of 1996 rumours about frequent board meetings started to circulate. The main operational shareholder was Burda, and the costs and complexities of the operation were beyond anything that the company had anticipated, and in the end it was the reluctance of Burda to continue investing in Europe Online which precipitated the end of the service. In fact one of the original founders of the service, Candace Johnson, purchased the name, and continues to run a Web site offering news and current affairs information.

The first few months of 1997 were still very difficult for the US services. CompuServe abandoned Wow! and disclosed some rather poor financial performance figures. AOL started running into law suits over its new unlimited access charging structure (which is only available in the USA), and problems of providing reliable service access. Talks between AOL and CompuServe with the objective of AOL acquiring the CompuServe information service ran up against some financial regulations that made the acquisition unattractive in terms of tax treatment. Meanwhile, in the UK, LineOne was launched as a joint venture between British Telecom and News International, publishers of *The Times* and *Sunday Times*. This service is notable for the fact that most of the content is sourced from News International, and that intelligent agent search technology is used. This service is being heavily promoted in *The Times* and the *Sunday Times*, with unlimited access to the service and to the Internet for a monthly subscription of £14.95. A service that was due to be launched by the BBC and ICL in February 1997 has so far failed to materialize.

Subscription figures for Europe are rather unreliable, but an indication of the overall situation in early 1997 is as follows:

Table 9.2   *European subscriber base as at early 1997* (author's estimate)

	Europe	of which UK
CompuServe	900,000	400,000
AOL	450,000	120,000
MSN	220,000	100,000

A number of national consumer online services has been established in Europe, mainly in the UK. UK Online was set up in 1995 with support from Olivetti, which also owned Italia Online, and provided services targeted at families, including games and educational content. This service never managed to get much beyond 10,000 subscribers, and was bought by Easylink, a UK ISP (Internet Service Provider), and continues to operate at a very low level of use.

Tel-Me, a service operated by Phone Link plc, provides a service of more interest to the business community, with detailed maps, company information, Yellow Pages and travel information, for example, but has failed to develop a Web interface and expand the range of content of the service.

In France there already is a mass market service, Teletel, but this was built around a dedicated terminal and a rather basic character set. Nevertheless there are around 7 million subscribers, but the factors that have created this level of adoption are complex and politically motivated. They have been expertly reviewed elsewhere,[1] and the only point to be made here is that no government in Europe is ever going to adopt the same very expensive strategy. The dominance of the Minitel terminal, in about 1 in 2 households, has severely inhibited the growth of either AOL or any other Internet service, though CompuServe, offering good e-mail and information services for business has managed to gain market share.

Faced with potential competition from Internet services, and from AOL and CompuServe, France Telecom moved quickly in early 1996 to lower the cost of the Teletel services, and to provide Internet/Teletel gateways. In addition the Wanadoo service, effectively a Yellow Pages service, was launched in early 1996, and Infonie was an entertainment service provided by Infogramme, a multimedia publisher, using a CD-ROM disc as the main service platform.

In the German market, T-Online, the PC-based evolution of the Deutsche Telekom Bildschirmtext videotex service, has now adapted its service to offer a Web front end, and has over 1.5 million subscribers, many attracted by the home banking services. Deutsche Telekom is hopeful that by the end of the decade the number of subscribers will match that of the French Teletel services, but with substantially greater revenues. To counter the combined threat from T-Online and AOL CompuServe has formed an alliance with germany.net, an Internet service provider with over 160,000 members.

Factors affecting the adoption of online services

The factors that will affect the rate of adoption of mass market online services are similar to those for Internet services, but with a few important exceptions. These factors are given below. Because there are a number of them, no one factor is going to determine the rate of growth of the market, but it is important to bear them all in mind when assessing the future of online/Internet services, and other new consumer information services that may be launched.

Installed base of PCs and modems

The penetration of consumer electronics equipment into European households is substantially lower than in the USA, but it is quite difficult to gain an accurate picture of the installed base of PCs in homes and small businesses in Europe. Published research is based on extrapolation from a sample survey, often from questions added into a more general consumer market research omnibus survey. In order to assess the market potential for online services it is not only necessary to identify PC ownership but also those PCs that are connected to a modem.

As a European average the penetration of PCs into households is of the order of 15%, but this includes all PCs and there are no doubt a substantial number of older models, such as Amstrad, Atari and Amiga, that are unlikely to be used for online service access. A more realistic penetration, therefore, is probably about 12%, with a substantial bias towards the UK and Germany, where the figure may be as high as 20%. Only about half these households will also have a modem, and so the current market potential for online services, and also Internet access, is about 10 million households. Another complicating factor is that French households are unlikely to add a modem to a PC until there are substantial benefits in dispensing with the Minitel terminal.

Teletext

Teletext services, in which data is encoded in the vertical blanking interval in broadcast television signals, have been widely available in Europe for over two decades, and there are probably over 60 million television sets that can display teletext information. The Sky satellite channels also have a teletext capability. The range of information on these services is quite wide, including news, weather, sports results, TV listings, travel information and other leisure information. It is also possible to provide a limited degree of interaction through the use of touch-tone telephones, and in the UK there have been some trials of online shopping through teletext services. Because of the localization of the commercial television companies it is feasible to produce local advertising and news services. One recent development has been to put personal messages and advertisements on the service.

One of the most successful areas for UK advertising on the teletext services has been that for holidays, and Teletext claims that over 20% of all holidays are sold over this network. This is an area that the B-Sky-B Intertext service is also planning to develop.

These teletext services represent a substantial challenge to the consumer online services that does not exist in the USA. Instead of having to dial in to an online service for sports results, weather, railway timetables and news, teletext services offer all this free, without moving from the television. Over the next few years there will be enhancements to the teletext decoders which will enable a wider range of information to be accessed more quickly.

Telecommunications costs

Compared to the situation in the USA, the cost of accessing online services in Europe has always been high because of the tariff policies of the telecommunications operators. In the USA local calls are free, or virtually so, and this has caused many problems with the demand for telephone circuits, especially once the service providers announced unlimited access for a monthly subscription. Over the years telecommunications network planners have built up a wealth of knowledge about the average length of calls and the factors that influence duration and call volume. However online service access often results in calls lasting a great deal longer that the average voice call. In Europe at least the telephone company would gain additional revenue from the use of the circuits, but of course this is not the case in the USA. Another issue that has to be taken into account is the ease with which additional lines can be installed, especially in the domestic market, to overcome the problems of extensive use of online services effectively cutting off the household from voice telephony. In Europe additional lines cost as much as the original line, a cost that many households will not be willing to pay.

Value-added tax (VAT)

One of the differences between the US market and the European market is the level of direct taxation on online services. Tax levels in the USA are usually around 5–7%, but in Europe they can often be twice that level. For the business user this tax can be passed on in terms of goods and services to customers, but consumers do not have this option, and (to take the case of the UK) currently pay 17.5% value-added tax on both online subscriptions and on telecommunications charges. Until recently the US companies were able to avoid adding VAT to their invoices, but this is now in the process of being changed by the European Commission to avoid unfair competition with European services.

Language

One of the most difficult problems to overcome in the development of a European online services business is that of language. Europe is fragmented into 40 distinct languages and language variants. Within the European Union native speakers of German (78 million) outnumber those of English (56 million) since the unification of Germany. As far as the online industry is concerned the problem is not only which is the first language, but also to what extent will users who do not have English as a first language be prepared to use English-language content. Over the next decade, possibly accelerated by the Internet, the use of English will continue to grow, but there will still be information, especially national news and leisure information, for which local language will continue to be important.

Information culture

Another important variable to take into account is the different 'information cultures' within each country. This is a rather broad term to cover the use made of daily, weekly and regional newspapers, readership of professional and consumer magazines, the use of book clubs, and the development of public libraries. The demand for news is being satisfied in very different ways in Europe, and this has an implication for the extent to which online news services will be able to compete with, or complement, the newspaper industry.

Pricing and billing

Just how price sensitive this market is going to be is still far from clear. The strategy in the USA seems to have been to keep the monthly subscription steady at around $10 per month, with the major change being the introduction of unlimited use for this subscription level. As has already been mentioned, in the USA the effect of sales tax is quite small, and can almost be discounted in any comparisons. That is not the case in Europe, where the valued-added tax issue is an important one in marketing terms. This presents particular problems for public libraries as they have to absorb the VAT element to a significant extent.

Billing is also going to be a difficult problem, as the number of currencies is almost certainly going to be greater than the number of languages supported. Even for businesses this is going to be an issue as the costs of raising small-denomination cheques or bank drafts can be larger than the value of the cheque itself. For a consumer a credit card or a charge card may be the only option, and many consumers do not like to have a payment on a credit card for which they have not individually signed. In the UK credit cards are very widely used, but this is not the case in Germany, and in Scandinavia in particular. In time this problem will be reduced in some European countries as the euro single currency is introduced.

Factors affecting the use of online services

There are also a number of factors that will tend to stimulate the use of online services. These include the following.

Electronic mail

One of the major reasons for the growth of the services in the USA was the availability of reliable electronic mail services, an evolution of the bulletin board concept that was such a stimulator to the purchase of PCs and modems in the late 1970s and early 1980s, and which led to the evolution of bulletin board services into online information services. In Europe the growth of electronic mail traffic has been very substantial. The discussion groups on the Internet have proved very popular, but are also prone to being misused, and there are often problems in identifying contributors. Within services such as AOL the identity of the subscriber can be ascertained, and the whole process of identifying and joining lists is made much easier. In addition there are 'real-time' interactive e-mail services that AOL in particular has made so popular. Adults may feel that these services are a very slow way of communicating, forgetting that children now have very good keyboard skills, and that parents cannot listen into electronic mail sessions in the way that they might overhear telephone conversations.

Electronic shopping and banking

If children and students are attracted by the e-mail and structured content of a mass market service then adults are beginning to see the benefits of electronic banking and shopping. Electronic banking has become very popular in many countries of Europe, in particular Germany, where the facts that the T-Online service is operated by Deutsche Telekom and that there is a high level of security that is built into the system have resulted in a very rapid growth of electronic banking. The Minitel services in France also offer home banking but there is much less interest in this service in the UK. Home shopping has not proved so popular.

Pornography

Parents are becoming increasingly concerned about the menace of electronic pornography. The service providers are equally as concerned, and CompuServe in particular has had some particular problems with child pornography in Germany. The reason for raising the issue here is that although technically it is not difficult to send this material across one of the online services, these services are very concerned about the damage to their reputations.

In general all the services are developing various ways that parents and others can control the type of material that their children are viewing. There are also services that claim to be able to offer a similar facility on the Internet.

Is there a future for mass market services in Europe?

There is no doubt that the mass market online services have had a very difficult time building up their subscriber base in Europe, for the reasons outlined above. Another factor for the problems they have encountered is that use of the Internet was already beginning to be established before they arrived (though admittedly CompuServe had been operating in Europe for some years), whereas in the USA AOL in particular had managed to build up a substantial subscriber base before the current explosion in Internet use occurred.

However, they have learned from their mistakes, and are starting to see levels of subscriber growth and use that should give them encouragement, if not a guarantee, that the mass market service format does have a future in Europe.

As such they need to be considered by libraries in all sectors as complementary electronic information services to direct access to the Internet, but to date the library profession, at least in the UK, seems to have paid little attention to these services.

Electronic service provision in public libraries

Many libraries are now establishing Internet connections and WWW sites without considering the complementary benefits offered by the mass market online services. There have been a number of surveys of the extent of Internet use in public libraries, but the extent to which the consumer online services are used does not seem to have been separately measured. In the 1995 survey undertaken by UKOLN (UK Office for Library and Information Networking) a question was asked about access routes to the Internet, with one of the options being CompuServe, but there were no other questions about online services. The survey did show the heavy use of Internet services for reference purposes.[2]

In principal there is, of course, much to be gained from having Internet access in a public library, but as the US 1996 National Survey of Public Libraries and the Internet comments[3] there are a number of levels of provision of access, which are (in a summarized form):

- making an Internet-connected terminal available;
- providing identification of relevant material on the Internet;
- accessing library services, including locating and reserving books and other material;
- providing interactive services that facilitate on-site and remote access to library staff and other library users;
- providing knowledge-based services, where the library provides on-demand customized services, and alerts readers to new material based on previous loan and search patterns.

In essence, a public library has to develop a policy that will determine its objectives, resources and performance in three areas:

- Expanding the range of resources in the library building to include electronic access to information, including printed information.
- Using electronic services to meet the needs of those who are unable to use the library premises.
- Teaching the skills of retrieval and knowledge management through the use

of electronic information services, and in so doing assist with the development of the skills of life-long learning with the assistance of electronic services. Let me look at each of these in turn.

Expanding the range of resources

The Internet may be a very incomplete information resource, but this is not apparent to searchers who, using a search site such as AltaVista, see that there are potentially thousands of documents that could satisfy their requirements. It is not until they start to look at the initial set of sites that the problems start to emerge, including:

- sites that have not been updated;
- sites that have lost links;
- sites that promise much, but are either incomplete or are 'spoiler' sites put up by people who just want to see their sites on a hit list;
- sites that are unnavigable other than by the person who created them;
- sites that seem to offer valuable information, but are compiled by an organization that has no apparent authority;
- sites that are compiled by companies who have an interest in biasing the site for commercial purposes;
- sites that change the material on offer so often (in particular magazine publishers) that a particular document may be accessible only for a month or less.

The search sites themselves need to be used with considerable care. Although they all try to impose some relevance ranking on documents identified, all to often, even for an information specialist, it is difficult to understand just why certain documents have been given the priority that they have. This is where the consumer online services have probably been neglected as complementary to WWW access over the Internet. The key benefits they offer compared to the WWW are:

- packaging – each provider wants to ensure that users find answers to the majority of their requirements from their service, so they have made considerable efforts to bring together a wide range of content, packaged to make it easy and enjoyable to use;
- editorial control – considerable care is usually taken to ensure that the material is of an acceptable quality, and is updated on a consistent and appropriate basis;
- technical support – all the services recognize that providing excellent customer service is essential;
- standard interfaces that are designed to be easy to use even when the service

has not been accessed for some time;
- reliable electronic mail, bulletin board and interactive messaging services.

In addition, because they are commercially oriented towards making a profit, their content, marketing and support are continually being monitored.

Because these services document the material that they offer, and usually have long-term relationships with publishers and other information providers, they are as stable a source of information as Dialog or LEXIS-NEXIS. In some areas, such as newspapers and reference works, they may well add to the resources of the library, or provide an index to library holdings. Library holdings that are available online through one of these services could be marked on the spine, so that users are alerted to the fact that there is a searchable version, which may encourage use of the print version, especially where the print version has inadequate indexes. These could include: newspapers, magazines, directories, dictionaries and encyclopaedias.

In the area of reference information, especially company information and travel information, the online services should enable the library to offer a wider range of services, in particular to the many small companies that form the economic base of so many towns and cities in the UK. The argument might be advanced that these companies should be able to access this information themselves, but the reality is that even the most easy-to-use interface does not help a manager who is concerned that he or she might be looking in the wrong place for information.

The provision of quality reference information goes beyond these rather obvious examples. One of the major problems with the WWW is that it is very difficult to obtain answers to the type of questions that users of most ages would look to their local library for a solution. To give a few examples, in all cases using the Advanced Search option of AltaVista:

- looking for biographical profiles of Harold Wilson, the former British Prime Minister, produced 80,000 hits;
- a search looking for any critical analysis of the J. B. Priestley play *An inspector calls*, which is a set text for GCSE examinations, produced 2000 hits, of which the first 200 were reviews of stage productions around the world.

And, most worrying of all:

- a search designed to find out the population of Paris not only produced 700 hits, of which none of the first 200 contained any numeric information, also produced, at document 31, a site that said the file 'may contain text that may be considered offensive by many viewers'.

Taking a lot of care over the search statements might have produced better answers, but at a considerable cost in time and effort.

Another benefit of these services is the fact that they are available in other languages, and therefore offer the opportunity to search non-English resources, and to build up networks with correspondents in other countries.

Using electronic services to meet the needs of off-site users

The use of electronic mail services to provide a link between the library and its community of users could be very considerably enhanced by using the online services. Many libraries are now starting to develop their own WWW sites, or using pages on a county or other regional site, but these take considerable resources to establish and support.[4] Given the widespread use of AOL and CompuServe by students and adults it would seem more sensible to link into these services rather than invent something new.

These services would also enable the needs of disabled users to be better served and, of course, given the links of services such as AOL into the schools, there should be some interesting opportunities to link schools into the local public library.

Libraries have always seen themselves as an important focal point for community activities in the UK, and there would seem to be some opportunities to replace the lists of societies on cards on the library wall with electronic access to an even wider range of contacts.

Teaching information skills

Although every justification can be made for libraries to offer training in the use of the WWW, there is also a strong case to be made for similar training in the use of mass market online services. The content is consistent, and the interface is also consistent, so there is an opportunity to set up some standard searches that can be used for self-instruction, and link the results into material that is available in the library.

It is important to demonstrate how electronic access complements other access methods, and also the limitations of these services in many areas, particularly to to students, who might otherwise think that everything they need is available on the Web.

At last there seems to be a recognition that these skills need to be taught at school, and there would seem to be a real opportunity here for libraries and schools to work together for mutual benefit, especially when school library resources are stretched or non-existent.[5] Most schools are very reluctant to offer students access to the WWW without very close supervision, and here the high degree of control included within a mass market service renders these much more amenable to use in schools.

The need for a policy framework

The private sector often complains that public libraries are not entrepreneurial, and are not willing to create closer relationships with the private sector. The problem here is that often it is not the individual librarian who is at fault, but that there is no overall policy from central government for the way in which electronic access to information should be developed (which usually requires investment), and therefore no policy framework at a local authority level that enables decisions on resource allocation to be made and justified.

This problem will be exacerbated in the case of mass market services, where there could be considerable benefit from working with these services on a nation-wide basis. Such initiatives can take place only within a policy framework, and to date many of these are geared only towards the provision of Internet services. To give an illustration from the Danish government's policy statement:[6]

> The goal of implementing 'the Info-Society for All' entails increased requirements on our libraries' efforts to present information to the individual. It is therefore rec-ommended that local councils incorporate IT into the finances of their public libraries in order to support continued development of the application of IT in this sector. All public libraries should give the general public access to the Internet by no later than the end of 1997.

This is a very laudable objective. However, the problem with policy statements in the public sector is that once they have been promulgated it is very difficult to argue after the event that the words used actually meant something else. Negotiating an access agreement with a mass-market service is going to be much more difficult to justify upwards to a local authority if the overall policy statement mentions only the Internet.

Implications for library managers

In the research for this chapter I have looked at a range of policy statements on the way in which information technology and electronic information services should be used to create a better society. The European Commission is prepar-ing a Green Paper on the role of libraries in the information society.[7] The Green Paper's main purpose will be to stimulate discussion towards a coherent approach on how, within the context of the evolving information society, libraries can best serve the needs of European citizens by providing mediated access to the grow-ing wealth of digital resources. Already the national policies of a number of mem-ber states have been collated. However, the best of the policy documents is the *Strategic agenda for the Ottawa Public Library*, published in June 1996, and any library in the public sector would benefit from reviewing this document.

A section on 'The library worker of the future' states the situation with clarity and vision:[8]

> The paradigm is shifting. Our world is increasingly built on information. Libraries will be the electronic doorways to information. Library workers of the future will be the navigators, the facilitators and the mediators of the digital revolution. They will help people retrieve, organise or develop the information that they need. Library workers will be as comfortable with computers, networks and databases as they are with books, tapes and story-times. They will need to train and retrain constantly. They will have skills and strategies to meet the needs of people from different cultures, age groups, social and economic backgrounds, and levels of ability.

The case that I have been trying to make in this chapter is that mass-market services have a role to play in enriching the resources that a library can make available to its users. To date they seem to have been ignored as far as service availability, policy formulation and implementation and training requirements are concerned

Kovacs has set out a detailed schedule for a certification in Internet training which sets out 36 competencies, at a level of, for example, 'a detailed knowledge of how to work with an established 56k or higher dedicated Internet connection on one or more computer platforms'.[9] In this list there is just one passing reference to the ability to explain the relationships between the Internet and online services. Given the millions of subscribers to mass market services in the USA, the lack of a specific reference to these services (and it could well be that the reference is to bibliographic online services) is difficult to understand.

The justifications for ignoring the possible benefits of mass market online services are probably:

- they will be overtaken by the Internet;
- they are only really for games and other leisure activities;
- they cost money.

To take these in order, it seems unlikely that these services will be submerged by the Internet, at least in the near future. They have a strong subscriber base, and now that they facilitate access to the WWW through their own interfaces, they can provide the best of both worlds. To regard these services as providing only games and other entertainment content is an indictment of a profession that should always be looking for new ways of providing a wider range of services. In this respect it is interesting that, without doing a rigorous search, there do not seem to have been any substantive articles on these services in periodicals for the library profession. Even the PC magazines tend to evaluate the services only as Internet service providers, and do not look in any detail at the content of the services. The final point, the fact that accessing these services will add to the burden on a library budget, is certainly a point that needs addressing, but the opportunity here is to approach the service operators and develop new types of relationship to the mutual benefit of both parties.

Conclusions

My objective in this chapter has been to raise the awareness of the potential value of mass market online services in three areas:

- as a complementary source of information to the Internet, and other electronic reference services;
- as a means of teaching information retrieval skills on a stable and editorially consistent platform;
- as a means of creating electronic communities among the users of libraries.

The actions that need to be taken are:

- the education of the information profession about the benefits and limitations of these services, with articles in the professional press and presentations at conferences;
- ensuring that policy statements at all levels do not exclude the use of these services in libraries because of the use of the term 'Internet' in setting parameters for service access;
- building relationships with the service providers;
- ensuring that surveys of the use of new electronic services include the option to report on the use of mass market services, so that use can be captured and analysed, and that libraries that are not using these services are at least prompted to reconsider their decision.

On the horizon there are more new services appearing, including interactive television and the delivery of online services using the television as the interface. The purchase of WebTV by Microsoft in early 1997 would seem to indicate that this technology may have much to offer. There are also important developments in the area of the cable delivery of television and interactive services, and the imminent launch of digital television. The impact that these, and other technologies, on the use of libraries is far from clear, but it will be important for the information profession to monitor the development of these services over the next few years, and see where they fit with existing library services.

It may be that all these services do is raise awareness of the enormous heritage of the cinema and television. If *Citizen Kane* is being broadcast on a cable channel, then efforts ought to be made by the library community, in alliances with other interested parties, to highlight biographies of Orson Wells, or of Randolph

Hearst, on whom the film was based.

To ignore the products of digital consumer electronics as consumer toys could be a grave mistake, both for the profession, and for society at large. The library profession has a tremendous opportunity to reach out to new users and offer new services to regular users, but it will take courage and vision on the part of the information profession, on the policy makers and budget holders, and on those who train and educate the profession.

Go back to the statement from the Ottawa Public Library strategy I quoted earlier (see page 237), type it out (or should it be word-process it out?) and put it somewhere visible. Then every day see whether you and your colleagues are alive to the vision and the opportunity.

References

1   Housel, T. J. and Davidson, W. H., 'The development of information services in France: the case of public videotex', *International journal of information management*, **11** (1), 35–54.

2   Ormes, S. and Dempsey, L., *Library and Information Commission public library Internet survey: first public report*.
    <http://ukoln.bath.ac.uk/publib/lic.html>

3   1996 National Survey of Public Libraries and the Internet.
    <http://istweb.syr.edu/Project/Faculty/McClure-NSPL96/NSPL96_3.html>

4   Kendall, M., 'Web for the community', *Library Association record*, **99** (4), 1997, 212–4.

5   Herring, J., 'Enabling students to search and find', *Library Association record*, **99** (5), 1997, 258–9.

6   *The info-society for all – the Danish model*.
    <http://www.fsk.dk/fsk/publ/1996/it1996-uk/cap1.htm#1_cap>

7   Material relating to this Green Paper can be found on
    <http://www2.echo.lu/libraries>

8   Ottawa Public Library Board, *Public library service beyond the millenium: a strategic agenda 1996–2001*, June 1996,
    <http://www.opl.ottawa.on.ca/english/new/stratage.htm>

9   Kovacs, D. K., 'Internet trainer certification and training for librarians', *SLA business and finance bulletin*, (105), Spring 1997, 47–52.

Further reading

White M. and Coyne, M., *Mass market online services in Europe*, 3rd edn., London, TFPL Ltd, 1997.
    <http://www.tfpl.com>

10

EDUCATION AND TRAINING FOR INFORMATION PROFESSIONALS IN FACE OF THE INTERNET AND WORLD WIDE WEB

Pieter van Brakel

DEPARTMENT OF INFORMATION STUDIES, RAND AFRIKAANS UNIVERSITY, SOUTH AFRICA

Introduction

The advent of the Internet and consequently, the global information infrastructure being developed, together with PC-based hardware and software developments such as faster, multitasking end-user workstations and friendlier point-and-click graphical user interfaces, necessitate a completely different approach to the education and training of the information professional:

- Information science (IS) programmes can no longer ignore the fact that, because of information technology, today's end-user has 'graduated' to the status of self-sufficiency in solving his or her immediate information needs.
- Thousands of World Wide Web sites exist, creating an exciting information infrastructure for retrieving as well as publishing any type of document, including multimedia formats.
- Web-based retrieval mechanisms have grown in only two years from a small and very unrefined number of indexes to large, sophisticated search engines, covering various subject fields, reaching the content of thousands of Web sites represented from all over the globe and reflecting already many of the search facilities built into the command driven systems of traditional online database vendor systems.
- Authoritative publications, such as peer-reviewed journals, subject reference works, research reports or conference proceedings, are successfully finding their way to the Web as electronic documents being retrieved by search engines and cited by other authors.
- Pupils are already citing Internet resources in their school projects. In certain

subject areas university and college students can complete a research assignment without the necessity of using any paper-based information sources at all.

- Accessing e-mail and Web-based sources from home is no longer a dream; the many Internet providers have already developed competitive pricing structures for giving home users and private enterprise access to various Internet facilities.

These and other trends are responsible for the fact that many conference papers and journal articles (and even a few books) have been published during the last decade about the turbulences occurring in and around the traditional information profession and, naturally, the consequences these may have (or indeed have already had) on the nature of education and training programmes in information science programmes.

Although it is required from any profession, as a growing entity, that the education of its potential workers/employees should change by practice according to demands, the intensity of the demands for change in IS education has increased remarkably since the early 90s. One of the reasons for the increased pressure for change is that IS is engaged in a struggle with other professions to obtain a visible and viable share of the information industry, or rather, information marketplace.

Reasons for what can be called a survival struggle will be discussed later in this chapter, but probably the most prominent reason is the fact that information handling skills are no longer the territory of the information professional alone. The increasing strategic importance of information to an enterprise – or society as a whole, for that matter – is another reason. Improved personalized communication and workstation technology, as well as the increasing availability of information delivered in electronic format directly to the end-user, are other reasons why the information professional is involved in a survival battle. Van House and Sutton[1] are taking this argument further by stating that the struggle with other professions is for jurisdiction over both those information functions that have traditionally been the problem domain of IS, as well as those emerging information functions brought about by changes in society and technology. The traditional services and tools designed by IS to address the information problem are well known, but are summarized here to form the background to later discussion (the present author's own interpretations and examples are added where applicable):

- Information retrieval: establishing the principles and methods for the organization and retrieval of information, such as knowledge representation, establishing and addressing of the user's needs, and matching the two.
- Intermediation: interpreting information needs and behaviours, information

production, the flow and uses of information, as well as the methods of inter-action between the user and information.

- Technology: studying hardware and software of computer-based systems to support information handling processes.
- Social context: scanning and describing the social, political, economic and organizational environments that affect information production, information flow, uses and information behaviour.
- Domain knowledge: studying the content of the information store as it is found in different information formats, from paper-based to multimedia.

This knowledge base has been developed by information services along four dimensions:

- Toolmaking: developing systems to identify, evaluate, organize, retrieve and disseminate information.
- Utilization: applying the tools developed for day-to-day practices, such as information storage, organization and retrieval.
- Agency (or service): acting as intermediaries or directly on behalf of end-users and education users to become more self-sufficient in information handling skills.
- Management of organizations: designing, managing and operating information organizations, units and systems.

The above functions and tools reflect those that traditionally distinguish the work of the information specialist from other careers. However, the new electronic environment, and specifically in the face of the Internet, necessitates that this extremely dynamic and highly competitive marketplace is constantly moni-tored for change. The purpose of this chapter is exactly that: to investigate the latest developments in the electronic (Internet) marketplace, to put these into perspective, and to indicate how IS programmes should react to these develop-ments. The chapter could therefore contribute to the first phase of any curricu-lum change – the situation analysis.

Because of many variables, such as different market needs, target groups, products, course structures and policies of specific tertiary institutions and IS departments, only global changes can be suggested here and only general conclu-sions with regard to the content of IS courses can be made. Individual IS depart-ments might like to consider the ideas mentioned in this chapter, compare them with their own courses and hopefully find some of them worth implementing.

Before current developments and their impact on IS programmes are dis-cussed, the situation with regard to a new (economic) marketplace and the pro-posed role of the information professional will be addressed.

The new electronic marketplace

The departure point for this discussion is that information is seen as a resource when evaluated or compared to any other resource such as water, industry or human resources. Various authors have discussed the general as well as unique characteristics of information as a resource.[2] This leads further that, because information is a resource, it should be seen as an essential product or commodity for what can be described as electronic commerce. In general, electronic commerce includes any form of economic activity conducted via electronic links or connections.[3] Electronic commerce is, of course, more than the mere use of technology. It is the seamless application of information and information technology, from its point of origin, along the entire value chain of business processes conducted electronically and designed to strive towards reaching a specific business tool, up to the end of the process.[4]

Within any economic system, electronic commerce should be evaluated in the context of markets, that is, places of exchange. A market is typically where different groups, such as consumers, come together to exchange goods or services. When a specific market is competitive, it is characterized by:

- many buyers and sellers;
- homogeneous products;
- easy entrance to and departure from the market;
- low switching cost for consumers who wish to choose among suitable goods from competing firms;
- availability of 'perfect' information (perfect information implies that consumers will have all the information – for example via different information formats – they need to make informed, rational decisions about which goods or services to purchase in the marketplace).[5]

If the above explanation is extended beyond the typical situation of buying and selling goods, 'perfect' information also reflects further reasons why information should be seen as an essential commodity or resource, such as for the purposes of decision making, planning, research, training or report writing in general. The need for or involvement in information has been increased with the advent of the Internet. Any WWW statistics file will indicate the phenomenal growth in the number of users and of Web sites currently active in the Internet environment.[6]

As the extent of electronic (Internet) commerce increases, the current information infrastructure still trails behind. Pattinson[7] described the situation in 1995 as follows (his various statements have been augmented where necessary to reflect the status of developments in 1997):

- Limited Web site search mechanisms and processes, inhibiting ease of access and use. (Many search engines have been developed since 1995, such as AltaVista, Lycos and Magellan. These and other search engines concentrate on simplifying the retrieval process. As will be seen later in this chapter, large online vendor systems, for example Medline, KR's DIALOG or Data-Star, are opting for WWW-based search interfaces as an alternative or supplement to their command languages. Although most of the search engine's graphical user interfaces (GUI) are relatively friendly, precision ratios are still very low.)

- Slow access time and slow downloading of images, specifically in video and audio form. (Depending on the time of the day, downloading, especially of very large files, can be very slow. Lines are being upgraded all the time, but the interest in using the Internet for transmitting data and information files is growing to such an extent that any upgrade does not last long before the climbing usage figures have eliminated the effect of any upgrade in line speed.)
- Lack of security for transferring and processing financial transactions within the electronic commerce environment. (Electronic security measures, for example to secure the electronic transfer of money, are being researched and developed extensively at the moment. The implications for information and the involvement of the information professional will be discussed below.)
- Uncertainty in many countries regarding policies for investment, ownership, technology selection and making available for the general public access to the new information infrastructure. (Information infrastructural developments in Europe and the USA are being monitored by most and especially developing countries. They all realize ultimately that no country can take the risk of not forming part of the international electronic commerce and, specifically, information infrastructure.)
- Major corporate rivalry in the development of technology and standards within the new infrastructure.
- Concerns on how best to connect to and implement the new infrastructure within firms. (These concerns can be eliminated when information professionals form strategic partnerships in the development of their organization's infrastructure. More detail about such an information partnership will be discussed below).
- Resistance to implementation on cultural grounds. (This is a reality that will not be eliminated easily.)

It can be said that, in general, financial transactions, for example, via in the World Wide Web, have grown to such an extent that role players in the information and electronic commerce fields are positive and enthusiastic about the financial possibilities of trading via the Web. In electronic commerce the traditional marketplace interaction between the physical buyer and physical seller has therefore been eliminated. Rayport and Sviokla[8] call this new environment the *marketspace*. The following key elements within marketspace activity illustrate that electronic information forms an essential part of marketspace:

- **Content**: this refers either to the physical product extended by information services, or the information itself, with the emphasis on the services being offered rather than the physical product. (The authors' viewpoint on information as service should be extended, by adding that information delivered or 'sold' should be repackaged and/or value-added as well.)
- **Context**: addresses the electronic channel or product/service outline.
- **Infrastructure**: the electronic infrastructure operators. (Within the next few years many of the technological constraints surrounding today's information infrastructure will be solved.)

The above thoughts about the status of information in this fast changing marketplace, or rather marketspace, should be narrowed down to the workplace (or is it workspace?). The current position and role of the information professional in providing information to various categories of clients is changing at an alarming rate. In some instances the re-engineering or redesigning of processes in organizations has seen the downscaling in importance of the information department. Furthermore, in the business environment, for example, access to electronic information services is shifting from the corporate information centre directly to the desktop of the end-user.[9] This implies that, since the introduction of the Internet and specifically the versatility of the multimedia and hypertext approach to information published via the Web, the end-user has found a way to become more information independent. Desktop access to information in an enterprise supports the idea of innovation and change:

- Creative use of technology and media transforms business by presenting new ideas in a new way.
- An information infrastructure brings a powerful competitive advantage to a company; it empowers employees and assists them to be more productive.
- A smaller number of employees can deliver a higher quality of service at less cost.[10]

The information professional's potential role in any electronic partnership will, without question, diminish, and will eventually be reduced to being merely the 'keeper' of paper-based documents. Alternatively, the many challenges offered by the digital, global environment could be grasped by the information profession, involved in a re-engineering process, and consequently still playing an essential role regarding the flow of electronic information. IS programmes should be adapted to address these challenges and prepare future information professionals for what has become an extremely demanding and diversified workplace.

A new but challenging role

Existing information professionals do not go back to IS schools to learn about all the latest developments in the electronic information environment. If they want to be re-engineered and thus survive, they should further their skills via good quality continuous education programmes, short courses or postgraduate work that are designed to assist the professional in moving from the traditional inter-mediary approach (finding and providing information sources), to one which also integrates new information technologies for an organization and assists end-users in the organization to become even more information independent. The infor-mation professional, in a new role, performs the creative tasks of information product development and product synthesis. The changes (retooling) taking place in the corporate environment are challenging the information professional to retool his or her skills to provide information solutions, not just information or information sources.[10]

According to Peters[11] there are several areas in which today's information pro-fessional can develop new skills and strategies in order to change, survive and continue to compete in the world of electronic information:

* Information 'anxiety' amongst corporate knowledge workers. Anxiety, or uncertainty about what they (knowledge workers) don't know, and further, about what they don't know regarding the decision-making resources that are available to help them learn. The information professional can help workers overcome this anxiety.
* Intellectual capital and knowledge management. Intellectual capital is nowa-days increasingly being referred to as the new corporate asset. Using informa-tion resources to create a knowledge base to support the development of intellectual capital presents an important new strategic marketing opportunity for information professionals. They should seize the opportunity to help knowledge workers maximize the return on investment with decision-making information.
* Information resource audit. If correctly executed, an audit should be a strate-gic opportunity for information professionals to maximize the return on the investment of their organization's intellectual capital.

It may be more than a coincidence that discussions and developments such as organizational restructuring, retooling of staff and end-user delivery of informa-tion are taking place at the same time as a phenomenal evolution in the access to local and external communication networks via TCP/IP protocol or the Internet occur. Speh's contribution[12] in this regard supports the viewpoint that it is the Internet (and electronic commerce for that matter) that is having a profound effect on the thinking behind the future role of the information professional:

- The input for knowledge management is business information, which can become knowledge capital if cleverly managed. The information professional can eliminate the daily risk of making bad business decisions from the use of 'too much' or the 'wrong kind' of information.[11]
- The Internet can assist us to draw upon cross-functional expertise to solve operating problems (it supports communication on a global scale).
- The Internet can help with the integration of new tools and methodologies and to experiment (it is a tool where new strategies and methodologies can be tested on a very diverse audience).
- It can assist companies to import knowledge from the outside world (the Internet already competes with traditional and expensive online database services).

This section described some trends with regard to the nature of the new marketplace being made available by the advent of the Internet, as well as the new demands being placed on the role of the information professional in the learning organization. In this regard the conclusions made by Van House and Sutton[13] form a valuable introduction to the following sections:

- Survival of information science education does not necessarily mean the survival of current programmes and certainly not their survival in their current forms. It means survival of the knowledge base, approaches, values, practices and tools that must be applied to new problem areas.
- IS education needs to (finally) decouple itself from the 'library' concept. Abstraction, reduction and the creation of new knowledge to address new information problems are essential for the information profession to adapt to new demands.
- Many professions are involved in building new information tools in the form of computer-based systems. Just as many are concerned with methods of managing and delivering information. (The information professional's argument for jurisdiction will be to develop better tools and better solutions, especially in the electronic environment. Unique IS programmes should be developed to provide for these new skills.)
- 'Without a rapid response and fundamental change, IS education is likely to go the way of the pandas: cute, well-loved, coddled and nearing extinction'.[13]

The following sections will report on the new information services and facilities being brought about by the Internet and the WWW. An introduction to each topic

is provided, supplemented with **goals** and **actions** for information science education and training which could act as guidelines (or 'idea generators') when bringing IS programmes on a par with current and anticipated changes. In all the cases,
a basic theoretical knowledge of the Internet infrastructure, its facilities and navigators is expected, including the World Wide Web. Detailed instructional objectives, learning content and practicals on basic Internet and Web searching has
been discussed elsewhere.[14]

The changing scholarly communication scene

Scholarly communication is traditionally divided into informal and formal (or
published) sectors. Opportunities created by electronic means created various
informal applications, such as electronic mail, electronic conferences and electronic bulletin boards (listservs). Exciting and more effective methods of informal communication are now possible when compared to previous paper-based
methods such as personal letters or the distribution of preprints. Formal communication, an essential part of the structure of scholarly communication, is also
effected by new electronic means. The scientific journal is a good example; since
its inception in the middle of the seventeenth century it has been accepted as
the most important means of reporting on experimentation and research results.

Informal communication

Electronic mail

Electronic communication facilities can benefit both the intermediary as well as
the end-user sectors. Information professionals have, for the first time, better
access to the informal or more personal channels of communication, by applying
the opportunities brought about by e-mail and discussion groups. For the first
time the information professional can actively monitor the activities of a specific
discussion group on behalf of specific end-users or groups of clients. Apart from
improved communication via e-mail with other information professionals across
the globe, various applications exist in their contact with clients, such as current
awareness to groups, personal notifications and SDI results to individual clients.
Even full-text electronic journal articles can be retrieved via e-mail databases.

New e-mail applications are being added from time to time. Apart from receiving bibliographic references retrieved from SDI or retrospective searches via e-
mail, it is now also used for distributing various news service options, for example
NewsNet's Smart-Mail (**http://www.newsnet.com**) and the Information Access
Company's SearchBank (**http://www.iacnet.com**). The following features from
these systems indicate the essential part e-mail has to play in any information
environment:[15]

- SmartMail delivers news headlines and summaries to each client's e-mail box at least twice a day. These include headline links that seamlessly connect to NewsNet on the Web for the full text of the news articles.
- SmartMail can also deliver tables of content from new issues of publications offered by NewsNet, with links to the full text.
- SearchBank's Web service allows end-users to electronically transmit the text of articles or citations to any valid e-mail address.

IS programmes

Goal:
- To expose the possibilities of e-mail as an invaluable medium of transmitting scholarly communication.

Actions:
- apply the general functions of at least one e-mail software package to send and receive mail items;
- study a number of e-mail news delivery systems; obtain experience in using at least one representative delivery system;
- deliver a prototype SDI service by posting information items to a group of end-users; items to be based upon URLs found via Web search engines;
- search for e-mail addresses by using various methods, including FTP sites and Web search engines.

Discussion groups: mailing lists; listservs

The literally thousands of mailing lists and listservs on every topic imaginable implies that the information professional has access to a very wide range of active databanks which provide, on a regular basis, informal information on relevant topics. End-users may find it difficult to identify and evaluate relevant discussion groups, although various online tools and Web sites could provide valuable assistance, for example:

- CataList: A catalogue of listserv lists (**http://www.lsoft.com/lists/listref.html**).
- An indexed Web site can be found at Indiana University (**http://www.nova.edu/Inter- Links/cgi-bin/news-lists.pl/**) – it is a keyword searchable database of nearly 12,000 listservs.[16]
- New-List: This is a listserv where owners of new e-mail-based discussion groups announce their new lists (**new-list@vm1.nodak.edu**).[16]
- Broeker's *Reporters's guide to Internet mailing* lists is a detailed step-by-step guide to finding and using mailing lists (**http://www.daily.umn.edu/~broeker/guide.html**).[17]

- Kovacs' directory[18] concentrates on scholarly and professional electronic conferences.

End-users should be assisted in identifying and subscribing to an applicable listserv. The following criteria should be applied before subscribing: Does the information from the group have value to me? Do I have the time to assess all the mail I would get? Is most of the discussion relevant to the main theme of the listserver? Is the information received usually accurate? Do the participants seem knowledgeable about the topic?[19] When effectively applied, a listserv can be invaluable. It can be used for monitoring current trends, finding advice on problems, acquire data and information for research purposes and be updated (current awareness) on recently published developments.[20]

IS programmes

Goal:
- To investigate discussion groups, with special reference to listservs, as an effective informal information delivery channel

Actions:
- browse indexes for messages about a specific topic; download various sources, for example full text journal articles or current awareness bulletins;
- identify, subscribe and unsubscribe to listservs according to topic (using indexes to news groups, or search for applicable URLs);
- take part in designing, implementing and moderating an experimental listserv for a specialized group.

Formal communication formats

Formal communication formats are typically represented by primary and secondary publications, such as conference proceedings, scientific journals, monographs and indexing and abstracting journals, to name but a few. A total lack of quality and bibliographic control is currently an issue because of the fact that anyone with an IP address, a modem or access to a LAN, could 'publish' via the Internet. Many of these 'manuscripts' and other informal publications found on the Internet do not necessarily represent the typical formal formats identified above, but cannot be ignored because of the up-to-dateness and quality of information they might communicate. They are already accepted in the learned communities as information sources, although the end-user should be extra cautious with regard to normal criteria such as authority and data integrity.

Harnad,[21] well-known for his contributions on scholarly communication, proclaimed that the Internet is definitely fit for serious science and scholarship.

Only peer reviewing on the Internet should be extended. On the issue of the Internet generating so much information that it will be impossible to distinguish signal from noise, he remarked that powerful search tools would be created in due course to optimize access to the scientific literature. His 1995 prediction was correct, as the developments and ratio of development of search engine technology were of such magnitude that the today's typical search engine demonstrates a much higher sophistication level than the typical 'library' based system of the past. Ranked search output, hyperlinks to sites or meta-searching are but a few examples. Tenopir and King's recent study[22] on managing scientific journals in the digital environment found a small but growing number of high-quality titles. In the 1996 edition of the *Directory of electronic journals, newsletters and academic discussion lists* a total of 352 scientific Web journals are listed. An estimated 84% of these are refereed.

This growth ratio has shown that the Web offers a positive environment for electronic journals to become a success factor. Their major strong points are the combination of multimedia capabilities, interactivity and provision to browse for relevant articles via different entry points, for example, author, title or abstract. In the near future it might also be possible for a publishing house to maintain a local search engine to provide accessibility to its journal content via keywords. Other unique features distinguish them from their paper-based equivalents, such as the following:[22]

- Web journals are typically complete entities, not mere collections of articles.
- They may already include the full editorial and subscription information, instructions to authors and readers, as well as copyright and restrictions regarding further use.
- Articles can accommodate multimedia, complete graphical and tabular information, and links to related or cited material.
- Online forums for discussion could be included. This could be either between readers and authors or in the form of letters to the editor.

Sources to identify electronic journals are still in their infancy. In comparison, their printed counterparts are being indexed by publishers and libraries, and various other sources are electronically making paper-based journals accessible, such as: second-party distributors (document delivery systems); third-party distributors (online and CD-ROM vendors); gateway organizations that provide hardware, software and telecommunications only; subscription agents; information brokers; and multi-type library cooperative networks.[22] Pricing policies and structures vary from electronic title to title. For example, subscription can be based upon individual articles, site licences, database fees, and/or a combination of these. Information professionals, and therefore IS departments, should accept the fact that Web journals will continue to grow, not only in the number of titles but also in quality and thus authority.

Besides the increasing popularity of personalized news sources (discussed below), another major area of development is Web-based reference sources. These sources already cover a variety of different subject areas. Examples of titles are Infoseek's *Bank and market rates*, *Webster's dictionary*, *Roget's thesaurus* and *Bartlet's quotations*.[23]

Critical decisions await the information professional regarding pricing, archiving, resource sharing and assistance to end-users to enable them to provide the best and most cost-effective means to access the content of the primary sources on the Web.

IS programmes

Goal:
* To investigate the role the Internet and specifically World Wide Web can play in the formal scholarly communication process.

Actions:
* search the Internet (including WWW, FTP, Gopher and Archie sites) to identify and categorize the formal electronic information channels;
* devise ways and means (including policy) to incorporate formal electronic channels into information work (indexing, for example, of URLs; repackaging; value-adding);
* investigate the validity of the electronic scientific journal (identify criteria for evaluation; access methods; optimal end-user workstation configuration);
* find and describe the methods to identify channels to formal electronic sources.

Impact on traditional online searching

'Online searching', previously 'online database searching', is the term commonly used to describe the most typical area of the information professional's work. This includes all levels of online searching, that is, from the spectrum of the information broker, who renders information services at a fee, to that of the professional employed by a tertiary or private company, and responsible for online searching in a highly specialized subject field. Regular conferences are being held over the years on online searching, such as the International Online Information Meeting, which held its 20th meeting in December 1996. A similar regular conference, the National Online Meeting, is being held in New York every year. Although the definition of online searching has been expanded over the years to include topics as varied as CD-ROM interfaces, network technology and the like, the term still corresponds with the description formulated by Haygarth Jackson ten years ago:

> In online searching for the retrieval of information, the searcher at a terminal is con-
> nected to the computer which holds a collection(s) of data in machine-readable
> form known as a database(s). The searcher interacts with the computer and poses a
> series of queries, in the form of search terms or indexing terms which will corre-
> spond with those in the collection of data in the computer store. The computer
> responds by listing items identified by these search terms. The searcher can then
> adapt the search according to the response from the computer.[24]

The definition obviously addressed the 'traditional' view of online searching. But
how does this differ from online information retrieval activities when using the
Internet? The first point to remember is that the Internet provides the facilities
for the development of a complete information system (or systems) in its own
right. One cannot compare the Internet's navigation facilities with traditional
online searching: that is, manipulating the content of large bibliographic and full-
text databases interactively. Wittig and Wolfram[25] argue that where the traditional online systems permit timely retrieval of information from large *centrally*
located bibliographic databases, the latest Internet-based storage and retrieval
tools permit access to *decentralized* resources.

Koenig emphasized the trend that the location *of* information becomes less
and less relevant, 'as we move information around more and more readily'.[26]
Basili[27] is more specific in reminding us that traditional online database systems
have a star-shaped architecture where the local PC links up with the service-sup-
plying computer (the vendor). The local computer is completely subordinate to
the central computer in terms of both query language and type of service. In a
single session only one vendor is accessed and an online search is thus limited to
the databases of that vendor alone. In the case of the Internet the connection is
reticular, because it (the Internet) consists of a constellation of interconnected
nodes in which in one network session (for example a World Wide Web's) it is
possible to execute a search for information that can move from one node (system) to another.

These differences still conform to the 'online' idea. The Internet navigator's
searching – for example via Gopher, Archie and the Web – can be regarded as
'online searching', because as indicated in the above definitions, processing is
executed in an online mode (albeit via TCP/IP and a client-server architecture).
There is also interaction via an interface (i.e. browser), with the main purpose of
solving an information-retrieval problem. The Internet could therefore be seen as
a fast-growing online infrastructure, consisting of a wide variety of navigators and
search services.

The following developments have been identified as critical in depicting current and future trends in the online searching environment. Goals and actions will again be provided as guidelines or for stimulating thoughts regarding IS curriculum development.

Web interfacing by commercial online vendors

It can be expected that all the large international online vendor systems, such as Knight Ridder's DIALOG and DataStar, or Medline, with their typical sensitivity towards the needs of their clients, will slowly employ the extremely versatile capabilities of the Internet and the Web. Most of them have already made provision for client access to their databases via Internet's Telnet. During the second phase (since early 1996), which occurred alongside the growing interest in the Web by the commercial sector, vendors such as OCLC have begun to participate by developing Gopher sites or home pages for marketing purposes or to provide more information about their databases. DIALOG's home page, for example, links to its *Chronolog newsletter*, as well as *Blue sheets*, which consists of descriptions of its databases (see **dialog.krinfo.com**). The next and final phase of online development should be to design a Web interface to enable online clients to search the content of the various bibliographic and full text databases in 'search engine' mode (as discussed below).

Online vendors' moving towards Internet access has reached the stage where Web interfacing will be the standard. With client/server architecture and the Web's support for forms, a new model of online interaction is developing.[28] Instead of the traditional interactive search mode, well known to online searchers and necessitating a high level of hurried skilfulness to download search results as quickly as possible to keep the bill as low as possible, searchers (as well as end-users) can now take their time to fill out the form before submitting it. The Web browser/client connects to the server and disconnects again as soon as the results are being displayed to the searcher. In a news item in the November 1996 issue of *Information today*, under the caption 'Database race to the Web', the first paragraph describes the nearly frantic scrambling for Web presence as follows:

> The Internet's World-Wide Web is rapidly becoming the platform of choice for information delivery, as demonstrated by the numerous databases and information services that have announced Web access in the past few months. With the convergence of enabling technologies, delivering an acceptable multimedia experience to the end-user over the Internet is now possible.[29]

In the light of the importance of online searching, this 'database race to the Web' will also effect information science education programmes. These effects will be highlighted below after the current trends in the race have been evaluated.

Examples of vendors moving towards Web interfacing

Since the mid-1970s various role players have arrived on the online scene, for example the database producer, the database vendor, the telecommunication provider, and, last but not the least, the online searcher (who can be an information professional or an end-user). The increase of Web-based facilities for information publishing and retrieval, however, is responsible for the fact that the distinction between the different role players are not that clear any more. In one scenario, the end-user can publish his or her personal PC-based database on the Web (the end-user acting as a database publisher). In another scenario, database producers may opt to purchase or develop a search engine and, instead of leasing or selling their database products to online vendors as in the past, make these database services available directly to end-users via the Web. It is still too early to speculate about the medium- and long-term future of the online vendor, but in the light of the possible direct Web access to database publishers, there is a strong possibility that the influence of this important role player on the online industry might eventually diminish. The following examples are being discussed in an effort to indicate the current state-of-the-art. It was not always easy to distinguish if a specific product originated from a vendor or a producer. Furthermore, not much information (such as comparisons between or evaluations of Web interfaces) has been published yet. These examples are briefly discussed here to form the backdrop for suggestions regarding the goal and actions for IS educational programmes.

Medline

Medline was one of the first online vendors to report its Web-based interface.[30] The interface was developed by Infotrieve and provides access to Medline using natural language as well as Boolean searching. The search results, a list of bibliographic references, is ranked by relevancy to the search topic. A point-and-click ordering system is also included in the interface to allow the user to purchase a copy of the full text of a specific article. The Infotrieve interface can also be used to access internal as well as external databases from different platforms. The service can be accessed at **http://www.infotrieve.com**. Like all the other vendors, the Medline databases are not for free; access is via a login code and password and for subscription holders only.

UMI's ProQuest Direct

In October 1996[31] UMI announced the availability of its ProQuest Direct online system on the Web. This intends to be an information system combining the search facilities for its electronic sources and information delivery in a single, easy-to-use desktop package. End-users interested in full text information can order documents directly from ProQuest Direct and have them sent or faxed by overnight service. The interface provides access to all UMI's databases, including indexes to 17,000 periodicals, 7000 newspapers and 1.4 million dissertations.

CAB International

CAB International (CABI), the US Centre for Agriculture and BioSciences, and SilverPlatter Information Inc. have signed an agreement to create Internet access to all 13 CABI databases from over 11,000 journals covering subjects such as agriculture, health and disease. End-users and information professionals will use SilverPlatter's SPIRS interface, which is the same being used to search the firm's CD-ROM databases. SilverPlatter's Internet interface is based on its Electronic Reference Library (ERL) technology, which is a client/server approach that enables multiple options for both searching and operating platforms.

LEXIS-NEXIS

This database vendor has begun releasing a series of products that will allow its customers to use any WWW browser to find information in its various databases. The first product, LEXIS-NEXIS Advantage for the Web, allows a legal professional with a subscription to search for state legal material, such as case law and statutes. The company anticipates that the majority of its legal clients will have Web access by the end of 1997.[32] The Web interface service is complementary to the firm's traditional online service. The company will also offer Web searching of the service via credit card transactions for more casual users.

Ovid Online

According to Jacsó[33] Ovid Technologies, Inc. was the first online vendor to develop a fully functional Web interface that can manage search sets, display thesauri and search large databases such as Medline and EMBASE with ease. The following main features are included here to serve as an indication of possible trends to be expected in this environment. A basic and advanced search mode has been provided for the Ovid Web Gateway. Typical Web search engine features have been included, such as check boxes for field searching, with navigational buttons to help the user to move around. Browsing has been made easy too: the index terms can be selected by mouse, with posting information (number of references) shown next to the word. Selected terms are automatically combined in an OR relationship. A search is then activated by a mouse click. A more experienced end-user may bypass the indexes and search directly by term.[33] Field restrictions are still limited, for example to the title field. Commands must still be used to apply other field limits. To increase search efficiency, a Java client has also been introduced in an effort to reduce traffic on the Internet or an Intranet by optimizing communication between server and client.[34]

Knight Ridder's DIALOG and DataStar

Web interfaces for both Knight Ridder company's vendors were launched as DataStar Web and DIALOG Web in late 1996 and early 1997 respectively. As could be expected from Knight Ridder, the quality of both interfaces should be of high standard, or at least on a par with the Ovid interface described above. Searches are still performed in the original command language, such as combining and limiting. Search results can be downloaded directly via the browser software. Documents can be saved in either HTML or tagged format. More specifically, valuable links were established to DIALOG's *Blue sheets*, all the systems' databases could be browsed by topic while the database directories simplifies database selection. Search strings are entered in the applicable box, in typical GUI fashion. Functional hyperlinks can be made to various other files, such as the *Blue sheets*, ERA (the Electronic Redistribution and Arching site), KR SourceOne for document delivery, or to the Alert service for SDI.

Web interfacing by online vendors supports end-user searching – such searchers being already acquainted with Web-based search engines such as Excite, Yahoo!, AltaVista and many more. The cumbersome menu-driven systems and consequently end-user orientated marketing approaches of the mid- to late-1980s did not succeed in selling online searching to end-users. Web-based access can thus be seen as the watershed between past and future database search techniques.

IS programmes

Goal:
- To explore Web interfacing technology, with special reference to current online vendor approach to optimize database access to the end-user via Web-based hyperlinks.

Actions:
- create a database of those database vendors that provide Web-based access and interpret the specific links from these pages, such as FAQs, manuals, newsletters, pocket guides, document delivery options, available databases, search features and help desks;
- establish the nature of the search engines and/or interfaces of the different vendors and develop criteria or variables to evaluate their quality (as compared to or supplementing the command language approach).

Database producers opting for Web interfaces

In the introduction to the previous section, mentioned was made of the expected trend that database producers or publishers would in future decide to make their products available directly to customers (information professionals and end-users). The end-user will be an important target group, as current friendly search engine technology is already a familiar application for the serious as well as the casual end-user. An investigation regarding trends in this area indicates that the producers of the well-known bibliographic databases have yet to begin exploring Web interface possibilities. In contrast with these traditional bibliographic databases, it is the full-text business news or financial database producers who were quick to explore and invest in the Web in an effort to break new ground, as is shown below.

Bibliographic databases (journal indexes or abstracting journals)

Very few and still experimental Web sites could be traced. In September 1996 Notess[35] reported about three titles, namely the multi-disciplinary *ERIC* database, the US Government Printing Office's *Monthly Catalog* and *DOE Reports*.

The ERIC Clearinghouse on Information and Technology sponsors the AskERIC Web site at **http://ericir.syr.edu/Eric/**. A typical Web form interface has been developed, on to which the searcher's input can include Boolean operators and field limitations. As with the typical WWW search engine, results can be ranked according to relevancy. However, the database coverage is still very limited as it only goes back to 1991. Further limitations are that no nested search statements are permitted, no online thesaurus is available and, as search results cannot be saved as sets, no further combinations to narrow down results can be made.[35]

The GPO Web site can be found at **http://www.access.gpo** and *DOE Reports* at **http://www.doe.gov**. The advantage of visiting the GPO site is that bibliographic records are updated daily. An important limitation is, again, that the retrospective files are small as they are available only from 1994 onwards. The same search limitations, when compared to online services, prevail.

The above examples were described to indicate the possible beginning of a trend where an individual database producer makes its database available to end-users via a Web interface. Although not many examples of producer interfaces could be traced, an IS curriculum should include goals and actions to at least make the potential information professional aware of such a possibility.

IS programmes

Goal:
- To stay abreast of developments with regard to the use of the Web by commercial database producers for such services as indexing and abstracting.

Actions:
- create a database of database producers with a Web presence;
- access various producers' home pages and evaluate the Web interface and search engine being used (if any).

Specialized business and financial news delivery services

The premise of this chapter's discussion on the effects of the Internet on IS programmes is that, as explained above, the emphasis of the Internet marketplace is not necessarily towards transmitting scholarly communication, but more prominently on business and financial data and information such as news, forecasts or financial transactions. It is difficult, and sometimes impossible, to categorize these products because they vary in content (from indexes to full text) and in purpose (concentrating on adding value, or updating links to applicable Web sites only). The following examples indicate the importance of being aware of the existence of Web sources in the business arena:

DunsLink

DunsLink on the Web was announced in late 1996 by Dun & Bradstreet Information Services.[29] This site (**http://www.dbis.na.com**) provides customers with access to its information services on US companies and thus allows them to retrieve the company's most popular reports on US businesses, such as the *Business information report*, *Payment analysis report*, *Supplier evaluation report*, *Comprehensive report* and selected *Credit score* products.

DJIN

The Dow Jones & Company's Investor Network (DJIN) has been available since January 1997 to customers via the Internet.[29] It offers exclusive interviews with corporate officials, stock outlooks by top analysts, important financial news events and corporate presentations. A unique added feature to this site is that the content will be available in audio format, with video (both still-frame and full-motion) to follow suit. DJIN clients will have the ability to listen to events as they occur and to retrieve events that are stored in its recorded database, which contain more that a year's past broadcasts.

Investext

A similar, but very specialized example, comes from the Investext Group, a unit of Thomson Financial Services and which offers a series of industry-specific research databases via the Web.[29] The service provides business professionals with access to a large collection of company, industry and competitive intelligence research. The information is available according to specific economic sectors such as BioMed Strategies (**biomed.securities.com**) which covers the biotechnology, pharmaceutical, medical and health care industries; Telecom Strategies (**telecom.securities.com**) for telecommunications, broadcasting and cable industries; and Computer and Electronics Strategies (**electronics.securities.com**). The latter offers research on the software, computer, electronics and semiconductor industries. Each database offers executives with industry-specific information needs to make decisions regarding strategic planning, competitive intelligence, marketing, product development and business forecasts.

Although the financial and business sectors were traditionally a relatively specialized area, Internet commerce (as discussed above) has widened the possibilities of information professionals becoming involved in this sector.

IS programmes

Goal:
- To study the prominent features of business and financial information services available via the Internet and the Web.

Actions:
- explore the business and financial information sites (including financial newspapers), categorize them and maintain a database according to type of service available, access methods, costs, target groups, coverage and emphasis;
- subscribe to some of the main categories of services to obtain a working knowledge of rendering an information service to a selected group of clients (end-users).

Specialized newspaper databases

This category could also be grouped under the previous heading, but because of the prominence of newspaper databases, limited mostly to the business environment, it is discussed here as a separate trend. Online news and specifically business news has been not very difficult to get during the pre-Internet era. Vendors such as DIALOG, FT Profile and Mead Data (NEXIS) were prominent providers of full-text news from important newspapers such as the *Financial Times*.[36] Today many of these vendors are still prominent in providing financial and business news, either in the form of specific newspaper titles, for example the *Financial Times*, or specific news delivery services, such as those described in the previous paragraph. The Internet, and more specifically the Web, provides the ideal infrastructure for developing multiple and even multimedia news services.

Irrespective of all the available specialized alerting and real-time services, the complete Internet newspaper is also gaining ground. The strong points above their online counterparts lie in the fact that their Web-based interfaces and protocol allow for multimedia such as graphics and colour, updating of information is better (events can even be updated interactively) and hypertext linking can provide a versatile and imaginative value-added service. The following international business newspapers are already available via the Web[36] – all the examples providing continually updated full-text news stories:

- *Wall Street Journal* Interactive Edition (**http://www.wsj.com**)[37]
- *Guardian* (**go2.guardian.co.uk**)
- *Financial Times* (**http://www.ft.com**)
- *Times/Sunday Times* (**http://www.sunday-times.co.uk**).

The task of the information professional to select the best news service for a specific client group is becoming increasingly more difficult, as well as understanding the delivery technology, its potential costs and compatibility with other systems, such as groupware (Lotus Notes) and operating systems (for example Windows95).[36] For a comprehensive overview of the different categories of news resources, see Notess.[38] No separate goal and actions will be provided here, as this section belongs logically to the previous subheading (Specialized business and financial news delivery services).

Web interfaces for intelligent gateways

The early 1980s saw the development of the intelligent gateway, that is, an intermediary organization acting between the end-user and various online vendors (for example EasyNet). The idea was to assist the end-user by means of menu-driven options to create a search strategy and choose a database. The gateway would then select an applicable vendor, connect, execute the search, logoff from the vendor and displays the postings file to the searcher. A menu would then, *inter alia*, prompt the user to either adapt the strategy or download the results in a specific predefined format. Cumbersome menus, which added to the data communication and search fees, are now replaced by a Web interface, allowing for imaginative possibilities to search in the same way as via a typical Web search engine, that is, filling in a search form and linking to various search options.

Telebase's introduction of a Web presence for EasyNet (Version 2.0) is a good example of how a traditional menu-based online gateway could be transformed to the Web environment (**http://www.telebase.com**). The new Version 2.0 has a new pricing scheme with subscription fees and no longer per-minute charges.[28] EasyNet's Web gateway is still in its infancy – its future developments should be interest to monitor, as it is in direct competition with the current Web search engine. Meta engines, which will be discussed below, can be used to search more than one standalone engine simultaneously. In future a single search engine could theoretically include the databases of more that one online vendor during one search.

AT1 (for 'at one') represents another concept of providing easy access to end-users via a gateway. Designed specifically for the Web, the AT1 gateway (**http://www.at1.com**) was launched in December 1996 as a 'unified index of commercial online services', including DataStar, DIALOG, Questel-Orbit, Newsnet and AOL.[39] These commercial systems are called 'hidden' databases because they are beyond the reach of Web spiders or robots (discussed below). It is claimed that AT1 provides a single index to about 5.7 terabytes of information, made up by the 'hidden' or commercial databases loaded at the large database venders. Initially a search of AT1 will lead to the abstracts of relevant articles, together with links to the servers where they can be found. In Phase two, planned for mid-1997, users will be able to access the actual database directly through AT1.[39] An interesting development is that AT1 uses unique 'beacon' software which enables any online publisher using PLS (Personal Library Software) search and indexing products to create and send an index to the AT1 hub – the central server that manages all searches for the end-user. It also provides one-at-a-time access to the 'searchable' part of the Web, that is, the known search engines such as AltaVista, Excite, Infoseek, Lycos, Webcrawler and Yahoo!.

IS programmes

Goal:

- To establish the trends and functions with regard to Web-based intelligent gateway systems.

Actions:

- identify all the intelligent gateways that have developed a Web interface to simplify access to its services;
- access examples of the various categories of intelligent interfaces and evaluate their services in terms of search efficiency.

Web interfaces to local databases

With so many enterprises present on the Web, representing just about any topic of human interest, the need to organize its own or external URLs to representative sites can quickly arise in any organization. One solution is to create and maintain a local or personal database for sharing useful Web site information. Ribbler[40] reports about such a Lotus Notes database. People in the company submitted their most useful Web sites for entry into the database. After the file's initial design it will be updated by anyone wishing to add or delete information on the site. File integrity was considered less important than maintaining a working file that could be changed by any of the end-users of the intranet.

The local database being described in the previous paragraph can come into its own right if it is also published on an extranet, or even on the open Web environment. Although not yet widely available, software tools to do this are already on the market.[41] Given a full Internet connection, hardware and software resources, anyone can therefore publish a searchable Web-based database which is accessible worldwide. Inmagic Inc.'s DB/Text WebServer provides a Web interface for an internationally acclaimed database software, DB/TextWorks. The general approach in creating a Web database requires that Web server software and database software run simultaneously. The remote user starts a search by interacting with an HTML form that contains the same elements as the normal search engine, such as text areas, check boxes and radio buttons. The query is passed to the database engine and the results are returned, formatted on-the-fly into Web page format, which is then sent to the end-user.[41]

These developments indicate the ease with which anyone could use the Web to publish various formats of data and information. This does not exclude the information professional. In fact, it emphasizes the necessity for this group to keep track of developments in this area to enable them to be in a better position to render high-quality information services.

IS programmes

Goal:
- To investigate the current status and application possibilities of Web interfacing for local databases.

Actions:
- identify the titles of interfaces designed for a local Web site or to be used in an intranet environment;
- experience the application possibilities of publishing a local database with a given purpose on the Web (for example, market trends for a specific product; database of articles of a specific scientific journal);
- study a representative product and install and maintain it to acquire a working knowledge thereof;
- establish criteria to evaluate at least one interface to a local database.

Current awareness and electronic document delivery

A well-known facility provided by the online vendor is to save a search strategy (search terms and Boolean logic) in one of its databases after a bibliographic search has been successfully performed. One limitation of this approach is the cumbersome full-text support offered by the vendor. Before logging out, documents found in a retrospective search could be ordered by using the correct command, but the full text for SDI results, (received by e-mail), had to be supported by the end-user's information centre or ordered afterwards from the database vendor's full text provider. The last couple of years has seen considerable growth in commercial electronic document delivery services (EDD), that is, a private enterprise having access to a large number of scholarly journals and providing a faxed or condensed copy of a specific article upon request and at a specific fee. The Internet, and especially the World Wide Web, provides the infrastructure needed for these developments. Price *et al.*[42] sketch a more comprehensive picture of the reasons behind the explosion of commercial EDD services (the authors depict these reasons as being market forces and enabling technology):

- Journal subscription rates increased at a higher rate than inflation.
- Improvements in high speed telecommunication networks, enabling:
  - the transfer of large compressed data files and
  - increased use and accessibility of end-user bibliographic databases.
- Proliferation of published information, resulting in:
  - libraries no longer being able to maintain complete collections.
- Increase in demand for information and documents, as academic institutions have expanded and patterns of teaching, learning and research have changed.

The awareness by the end-user of the availability of electronic document delivery and the demands to make these more user-friendly, should be emphasized here as probably one of the most important reasons for the development of the retrieval ability built into recently marketed EDD systems, which could be categorized into the following broad groups:

- non-collection-based services (for example OCLC, Infotrieve, Swets & Zeitlinger);
- collection-based services (British Library DSC, UMI, ISI, Knight Ridder/UnCover);
- specialized collection-based services (IEEE/IEE, Disclosure, ADONIS, BIO-SIS).[43]

The end-user's growing familiarity with the various techniques of finding information in the Web, either by browsing (following hypertext links) or by keyword searching (using Web search engines), have put new demands on the facilities provided by EDD systems, for example more powerful searching, a friendlier accounting approach, a Web-based interface (using HTML forms instead of menus) and, last but not the least, an SDI service. The latter indicated the fulfilment of a longstanding ideal, that is, combining a SDI profile with a facility to easily acquire the full text of documents retrieved.

SDI/EDD companies have started to market their products as a one-stop service to the end-user, that is, searching for an update on the latest references on a specific topic, then ordering the document at a fee. Various review articles can be studied for more information on recent pricing structures and URLs to these systems (see, *inter alia*,[44–5]).

Further SDI/EDD developments – for example, more direct access by the end-user and an increased journal title base – should have an effect on the content of IS education programmes. They will also have a direct impact on the journal subscriptions of the typical scientific/academic information centre, as well as the distribution policy as far as paper-based versus electronic document supply is concerned. The expanding availability of electronic journals (discussed above) is another impact factor with regard to document delivery. The full-text of an increasing number of titles is being published via the Web. This represents a second option to acquire the full text of an article. These journals have a much better browsing facility, are already being linked from article title to abstract to full-text, and can accommodate data and information in multimedia format. In contrast, EDD systems still act as a 'clearing house' for a large number of titles on any specific subject area. Only the future will reveal how these two approaches will support or supersede each other.

IS programmes

Goal:
- To access and evaluate the search and retrieval facilities of a number of the large commercial electronic document delivery services.

Actions:
- identify and catagorize commercial EDD services according to such variables as the type or organization, purpose, international accessibility and type of full-text delivery options (for example, fax or compressed files);
- study the nature of EDD services to be able to create a set of evaluation criteria to establish which system is the best for specific circumstances, such as scope, journal coverage, costs, user friendliness, search and retrieval facilities
- establish the most effective ways to use EDD services in conjunction with vendors' SDI services, to be able to consult clients regarding the best systems for a specific situation.

The next section takes SDI/EDD technology one step further, namely, developments labelled as 'push' technology. Information professionals are experienced in the 'pull' method of information delivery whereby a search need or query is identified, a strategy formulated, a vendor and database selected and manipulated and the results pulled out. Push (or 'smart pull') technology implies that relevant information is selectively and automatically pushed to the end-user's workstation via an applicable service or vendor.

Personalized current awareness services

Various terms are used to describe recent developments regarding, amongst others, the need to address the Internet's and especially the Web's information overload. Web information retrieval has become synonymous with 'browsing', that is, the inability to search for a very specialized bit of information. Although ranking is incorporated as a basic feature of most search engines, this feature only emphasizes the weak point of search engines: high retrieval ratio; low precision ratio. Additionally, the Web environment has yet to provide facilities whereby the end-user can subscribe to an SDI service that offers the same sophistication level as the SDI features found in the commercial online vendor systems. A step in this direction, i.e. to address the personal information needs of end-users, may be found in intelligent agents, which have the potential to transform the nature of Web browsing and make it a more personal, productive and effective environment for both end-users and database producers.

Although it is not easy to classify or organize these 'push' technologies, two broad groups can be identified: firstly, the personalized agent that reacts to the end-user's choices in terms of topics to be searched, and secondly, customized news delivery when subscribing to any one of the large international news wire services.[46] Other terms used for describing this category of Web-based services are, for example, knowbots, softbots, taskbots, interface agents, personal agents or network agents.[47] The umbrella term 'Web casting' is increasingly used to group together all the different approaches.

The software being used for these agents can be categorized roughly into two main groups, namely anchored and mobile agents. The first group resides on either the client or the server side. These programs function alongside the browser to automate browser search sessions. Mobile agents have shown greater promise: these agents can move from Web server to server to find information on a regular basis.[46] Intelligent agent software can keep an automatic eye on topics and sites of importance to the end-user. When information is found, for example a new URL or content of a specific node, it delivers the information to the end-user.[48]

At this stage it might seem as if the term 'personalized current awareness service' could best describe this development. A customized news service is a subset thereof, which can vary from the basic agent software referred to above to high-end services such as MAID, Reuters Business Information and Financial Times Information.[49] The emphasis is on providing financial news to business people so that they can track developments in their own or in other industries. The following few examples indicate some of the features offered by customized current awareness services:

- **PointCast Network**: this downloadable client software (**http://www. pointcast.com**) lets the end-user select from a variety of types of information, including news, company information, industries, sports, lifestyles and weather. It then delivers updated reports and images, which the user can browse interactively. Its graphical screen-saver mode displays hyperlink headlines from the selected topics, turning the end-user's workstation into an information kiosk.[50] Other examples of Web delivery systems worth investigating are AfterDark Online (**http://www.afterdark.com**); AphaConnect StockVue (**http://www.alphaconnect.com**); BackWeb (**http://www.backweb. com**) or My Yahoo! News Ticker (**my.yahoo.com**).
- **Reuters News Explorer**: launched late 1996, this is a personalized awareness service that provides customized news to individuals on an intranet. End-users define their interests according to a few search terms and the Muscat search engine selects relevant articles from Reuters' global news-gathering service, covering 2000 sources, including national and international newspapers, trade publications and news wires (**http://www.muscat.co.uk**).[51]
- **Financial Times Information**: a personalized service was to be launched during the first half of 1997. One of the key elements will be the near ubiquitous intranet access for users of the system of fresh news delivered every morning via the end-user's PC (**http://www.info.ft.com**).[49]
- **Excite Inc.'s News tracker**: instead of relying on predefined categories and keyword searches through news wires, this approach uses a personal agent to sort through the volumes of about 300 periodicals currently available via the Web.[46] As a current awareness tool, its coverage is larger than the Reuters' news stories. It promises a new alerting approach using free Internet resources.[23]

Newswire services are growing in importance and will soon be an integral part of intelligent agent or filtered current awareness services.[52] Another major development is that it is expected that 'push' technology will be incorporated into standard office software towards the end of 1997. Proof of this is found in Microsoft's *Webcasting White Paper* dated 22 May 1997,[53] providing technical detail of its Internet Explorer browser which can perform a scheduled 'webcrawl' of a specific site's content, checking for updated content and optionally downloading information for offline use.

Information professionals should be aware of developments in this important area, to be able to provide sound advice to their clients about the unique features of available agents and agent services. Information professionals can also utilize agents to cast for information on behalf of their clients and for keeping abreast of Web-based developments in a more productive way.

IS programmes

Goal:
- To acquire a working knowledge of the different end-user based personalized current awareness (Web casting) services.

Actions:
- identify and describe various intelligent agent software packages which could be installed by the end-user or information professional to search different types of current awareness services;
- create a set of guidelines to assist in choosing which personal end-user Web casting service should be selected during what circumstances;
- investigate ways and means to apply intelligent agent software when rendering an information service.

Search engines

Since its origin in 1992/3 the World Wide Web has grown at a phenomenal rate. Studying statistics sites (e.g.[6]) will prove the necessity of developing some kind of retrieval system to find information being published by the various formal as well as informal (even personal) Web sites across the globe. So-called 'search engines' were put in the field, basically consisting of, in the beginning, very crude software packages to locate resources in this very distributed environment. These are known at different names, for example robots, spiders, wanderers, crawlers or worms.[54] Basically, robots are programmed to retrieve WWW documents and index data, then store the results in a database. To find new sources, robots start with a known set of WWW documents, then follow the hypertext links to unknown (unvisited) documents. Algorithms are used to determine which of these new links to follow. Most robots periodically visit the same sites to establish if any changes were made since the previous sites and to update their indexes.[55]

Sing and Lidsky[56] have identified the following two broad categories of search engines – indexes and directories:

- Web indexes are huge databases containing structured information on millions of Web pages or Usenet news group articles. By using keywords, phrases and Boolean operators, the end-user can retrieve lists of Web pages that contain the requested search terms. Web indexes are built by Web robots. Examples of classic Web indexes are:
  - AltaVista (**http://www.altavista.digital.com**)
  - HotBot (**http://www.hotbot.com**)
  - Open Text Index (**index.opentext.net**)
  - World Wide Web Worm (**http://www.cs.colorado.edu/wwww**).

- Web directories are hypertext lists of Web sites, systematically organized into topical categories and subcategories. Specifying (clicking) on any of the categories leads to the Web site where the information is being stored. Web directories are being maintained by people, which implies that the relevancy ratio of search results should by higher. Examples of engines that are primarily directories are:
  - Magellan Internet Guide (**http://www.mckinley.com**)
  - Yahoo! (**http://www.yahoo.com**).

- The following services are hybrids of the above two categories:
  - Excite (**http://www.excite.com**)
  - Infoseek (**http://www.infoseek.com**)
  - Lycos (**http://www.lycos.com**)
  - WebCrawler (**http://www.webcrawler.com**).

It could be expected that combinations of these engines would develop sooner or later. This is exactly what happened: a number of meta-systems have recently been announced which let the end-user search several engines simultaneously. Like most single search engines these meta-engines each have their own advantages and disadvantages and since each search engine uses its own unique interface and search facilities, there is no commonly accepted way of performing even such basic functions as a Boolean AND.[57] A further disadvantage is, understandably, that the processing speed is extremely slow when compared to a single engine search.

Examples of such meta-search engines are:

- SavvySearch (28 engines) (**guaraldi.cs.colostate.edu:2000/form**)
- MetaCrawler (9 engines) (**http://www.metacrawler.com**)
- SuperSeek (10 engines) (**w3.superseek.com/superseek**)
- All4One (4 engines) (**http://www.all4one.com**).

Meta-engines can perform quick, single-term searches effectively. The end-user can normally indicate how many hits from each engine should be displayed. Items in the results list consist of links to the relevant site where the information is being stored.

The near future will see prominent developments in the area of local search engines, or rather, search engines that could be installed and used in a small environment such as an intranet. Acting like smaller versions of the familiar engines these local engines let users perform keyword searching at the same level of sophistication. There are already several search utilities available for Webmasters to include in their sites, ranging from simple freeware and shareware programs to high-powered commercial products.[58] One example, Netsearch from Recall Plus, was recently announced as a powerful, easy-to-use search engine for Internet and intranet applications. It runs under Windows95 and Windows NT and supports all the essential search facilities such as phrase searching, truncation, Boolean operators, word proximity, image display and multimedia support (**http://www.insoft.co.uk**).

It is imperative that information professionals are extremely self-sufficient in using all types of search engines. They should know how the main engines perform when tested against variables such as coverage, scope, search features, format options, retrieval and precision ratios (see [59] for an overview of current research on evaluation). This knowledge is needed for not only personal but also client-based searching.

Although search engine interfaces are relative easy to use, the busy end-user will still need advice on which engine to use for specific assignments or tasks. The battle of the Web browsers is surely not over – the information professional and end-user alike should be able to decide which browser is to be installed in a specific environment. In the early stages of Web development only browsers such as Mosaic, Cello, WinWeb and WinTapestry were available. Later Netscape appeared and recently also Microsoft's Internet Explorer. According to evaluations, Explorer 'is in many ways a technically superior product'.[60] The information professional should also keep track of the different plug-ins available for most browsers. These add-in component programs enable an end-user to access specialized multimedia content on Web sites, such as audio, video clips and animation.

IS programmes

Goal:
- To establish the various levels of Web search engines, and study and compare the wide range of engines currently available.

Actions:
- study search engines in general with regard to the existing categories or levels, typical search features, level of user friendliness, ease of use and search formats;
- create evaluation criteria and assess/compare different search engines;
- identify a number of meta-search engines and access some of them to test their search capabilities;
- investigate the application possibilities of local search engines;
- identify the names of search engine software designed for a local Web site or to be used in an intranet environment; assist in implementing and maintaining a local search engine in an intranet;

- establish criteria to evaluate a local search engine and test them on one or more specific examples.

Home page design and maintenance

The question often asked is to what extent the information professional should be involved in home page design, as well as the maintenance of a specific site. By looking at the requirements of maintaining a Web site – such as technical expertise, programming, HTML as well as managerial skills – the Webmaster, a new player in the Internet environment, is in a far better position to fulfil the responsibilities of installing, updating and maintaining a Web site. However, as the Web has grown into an environment in which individuals and organizations can become information providers as well, it can be argued that the information professional should be involved in both infrastructural facilities of the Web, that is an information system, and also, as a publishing mechanism. It is the latter application that necessitates a basic knowledge of HTML. Furthermore, knowledge of the principles of Web page design is essential for publishing purposes. Publishing is defined here in its broadest sense, that is, to use the Web not only for announcements or marketing of services, but also as a mechanism to deliver information to end-users or clients via a personal page. The information professional will in the near future need effective skills to be involved in one or more of the following:

- Methodology for designing a home page environment. This should include phases such as defining the problem statement, establishing constraining requirements, building a conceptual model, writing derived requirements, detailed analysis of specifications regarding elements such as page content and security, detailed design of individual pages and the last phase – developing the home page.[61]
- Basic, working knowledge of HTML: alternatively, knowledge of effective HTML converters and editors. Recently upgraded word-processing packages (such as Word97 and Corel's WordPerfect7) make provision for functions to save text in HTML format. Basic knowledge of other, specialized HTML applications, such as incorporating graphic, sound or video files in a document, should also form part of the information professional's skills.[62-3]
- Knowledge and experience in applying the Web as a communication mechanism. The information professional should show initiative by using his or her personal home page to create a set of nodes with which the end-user could access various value-added services, such as current awareness services, personal SDI, news, announcements, and so forth.

IS programmes

Goal:
- To design and implement a Web site to maintain and support various categories of information services to clients.

Actions:
- study the HTML mark-up language, as well as a number of compatible HTML editors, converters and word processing assistants (for example Word97);
- evaluate and apply basic home page design principles to create a prototype for a site of a given enterprise;
- evaluate the possiblities for the information professional of rendering an information service by using a personal home page and links to clients for value-added information.

Image indexing and retrieval

While image processing technology is improving, it becomes less complicated to publish images on the Web or integrate these with text-based publications (for example a scientific journal article). Therefore the need arises to find effective methods to index and retrieve images that are part of a database system. A conventional text based database consist of established fields such as author, title, descriptors or abstract fields. Some or all of those fields are searchable using sophisticated search functions (limits, adjacency or truncation), together with Boolean operators. Although a lot of development went into text-based database retrieval packages, the same approach (text retrieval) cannot be applied in a similar way as far as pictorial or image data is concerned. There at least two factors why images differ from text.[64]

- Images are decidedly multidisciplinary in nature: they contain a variety of features, each of which may be of potential interest to researchers from different disciplines. From which viewpoint should the image be indexed?
- Unlike text-based formats, images are not described explicitly by bibliographic entities such as titles, abstracts, prefaces or subheadings. As a result, viewers (thus indexers) have to rely on their own interpretation of an image and its subject content. Indexing could be difficult, specifically when dealing with graphics such as advertisements (different integrated pictures to convey meaning) or those that are symbolic of nature.

Research on the theoretical as well as the practical issues associated with image or pictorial information has been done in the past (for a comprehensive state-of-the-art review of research see [65-6]). With the advent of Web browsers and easy-to-use viewing software, not only displaying the images has become a lot friendlier, but storing them, incorporating them in an HTML file and then publishing them via the Web is no longer a difficult venture. However, finding specific images being posted on the Web is to a large extent an unresolved issue. Much of the research work currently being done relies on means to automatically analyse and describe an image's content and matching it with a search query.[67] Much of this work is based on the mathematical analysis of the pixel arrays that constitute a digitized image.

Facilities for searching for images on the Web are limited to only a few search engines. The basic approach to find images would be to identify one of the many image collections on the Web, for example Art Today with 5,000,000 images. It is currently not only cumbersome to find image sites, but also to identify images which adhere to a specific search query. Jacsó[68] investigated the approaches followed by search engines such as AltaVista, Lycos, SavvySearch and HotBot. Yahoo!'s Imager Surver (**isurf.yahoo.com**) seems to be a good example of the direction in which developments are pointing in this regard. A searcher starts by accessing an image collection or picture library, using Yahoo!'s established classification levels to reach the right subject area. Once the right images are found via keywords, an adjacent visual search button or thumbnail could be clicked to find more similar images.[69] A similar content-based approach is being used by a recently introduced search engine, WebSEEK, situated at Columbia University (**disney.ctr.columbia.edu**). It consists of about 300,000 thumbnails from multiple categories of topics.[68]

The availability of images as information sources via the Web emphasizes the necessity that information professionals should be fully aware of the problems and solutions of image information indexing and retrieval technology. With the emphasis on communication with end-users or clients via a personal home page, the information professional should also have acquired the knowhow to incorporate images into Web documents, as well as be able to advise and/or assist a client to find images on the Web.

IS programmes

Goal:
- To develop an awareness of images as important information sources.

Actions:
- identify and study the Web's search engine approach in retrieving images that are being stored via the Internet;
- study and apply the methods to scan, store and integrating images with the documents of a WWW site.

Security issues

Today, information technology forms a fundamental element in the operation of almost every enterprise. Even small companies use local and wide area networks, thus allowing different interest groups to access different public files of the company. The result is an increasing dependence on the availability, integrity and confidentiality of information being stored, processed and retrieved by a specific database system. Even in an information centre, a number of basic reasons apply why protection is required when connecting to the Internet or any external network.[70–1]

- Security is not built into the Internet itself; security of external networks can therefore not be guaranteed.
- Most of the host operating systems on the Internet have ineffective integral security measures.
- The large number of Internet users worldwide implies that there are many potential sources of abuse.
- Socially irresponsible users, competitors, disgruntled employees and ex-employees who have access to a network can misuse a loophole to attack the integrity of the organization's data, by means of:
  - loss of data on a Web site (through accident or malice);
  - intentional interference or re-routing of traffic in an attempt of cripple or crash the Web server;
  - altering of data on either the send or the receive side of a Web transmission;
  - misrepresentation by offering false credentials, passwords or other data;
  - repudiation – denial that an online order or transaction took place;
  - unauthorized altering or downloading of data;
  - unauthorized transactions, that is any use of the system by a non-approved party;
  - viewing of Web information by an individual not given explicit permission to have access to the information.

The best configuration for protection is a combination of an external router, connecting the Internet to a freestanding perimeter network, one or more hosts connected to the local perimeter network only, and an internal router connecting the perimeter network to the organization's internal network.[70] Any information professional should be sensitive to the security considerations when doing business via the Internet. This does not necessarily refer to financial transactions only, but for communication with systems, clients or end-users as well. Technical assistance for installing security precautions such as firewalls should be sought from the Webmaster or IT administrator, but the information professional should be aware of the fact that, although a firewall is a logical system that protects users of network services from attack by external parties, it is definitely not fireproof.

IS programmes

Goal:
- To develop an awareness of the importance of effective Internet security to protect the assets of an information centre.

Actions:
- study the theoretical issues with regard to security, such as financial security, data integrity and privacy;
- evaluate the various security measures currently necessary for an intranet and extranet;
- assist with identifying, installing and maintaining a firewall to protect the data and information of a specific environment from intruders.

Implications for managers

'Educators should have anticipated the power of the Internet and expanded course offerings earlier; trend courses that offer what's hottest today are not necessarily bad, so long as there are significant theoretical underpinnings'.[72] These words emphasize the message conveyed in this chapter, namely that the Internet, and especially the World Wide Web, should be seen as a major driving force for curriculum change in information science courses. The fact that the Internet has opened new ground for the end-user implies that a totally new approach is needed when educators decide upon goals and content for IS courses. In this regard Nicholas and Frossling[73] have observed that, since the advent of the Internet, growing numbers of end-users have greater access to information sources than some information professionals and have greater knowledge of some information systems (for example search engines) than information professionals themselves.

The new information-handling technologies and services brought about by the Internet, as described in this chapter, imply that deans of the faculties where an IS department resides should provide the necessary funding to maintain the latest networking and workstation technology within such a department. It implies, furthermore, that heads of IS departments should motive for and manage funds for a specific department's Internet technology according to a well-designed and well-maintained strategic plan. Only the very latest hardware and software should be used to enable IS students to acquire theoretical knowledge and advanced skills to enable them to experience the 'push' and 'pull' technologies made possible via the Internet.

Income to maintain as well as update the information technology of an IS department depends invariably on the number of students registered in a specific department. In cases where the number of students is small, or even dwindling, the problem could be addressed by broadening the client base of a department to include other target groups. This implies establishing new courses, offering information science as an academic subject across faculty borders or, in a few successful cases, moving the IS department to the business, economic and/or management faculty. Other but less successful efforts have been to motivate sponsorships from private enterprise, to share IT facilities with other departments or to liaise with the academic library or information centre to let students work on its IT facilities.

Managers (that is, deans and heads of IS departments) should seriously take note of the potential impact on their courses of the vast end-user orientated information retrieval services currently being developed via the Internet. In fact, all the developments discussed in this chapter could be accessed via user-friendly interfaces and WWW browsers. Two new avenues of thought should therefore be explored because of the ever-growing end-user climate, in an effort to attract more students and to render a service to the community in general:

- Design fresh information science degree courses to teach IS as an academic subject to end-users and no longer to information professionals as its main target group. (The so-called 'information literacy' courses that are sometimes offered to mainly first-year or elementary students are excluded from this proposal).
  - Current information science theory concentrates on information science as a science, emphasizing information handling skills such as identifying, evaluating, organizing, retrieving and managing information in various formats. It is only when IS theory is being applied that the information intermediary is involved. However, for the first time in man's history of information documentation electronic information is accessible in different (multimedia) formats and available to everyone with access to a workstation – and, inevitably, accessible without the presence of an information intermediary.
  - It is suggested here that such a 'new' venue, namely teaching information science to end-users, could follow a 'personal information management' approach. Briefly, this implies that general IS theory should still be taught, but instead of concentrating on the intermediary or information professional, rather than on the electronic work place, the theory of information management and specifically personal information management for effective decision making should be emphasized.
- In the digital information environment, IS courses involving, as suggested

above, the information professional and/or end-user will have more hope for success if they are decoupled from their traditional library science obligations. In most instances, IS departments, previously called library science (LS), then library and information science (LIS), are still also responsible for LS courses. The latter are typically geared towards the traditional library environment. In this growing electronic or digital information environment, fewer students are interested in following the traditional LS venue. In fact, a library-orientated career path has for many years been no longer a very popular choice. Proof for this statement can be found in the closure of many US 'library schools', and the current financial constraints of many traditional LIS schools around the globe.

Conclusion

The increased involvement of the end-user in manipulating his or her own information environment is being supported by the birth of various new information enterprises, rendering personalized information services directly to the end-user. Furthermore, different levels of intelligent agent software have been specifically designed to reside on the end-user's workstation, with the sole purpose of assisting in information gathering tasks by periodically scanning pre-defined Web sites for information. In the earlier parts of the chapter it was also stressed that the strongest end-user involvement came from the business and financial sectors, or, in other words, access to business information services is shifting from the corporate information centre directly to the desktop.[9]

More pressure on the very existence of the information professional is coming from another technology trend, namely outsourcing. Although information centre outsourcing activities are not yet streamlined, it appears to be a trend information professionals have to deal with in the near future. In the USA there are already several successful companies engaged in online searching as an outsourced service.[74] What is more is that studies indicate that the value management placed on traditional online database searching by information professionals continues to be in a deep decline: analysts have predicted that by the year 2001 database searching will have become the least valued of all corporate library services.[74] Eddison also believes that the focus on the development of end-user interfaces by the information technology industry is mainly responsible for the current emphasis shifts in the information profession.[74]

To be able to survive in the digital and thus end-user-orientated era, re-engineering might be the only solution. 'Re-engineering endeavours to break away from the old assumption about how we organize and conduct business'.[75] Ribbler[9] has listed a few but nevertheless critical elements about the nature of re-engineering by the information professional:

- In the re-engineering process the role of the information professional changes from one of producing data and information to one of integrating new information technologies for the company; and to
- assisting people in the organization to become information gathering independent; and
- performing the creative tasks of information product development and product synthesis – thus providing information solutions and not just information.

In this chapter, an effort has been made to describe the very latest trends brought about by the Internet in making information more easily available. All the new services covered are, with no exception, geared towards addressing the end-user's information needs. It is therefore clear that, from the above remarks about re-engineering, the information professional's needs for change should be strongly based upon inventing new venues to support the end-user. These alternative directions have been discussed under the goals and actions added after each discussion of a specific trend. They are intended to suggest alternative career paths that could be provided for in a certain IS programme. Intensive thinking and planning is now necessary to devise new ways and means to integrate the Internet-driven goals and actions so necessary for an IS course with the more traditional course content. For the digital environment, course content offerings should be completely discoupled from the traditional library-based context. This is essential to our struggle for survival with other professions for jurisdiction over both those information functions that have traditionally been the problem domain of information science, as well as those emerging information functions brought about by changes in society (end-users) and technology.

References

1   Van House, N. and Sutton, S. A., 'The Panda syndrome: an ecology of LIS education', *Journal of education for library and information science*, **37** (2), 1996, 131–47.
2   Eaton, J. and Bawden, D., 'What kind of resource is information?', *International journal of information management*, **11** (2),1991,156–65.
3   Wigand, R. T., 'Electronic commerce: definition, theory, and context', *The information society*, **13** (1), 1997, 2.
4   Ibid., 5.
5   Ibid., 3.
6   Gray, M. K., 'Internet statistics: growth and usage of the Web and the Internet', 1996.
    <http://www.mit.edu:8001/people/mkgray/net/>
7   Pattinson, H. and Brown, L., 'Chameleons in marketspace: industry trans-

formation in the new electronic marketing environment', *Internet research: electronic networking applications and policy*, **6** (2/3), 1996, 35–6.

8   Ibid., 37.

9   Ribbler, J., 'Delivering solutions: knowledge economy', *Online*, **20** (5), 1996, 12–13.

10 Ibid., 13.

11 Peters, R. F., 'Information partnerships: marketing opportunities for information professionals', *Information outlook*, **1** (3), 1997, 14–16.

12 Speh, M., 'Enabling a global community of knowledge', *Aslib proceedings*, **48** (9), 1996, 201.

13 Op. cit., Van House and Sutton, 145.

14 Van Brakel, P. A., 'Twenty years of training in online searching: integrating the Internet with the teaching programme', *Proceedings of the 20th International Online Information Meeting*, London, 3–5 December 1996, D. Raitt and B. Jeapes (eds.), Oxford, Learned Information, 1996, 57–64.

15 'Leading edge: hybrids are happening', *Information world review*, 123, March 1997, 2.

16 Robinson, K. L., 'People talking to people: making the most of Internet discussion groups', *Online*, **20** (1), 1996, 28.

17 Kennedy, S.D., 'The Internet as a communications tool', *Information today*, **14** (2), 1997, 39–40.

18 Kovacs, D. K., 'Directory of scholary and professional e-conferences, 10th revision', 1996.
    <http://www.n2h2.com/KOVACS>

19 Op. cit., Robinson, 29.

20 Kovacs, D. K., Robinson, K.L. and Dixon, J., 'Scholarly e-conferences on the academic networks: how library and information science professionals use them', *Journal of the American Society for Information Science*, **4** (4), 1995, 249.

21 Harnad, S., 'Electronic scholarly publication: quo vadis?', *Managing information*, **2** (3), 1995, 31–3.

22 Tenopir, C. and King, D. W., 'Managing scientific journals in the digital era', *Information outlook*, **1** (2), 1997, 15–16.

23 Notess, G. R., 'New databases from the Internet services', *Database*, **20** (2), 1997, 72–4.

24 Haygarth Jackson, A. (ed.), *Training and education for online*, London, Taylor Graham, 1989, 1–2.

25 Wittig, C. and Wolfram, D., 'A survey of networking education in North American library schools', *Library trends*, **42** (4), 1994, 626–37.

26 Koenig, M. E. D., 'Target 2000: some thoughts and predictions', *Online and CDROM review*, **18** (6), 1994, 364–5.

27   Basili, C., 'Subject searching for information: what does it mean in today's Internet environment?' *The Electronic Library*, **13** (5), 1995, 459–66.

28   Notess, G. R., 'New models of online interaction', *Online*, **19** (5), 1995, 87–90.

29   'Database race to the Web', *Information today*, **13** (10), November, 1996, 39, 44.

30   'Medline over the Web', *Information retrieval and library automation*, **3** (8), 1996, 3.

31   'Database race to the Web', *Information today*, **13** (9), October, 1996, 43, 50, 59.

32   'Internet and interface: new from LEXIS-NEXIS', *Information retrieval and library automation*, **32** (3), 1996, 1–3.

33   Jacsó, P., 'Ovid Web gateway: nobody does it better', *Online*, **20** (6), 1996, 24–31.

34   'Ovid: Java first, pay-as-you-go Web, journals online', *Information retrieval and library automation*, **32** (8), 1997, 7–8.

35   Notess, G. R., 'The Internet as an online service: bibliographic databases on the Net', *Database*, **19** (4), 1996, 92–5.

36   Scott, J., 'Online access to international newspapers and wires: a status report' *Database*, **19** (4), 1996, 42–9.

37   O'Leary, M., 'Database review: the Wall Street Journal meets the Web', *Information today*, **14** (3), 1997, 22–3.

38   Notess, G. R., 'News resources on the World Wide Web', *Database*, **19** (1), 1996, 13–20.

39   'At one with information on the Web', *Information world review*, 121, 1997, 9.

40   Op. cit., Ribbler, 19.

41   Beiser, K., 'Publishing text databases on the Web with Inmagic's DB/Text Webserver', *Database*, **19** (6), 1996, 45–50.

42   Price, S. P., Morris, A. and Davies, J. E., 'An overview of commercial electronic document delivery suppliers and services', *The Electronic Library*, **14** (6), 1996, 523.

43   Ibid., 524–31.

44   Mancini, A. D., 'Evaluating commercial document suppliers: improving access to current journal literature', *College and research libraries*, **57** (2), 1996, 123–31.

45   Op. cit., Price, Morris and Davies, 523–42.

46   Dragan, R.V. and Boscardin, F., 'Future agent software', *PC magazine SA*, **5** (3), 1997, 65–9.

47   Hey, J., 'Information professionals as intelligent agents – or when is a knowbot only a robot?' *Proceedings of the 20th International Online Information* Meeting,

London, 3–5 December 1996, D. Raitt and B. Jeapes (eds.), Oxford, Learned Information, 1996, 17.

48 Griswold, S. D., 'Unleashing agents: the first wave of agent-enabled products hits the market', *Internet world*, **7** (5), 1996, 55–7.

49 Lyon, J., 'Focus: what's the best way to read all about it?', *Information world review*, 123, March 1997, 15–16.

50 Hasset, C., 'The PointCast Network', *PC magazine SA*, **5** (1), 1997, 40.

51 Blake, P., 'Leading the edge: exploring the news', *Information world review*, 121, 1996, 17–18.

52 Ojala, M., 'The personality characteristics of newswires', *Database*, **20** (2), 1997, 14.

53 Microsoft Corporation, 'Webcasting in Microsoft Internet Explorer 4.0', 1997.
   <http://www.microsoft.com/ie/ie40/press/push.htm>

54 Dong, X. and Su, K. T., 'Search engines on the World Wide Web and information retrieval from the Internet: a review and evaluation', *Online and CD-ROM review*, **21** (2), 1997, 67–71.

55 Kimmel, S., 'Robot generated databases on the World Wide Web', *Database*, **19** (1), 1996, 41–2.

56 Singh, A. and Lidsky, D., 'Internet: All-out search', *PC magazine SA*, **5** (1), 1997, 52.

57 Notess, G. R., 'Internet "Onesearch" with the mega search engines', *Online*, **20** (6), 1996, 36–9.

58 Richardson, E. C., 'Add an engine', *Internet world*, **7** (5), 1996, 88–92.

59 Op. cit., Dong and Su, 77–9.

60 Kennedy, S. D., 'Joining the world of browser battles', *Information today*, **13** (10), 1996, 41.

61 Artz, J. M., 'A top-down methodology for building corporate Web applications', *Internet research: electronic networking applications and policy*, **6** (2/3), 1996, 65–6.

62 McMurdo, G., 'HTML for the lazy', *Journal of information science*, **2** (3), 1996, 198–212.

63 McMurdo. G., 'Web graphics for the lazy', *Journal of information science*, **23** (2), 1997, 149–62.

64 Baxter, G. and Anderson, D., 'Image indexing and retrieval: some problems and proposed solutions', *Internet research: electronic networking applications and policy*, **6** (4), 1996, 67–8.

65 Enser, P.G.B. 'Pictorial information retrieval' *Journal of documentation*, **51** (2), 1995, 126–70.

66 Berinstein, P., 'Images in your future: the missing pictures in your online

search', *Online*, **21** (1), 1997, 38–46.

67   Op. cit., Baxter and Anderson, 73.

68   Jacsó, P., 'Searching for images on the Web', *Information today*, **14** (3), 1997, 36–7.

69   Owen, T., 'Image surfer aims high but needs some refinement', *Information world review*, 123, March 1997, 5.

70   Doddrell, G. R., 'Information security and the Internet', *Internet research: electronic networking applications and policy*, **6** (1), 1996, 5–9.

71   McCarthy, V., 'Web security: how much is enough?', *Datamation*, **43** (1), 1997, 112–7.

72   Norton, M. J., 'Short takes in the digital revolution', *Bulletin of the American Society for Information Science*, **22** (6), 1996, 19–21.

73   Nicholas, D. and Frossling, I., 'The information handler in the digital age', *Managing information*, **3** (7/8), 1996, 31–4.

74   Eddison, B., 'Our profession is changing: whether we like it or not', *Online*, **21** (1), 1997, 79–80.

75   Lin, B., 'Managing in an information highway age: critical issues', *Internet research: electronic networking applications and policy*, **6** (4), 1996, 42–7.

Index